or be

D1513804

THE FUTURE OF MEN

THE FUTURE OF
MEN

MARIAN SALZMAN,
IRA MATATHIA,
AND ANN O'REILLY

palgrave
macmillan

PHOTOS
p. 7: Official Presentation of David Beckham in Madrid, © Dusko
    Despotovic/Corbis
p. 15: Daughter on Father's Shoulders, © ROB & SAS/Corbis
p. 31: Actor Alan Alda, © Mike Laye/Corbis
p. 53: 15th Annual GLAAD Media Awards, © Nancy Kaszerman/
    ZUMA/Corbis
p. 81: Audrey Meadows and Jackie Gleason on TV Set, ©
    www.corbis.com/Corbis
p. 103: Join the WAAC Recruitment Poster, © Swim Ink/Corbis
p. 123: "The Lord of the Rings: The Two Towers" Premieres in LA, © Frank
    Trapper/Corbis
p. 139: Bill Clinton Holding Saxophone, © Corbis
p. 163: Man on Stilts Looking for Way Out of Maze, © Images.com/Corbis
p. 187: Senior Man in Swimming Pool Wearing Cowboy Hat, © Claire
    Artman/Corbis

First published in hardcover in 2005 by
PALGRAVE MACMILLAN™
First PALGRAVE MACMILLAN™ paperback edition: September 2006
175 Fifth Avenue, New York, N.Y. 10010 and
Houndmills, Basingstoke, Hampshire, England RG21 6XS.
Companies and representatives throughout the world.

PALGRAVE MACMILLAN IS THE GLOBAL ACADEMIC IMPRINT OF THE
PALGRAVE MACMILLAN division of St. Martin's Press, LLC and of Palgrave
Macmillan Ltd. Macmillan® is a registered trademark in the United States,
United Kingdom and other countries. Palgrave is a registered trademark in the
European Union and other countries.

ISBN-13: 978-1-4039-7548-5 paperback
ISBN-10: 1-4039-7548-5 paperback

Library of Congress Cataloging-in-Publication Data
Salzman, Marian L.
    The future of men / by Marian Salzman, Ira Matathia, and Ann O'Reilly.
        p.   cm.
    Includes bibliographical references and index.
    ISBN 1-4039-6882-9 (alk. Paper)
        1. Men—Social conditions—21st century.   2. Masculinity.   3. Sex role.
4. Man-woman relationships.   I. Matathia, Ira.   II. O'Reilly, Ann.
III. Title.

HQ1090.S325   2005-05-16
305.3'01'12—dc22

                                                                2005045870

A catalogue record for this book is available from the British Library.

Design by Letra Libre.

First paperback edition: September 2006
10 9 8 7 6 5 4 3 2 1

Printed in the United States of America

CONTENTS

ACKNOWLEDGMENTS

IN THE BEGINNING

There never would have been metrosexual mania in summer 2003 without Schuyler Brown and Ryan Berger, both of communications group Euro RSCG Worldwide—she because she helped define "metrosexual man," undertaking a quest for the perfect metrosexual specimen in response to our research hypothesis, and he because he is a textbook case of metro-hetero manhood, not to mention an extraordinarily good sport for having allowed international television crews to accompany him on treks to Bliss for facials and manicures and to his home, to examine his treasure trove of clothing and accessories.

Ryan served for our team as the human face of metrosexual man. Schuyler, a phenomenal trendspotter, actually took metro to the next level, when she and her friends began talking about "emo man," ultimately featured in the *New York Observer* and the *Observer* (U.K.) in 2004, an extension of the metrosexmania of the previous year.

OUR COLLABORATORS

Several of the chapters of this book were drafted in conjunction with a coterie of strong writers, including "New Rules for the Mating Game," from our favorite social researcher/writer, Stuart Harris, of Bradford-on-Avon, England, and "Me Tarzan, You Jane: The Biology of Gender," drafted by James Harkin, of London. We have collaborated with Stuart since our days in Amsterdam at TBWA International and with James since we founded Young & Rubicam's Intelligence Factory. Stuart, a journalist, market researcher, and advertising account planner, has been with us in the trenches for a number of provocative trends, from initial thoughts on computer-mediated communities—and their pervasive power—in 1996, to the rise of religion in the late 1990s, to the initial question that fueled metrosexmania: Do men have a future?, in 2003. James consults as a social forecaster at the Social Issues Research Centre (Oxford); he holds a master's degree in politics from Oxford, and taught at Oxford University from 1996 to 1999, which is where we met him, through our efforts for the Intelligence Factory. He regularly contributes to the *New Statesman* and the *Independent on Sunday*.

Thanks to the power of www.craigslist.org, we hooked up with two other great freelance writers and thinkers. The first, Ian Sage Sherman, of Seattle, who was born and raised in Silver City, Nevada, who has lived in Moscow, Istanbul, and London, who attended Oberlin College, and who is working toward his MFA in fiction at the University of Washington, helped on several chapters, including portions of our chapters on influences (mass media and real-life role models). The second, Natalie Reitano, a New York–based professor of English, social commentator, and writer, contributed content and analysis, most of which is contained in our chapter exploring how men are handling the shift. We appreciate the contributions of both.

Jenny Burke, research manager at Euro RSCG Worldwide, created the timeline in chapter 5, provided enormous fact-finding support, and gave some much-needed order to a large chunk of the sea of endnotes that make up this book's research trail. She served as the steady rock for all three of us from 2002 to 2004, quietly finding the obscure fact or tossing out the big idea, always understated and with a smile. Jenny and Karina Meckel also deserve big thanks for helping us to identify and recruit the first wave of metrosexual men who joined us and the *New York Times'* Warren St. John for the much-reviewed dinner during which we tackled the future of men with research subjects for the first time.

THE POWER OF THE PRESS

Warren St. John, Marcus Warren of the *Telegraph* (U.K.), and other journalists who often covered our work on men and changing gender roles—and especially those who covered it early—empowered us to have the credibility to write this book. Jessica Kirsh and the team at CK Publicity in London, especially Alie Jowett and Bella Jowett, are really the ones to blame for the Summer of Metrosexuality 2003, since they were the ones who planted our "news virus" and watched it spread rapidly. It fell to them to micromanage our exposure as the story moved from London to New York, to Mumbai, Sydney, Johannesburg, Toronto, Chicago, Hong Kong, and even Sri Lanka, Bangkok, and Jakarta. And, of course, we owe a debt to Mark Simpson, the brilliant British journalist who had coined the term *metrosexual* years earlier, and to our wonderful friend and colleague Matt Donovan, then of Euro RSCG Sydney and now in the New York office, and Dan Pankraz, also then of Euro RSCG Sydney and now in New York. Matt and Dan started the whole darn thing with "that" word when they shot us an article on metrosexuals that one of them had seen in Wellington, New Zealand, at just around the time we had begun researching men and their lack of media *oomph*.

THE EURO RSCG LINK

Bob Schmetterer, Ron Berger, Lisa Fabiano, Annette Stover, Robert Fahmy, Peggy Nahmany, and Lillian Alzheimer were incredibly supportive of our research into metrosexuality and all our work on the present and future of men. Without their enthusiasm, the research would have amounted to nothing more than a one-time effort to jumpstart a specific new-business dialogue. (For the record, we did get that meeting!) We are also very grateful to the global colleagues who embraced our work on men, and localized it, including Mercedes Erra, Marianne Hurstel, and Nicolas Chemla in France; Patrick de Regt in the Netherlands; and David Jones, now in New York, but then working from a London base.

Romain Hatchuel challenged us to conduct the initial survey on men and their place, grounded in our observation that men are no longer CEO of the bedroom or the boardroom. He thought it just might open a few new-biz dialogues; little did he realize it would change the shape of our worlds, at least for several months.

Thanks also to our former colleague Mark Wnek for his insights and ideas. His comments on men, authenticity, and fatherhood resonate deeply.

RESEARCH, MORE RESEARCH, AND BUZZ

Alan Appelbaum of MarketProbe International provided a robust dataset from our surveys in the United States, the United Kingdom, and the Netherlands, and, working with Stuart Harris, we packaged the first two of several reports on gender convergence and the new man. Even before Romain kicked our study into gear, we had chatted with the late Debra Goldman, of *Adweek*, for her feature on men, "The Male Ego Takes a Beating." If Debra hadn't written that article, and if her editor, Alison Fahey of *Adweek*, hadn't published it, we're not sure we would have ever aggressively pursued this research lead. Her well-developed story on how men have become increasingly marginalized in the media reinforced our sense that men were a gender in serious transition.

Roxane Marini provided fact checking for several chapters and also helped with research. Lindsay Neiman, a St. Andrew's student who interned for our team during summer 2004, helped provide the youth perspective, and Rebecca Stokes lobbed in thoughts from London for a number of chapters. Thanks also to Helen Lepore for her help with trafficking all the input. And thanks to Owen Dougherty, Nancy Wynne, and especially Jim Heekin for their gracious permission to use data compiled and analyzed while Marian and Ira were working at Euro RSCG.

INTERVIEW SUBJECTS AROUND THE GLOBE

We are deeply thankful for the assistance of Lara Anderson, Priyanka Bajaj, Karishma Birdy, James Cullinane, Elisabeth Cuming, Cynthia Cyfert, Shama Dalal, Niels den Otter, Tim Dirgins, Katherine (Katie) Fey, Meg Folcarelli, Belle and Jim Frank and their wonderful offspring, Will Frank and Rebecca Frank (who ended up recruiting numerous college-aged respondents for us), Paul Fraser, Stuart Hazlewood, Jim Holland, Brent Kaiser (who connected us to the young-dad set in Manhattan, as well as the metro hetero crowd on the West Coast), Dik Klicks, Quinten Lange, Cathy Lasowski, Tamilla Mamedova, Elinor Mileti, Richard Notarianni, Madeline Park, Brenda-Lee Paul, Christopher Ross, Kshama Singhania, Jimmy Szczepanek, Rachel Taranta, Julius van Heek, Alex Wagner, and Friso Westenberg for sitting through lengthy interviews and/or answering our extensive questionnaires about men, women, men and women—and the future for men. (And thanks, also, to Fleur Dusée, Bernice Kanner, Karina Meckel, Jeanne Ponko, Shveta Raina, Sabine van der Velden, and Margaret Wagner for helping us unearth many of these people, and their unique perspectives.)

Many of our interview subjects are a result of our tenures at TBWA International, Young & Rubicam, and Euro RSCG Worldwide, for all three agencies have provided us with acquaintances and friends on every continent, and they opened up their address books with referrals, and cleared time to talk with us about this, our latest quest for insights and ideas about what's happening in the zeitgeist. Many thanks to you all.

Marian also wants to add a thank-you to new colleagues and friends at JWT, where she is now working. Of special note are Bob Jeffrey, Marc Capra, and Lew Trencher. And she and Ira both extend thanks to Paul Lavoie and Jane Hope, who are the genius behind Canada's most-awarded ad agency, TAXI, and who provided them office space and a spiritual home as each of them moved beyond Euro RSCG, Marian in fall 2004 and Ira in winter 2005.

We met our editor, Airie Stuart, of Palgrave, when she acquired and edited *Buzz: Harness the Power of Influence and Create Demand*, our last book, published by Wiley & Sons in spring 2003. We owe her a great thank-you for her support and brilliance in making this book real—and quickly. Melissa Nosal has also been immensely helpful.

The three authors collaborated on this book electronically during fall 2004, while Ira and Ann worked at Euro RSCG Worldwide and Marian spent her days as a freelance trendspotter and public speaker, and hanging around at TAXI and at mcgarrybowen, another New York advertising hot shop. While we wrote some of the book the summer prior, when all three of us were colleagues at Euro RSCG, the lion's share of the book is the byproduct of a decade-long working partnership that is one-of-a-kind. Even today, June 23, 2005, as we finish this book, two of us are in Connecticut, one in the northern part of the state, one in the southern part, and one of us is in rural Ulster County, New York. Yet, thanks to instant messaging and e-mail, we finalize this manuscript and reach out to say thank you to everyone who made this book possible.

—Marian, Ira, and Ann

INTRODUCTION

So it is naturally with the male and the female; the one is superior, the other inferior; the one governs, the other is governed; and the same rule must necessarily hold good with respect to all mankind.

—Aristotle (384–322 B.C.E.)

Well into the twentieth century, man accepted the deference of women as his due. His role was that of provider and protector. His authority over his family, over the workplace, over church, mosque, and synagogue was absolute. To what extent he asserted his authority over women depended on the individual man, his culture, and his upbringing, but there was no mistaking the fact that his dominion over the female of the species went largely unchallenged.

A lot has changed over the past half century, and nowhere is this more evident than in the changed—and still changing—relationship between the sexes. As we know, all through the twentieth century, and especially in the latter half, the movement for greater equality for women gained strength and speed. The efforts of such forceful figures as Gloria Steinem, Simone de Beauvoir, and Betty Friedan helped push the notion of feminism away from the fringe and into the popular press as social commentary, where it slowly but inexorably entered the public consciousness, public policy, our public and private institutions, and, ultimately, the public mind-set.

Now, in the early years of the twenty-first century, we live in what some have termed the postfeminist era. To a large extent (in developed countries, anyway), men and women have come to accept the basic equality of the sexes—in theory, if not always in practice. That shift in attitude in and of itself is of enormous import in terms of how society is structured, what and who is valued, and how men and women relate to one another en masse and individually. Women, to a degree at least, have gotten what they wanted: access to education, increased job opportunities, and more equitable social, political, and economic rights. But what of men? What have they gained or lost in the process? How are they faring in a society governed by rules and taboos that would have been anathema to their forebears? And how are social, political, and economic shifts currently under way likely to affect them as we move further into this new century?

This book is an attempt to understand what it means to be a man in the world today (particularly in the Western world) and to predict how the life of the modern man is likely to further evolve in years to come. As a team of trend spotters and social analysts, we are confirmed globalists by virtue of our work abroad; we are sociological in orientation and commercial in practice. The three of us have been employed for a number of years in keeping many of the world's leading companies ahead of the curve in understanding social trends and their implications for consumers and brands. We have helped introduce the world to a number of key social phenomena, including the emergence of "wiggers" in the late 1980s, the rise of female "singletons" in the mid-1990s, and the "metrosexual" in summer 2003. Each of those segments is important not just sociologically and culturally, but also economically. In marketing lingo, we'd call them "lucrative market niches."

When we first spoke about "wiggers" (a term we detested, but which stuck—particularly after Marian discussed it before a raucous crowd on the *Oprah Winfrey Show*), hip-hop was in its nascent stages. A lot of people weren't even aware it existed—and many of those who did assumed it would be fleeting. Today hip-hop culture is mainstream culture. Sean John, Baby Phat, Ecko . . . they're brands worn by all sorts of people. And such old-time companies as Levi Strauss & Co. have spent the past decade or so scrambling to come up with styles that will capture at least some sort of street cred.

Singletons also have been of enormous import in the worlds of business and marketing, and there are no signs that their socioeconomic power is waning. *Time* magazine recently devoted yet another cover story ("Are Friends the New Family?") to this group of people who are either forgoing marriage or postponing it to indulge in self first. Their economic might can be seen in the fact that single women are the second-largest cohort of homebuyers after married couples. So, our trends are not just "nice to knows" for cocktail-party banter, but, rather, the substance of which markets are made in the United States and beyond.

In our work over the years, we have witnessed and recorded a number of social changes among men, from the rise in male vanity to men's increased involvement in the home. Whether one looks at the growth of men's skin care and plastic surgery or the increasing number of men making decisions about interior design and home furnishing, it's apparent that men are affecting business in major ways. Advertising and marketing departments have had to change their approaches to men. That might suggest that men are more "important" than ever. All the while, however, we have been cognizant of some underlying themes that suggest that the consequences of the women's movement, the evolution toward information-based economies, and shifting social mores and values are having what we would describe as a negative, even debilitating, impact on men's position in society and within the family. Even more significant, these shifts appear to be having a negative impact on the male psyche, leaving modern men hesitant, disoriented, and, in many cases, more than a little depressed.

This book lays out what we consider the most important trends influencing the modern male and how he interacts with his mate, his children, his colleagues and friends, and how he thinks about himself and his place in society. As marketers with well over half a century's combined experience, we can't help but note this material's importance for companies looking to connect with the male consumer. Dramatic changes will be happening in how businesses react to the new man. This book will be useful not only to businesses but also to anyone who has an interest, be it personal or professional, in understanding the essential ways in which the twenty-first century male differs from his predecessors, the important issues and challenges with which he is grappling, and the current trends and influences that suggest more changes ahead in the coming decades.

As part of the research we undertook for this book, we completed more than seventy interviews with "real people," many of whom have strong, even strident viewpoints about male-female dynamics. A dozen of these people are homosexual men, who are already living a different future from the forty-plus heterosexual men with whom we spoke. The youngest contributor to this book is thirteen; the oldest, fifty-nine. Among our interview subjects: the Frank family of Haworth, New Jersey, made up of Jim (a magazine editor), Belle (a marketing expert), and offspring Will and Rebecca. Will is a student at the University of Pennsylvania in Philadelphia, and Rebecca is a student at Tufts University, in Medford, Massachusetts.

We spoke with the British writer Paul Fraser, who lives with his Dutch girlfriend in Amsterdam, the Netherlands. We talked with four young foreign students at Brown University, in Providence, Rhode Island, in great detail; among them were Shveta Raina, of Mumbai, India, and Tamilla Mamedova, of Istanbul, Turkey. Both of them connected us with their friends in the United States, in India and Turkey, and in London and Paris. Our former colleagues in Amsterdam, with whom our relationships date back to our days at TBWA International (1995–1997)—Fleur Dusée, Friso Westenberg, and Sabine van der Velden—connected us with Dutch nationals and expatriates living and working in Holland; those viewpoints are reflected in the interview excerpts we included in the final manuscript.

More than a quarter century ago, the term feminism summed up in a single word an entire range of changes and issues and feelings and phenomena that were beginning to surface; it put them all under an umbrella with a handle everyone could grasp. Now, we think it's high time to start focusing on the other half of the gender equation: men. **There have been various attempts to coin an umbrella term to serve for men as "feminism" has served for women. "Masculism" is around but hasn't sparked the popular imagination; "metrosexuality" has caught on, but clearly is relevant to only a section of the male population. So pending a catchier term, we propose to look at this issue as "the Future of Men."**

By the end of this book, we hope you will share our sense that society is seeing the emergence of a new "M-ness" or "My-ness"—a masculinity that men are defining and refining as their own. Their M-ness may take such forms as "my life as a modern man" or "my life as a man who lives in a world of men and women." What's important is that men are finally showing signs of beginning to reassert control over their own masculinity.

WHAT TO REMEMBER

1. The past half century has seen enormous and fundamental shifts in gender roles and gender expectations. While the focus has been very much on women, what they want, and how they are handling the shift, men have also had to grapple with fundamental social, political, and economic changes that have largely been outside individual control. As the activity of the women's rights movement has matured into the postfeminist era, many men are experiencing a sense of angst or dissatisfaction with their new roles in society, in the workplace, and within the family.

2. *The Future of Men*, our book and our ongoing study, is intended to explore the most important forces shaping men's present and future lives and to draw conclusions as to how recent and current shifts are likely to influence men's behaviors and attitudes in this new century.

1

THE GREAT GENDER SHIFT

However much we strive as individuals and as a society to be gender-neutral, it is virtually impossible to be gender-blind. Male and female are fundamental categories for human beings in dealing with one another. In every place and culture, people immediately identify others as male or female on first contact. Some sociologists would say we have to know a person's sex in order to know how to interact with him or her. Any parent who has brought a baby in gender-neutral clothing to a playground knows that among the questions he or she will hear is, "Is that a boy or a girl?" Only once that has been established does the stranger begin to interact with the baby. At least one study has shown that parents and others tend to smile more at female babies. It may well be that we can't even settle on a facial expression till we've ascertained what lurks beneath the diaper.

What does differ from place to place and from one era to another are the perceived normal characteristics of "maleness" and "femaleness," and how those affect individuals, their relationships, and society at large. The changes under way in this aspect of the male-female relationship were the impetus for this book. **In our professional and personal observations around the world over the last quarter century, we have spotted what we believe to be seismic social-psychological shifts taking place between the sexes. These shifts are driven to a very large extent by the dynamic interaction of science, technology, and economics, and are magnified by the increasingly omnipresent media. In one way or another, most major societies today have to come to grips with big changes in the behavior of men and women.**

In the West, there have been fierce debates, still raging, about which gender behaviors are innate and which are socially determined. What's nature and what's nurture in the sexes is still open to discussion and research, but what's certain is that the economy doesn't much care; it rewards people who can produce and consume, and it cares nothing about whether they button their jackets on the right or the left. Can they play? Can they pay?

The growing economic power of women owes much to the shift from land-dependent agrarian economies through factory-dependent manufacturing economies to intelligence-dependent service economies. The more women become fully qualified economic participants in their own right, rather than mere dependents of men, the more we all have to face fundamental questions about marriage, procreation, the role of family, and the changing force of "the tribe."

In our new world, life expectancy is steadily rising in most of the developed nations, and that, too, has its impact on marriage and procreation. People are no longer over the hill at forty, past it at fifty, old at sixty, and gone at seventy. We now have a vastly greater range of options in most areas of life, and a longer life in which to experience them, so there's less rush to get married early and it's more challenging to stay married for a lifetime. Late parenthood, second families, and even third families are far from unusual as couples separate and form new pairings. And more often these days than in the past, women are the ones with the wandering eyes.

Shifts in gender behavior are rarely greeted with unanimous approval. Okay, make that "never." The people with more financial, social, and political power (mostly men) tend to resist the shift of power to those with less (mostly women). The vehemence of male resistance varies from culture to culture, from the extremes of Afghanistan under the Taliban to the rearguard actions of male-solidarity movements in the United States. In the short term, it's clear that cultures that resist the rise in female power are losing out to those cultures that accept it, because the cultures that accept it are progressing farther faster on most fronts—health, economy, security, and technology, to name just a few. Only history will tell what the longer-term consequences may be.

PRIME CONDITIONS FOR WOMEN

Our observations have led us to believe that an increasing equalization of women's power occurs inexorably and "naturally" in modern service-oriented economies unless the authorities take specific steps to halt it, as happened in Afghanistan and is still happening in Saudi Arabia, Iran, and other strongly traditional countries. In most industrialized and modernized cultures, we're seeing a deliberate dismantling of gender-discriminatory legislation and the erosion of informal social practices that traditionally held women back, such as unequal pay for equal work, the glass ceiling, and men-only professional networking clubs and organizations. These discriminatory practices still exist, as a quick scan of male and female earnings statements would attest, but they are on the wane. And not necessarily because of altruistic tendencies on the part of the corporate elite. We are beginning to see proof that organizational cultures that promote women faster tend to do better: Avon and eBay, to name two well-known multinationals.

In the world of work, technology first made males' testosterone-driven muscle advantage less important, then irrelevant, and has now perhaps even made it a disadvantage. In the emerging networked economy of services and ideas, interpersonal and multitasking skills are becoming the must-haves, and they're female specialties.

At the darker end of the spectrum in the previously male-only sphere of deadly force—particularly terrorism—women are showing that here, too, they are willing to buck the "gentler sex" gender stereotype. The women fighters of Sri Lanka's Tamil Tigers have proved to be fearsome and ruthless, much to the fascination of the world media. In the Middle East, young women have carried out numerous suicide-bomb attacks. In Russia, the emergence of female Islamic suicide bombers has given rise to a new word: *shakhidka*, the female form of *shakhid*, meaning "the one who died for faith, a martyr, a witness."[1] Hostages who survived the school siege at Beslan spoke of several *shakhidki* (the plural) among the Chechen separatists who seized the school. The bombing of two airliners and a Moscow metro station were also pinned on such women.

WHO NEEDS A MAN?

Until very recently, biology itself was crucial in the division of roles between men and women. Only women could bear children, and only men could fertilize women. Men were bigger, physically stronger, and more aggressive, while women were smaller, physically suppler, and more conciliatory. Biology set men up for their basic job requirements in the business of life. A man's particular value was, first, his ability to protect his woman and children from wild animals and from other men, and, second, to secure resources in the form of shelter, food, and clothing so the family stayed healthy and its members were in good shape for the next round of procreation. These are the basic two levels of Abraham Maslow's Hierarchy of Needs (Safety and Physiological), and for much of human history, men have had a special role in protecting and providing. But no longer. Now in most of the developed world and even beyond, a woman doesn't necessarily need a man to protect her and provide for her. Police forces and civil society ensure basic protection, and the job market is enabling women to provide for themselves.

There are even indications that being a woman doesn't necessarily mean being smaller, lighter, and weaker anymore; all over the developed world, women are increasing in height, weight, and strength, and their sexual maturation is coming earlier. We hesitate to suggest that women's biology is taking its cues from their psychology and shaping them up—literally—to have more power. But it sure feels as if there's something more substantial happening than the effects of improved nutrition.

So it seems that what always appeared to be the "natural" division of roles and power between the sexes has been rolled back to the most basic elements of egg and sperm and the "under the hood" biochemistry of hormones and pheromones that goes with them. But even the power lines laid down over the centuries by the dictates of egg and sperm are undergoing major shifts. First, contraceptive science gave women control over their own fertility ("to breed or not to breed?"), effectively giving them the power to switch their sexual partner's fertility on and off. And now the various techniques of artificial insemination are giving women the option to be fertilized without a man being physically present. A woman can now get hold of the genetic inheritance she wants from a man's sperm without being obliged to take the man himself—she can buy the bun without having to buy the bakery, so to speak. In fact, sperm is now available as a commodity to be bought and sold, online or offline. It's a buyer's market, in which the buyers (women) can even specify the attributes they want the sperm to confer on their offspring, including skin color, hair color, and desired physical and mental attributes.

Science hasn't yet come up with a way of producing sperm without men, but why bother? Cloning technology may eventually make sperm unnecessary. Science has not yet made men obsolete, but it has gone a long way toward separating the message (genes) from the medium (the man). The potential impact of this development is vast; just think what happened to the music industry when MP3 technology separated the message (music) from the medium (CDs).

Regardless of legislation and social concerns, women are now potentially getting no-strings-attached options on men's last remaining biological trump card: their sperm. And regardless of whether individual women choose to exercise that option, the fact that they could do so is both a symbol and a manifestation of the shift in the balance of power between the sexes.

Going forward, this means that women with resources can choose to treat a male partner/spouse as an option rather than as a necessity. A woman with an education and reasonable financial resources doesn't need a man to protect her, or to provide for her, or to procreate with her. This is certainly the viewpoint of a number of the women with whom we spoke in researching this book. Cathy Lasowski, an American baby boomer based in Paris, is unmarried, but currently partnered. In her view, men are not so much a necessity as an optional add-on. "Most women want men," she says, "but they don't need them for the old-fashioned reasons: money, family, and children. You can have all those things (and often in a less complicated way) without a permanent man. Why? Because once you learn you can do it for yourself, the tradeoffs/compromises you are willing to make to find a man to 'take care of you' become unacceptable."

Cynthia Cyfert, twenty-four, a secretary living in Hoofddorp, the Netherlands, is even less inclined to consider men a life requirement, though she does concede that they have their uses: "Women need men today just like they need a hole in the head! Women are much more independent—but they still need someone to carry out the garbage!"

The men we spoke with were apt to believe that women do need men, but primarily for such basic biological functions as procreation and sex (neither of which requires a committed relationship), rather than because men fulfill any particular emotional needs a woman may have. In contrast, both men and women feel strongly that men need women to fulfill a variety of needs that men would be unable to fill any other way. "Men need women for love, support, sex, and comfort in a way that women don't need men," avers Cathy Lasowski. "Whereas women have friends, family, and media networks to connect to, most men simply don't seem to have that web of connection to keep them going." Elisabeth Cuming, a public policy student at the University of Chicago, agrees. "Men need women more than women need men," she says, "because women are as capable of getting by in the workplace as men are, but men are less capable of expressing their emotions or of forming close relationships with other men, so they need women to bring that aspect to their lives."

Cuming's point receives support from Niels den Otter, twenty-three, a sound designer and composer in Amsterdam. "We men need women," he says, "if only for the simple fact that women are better organized. Personally speaking, it's easier for me, when talking to one of my best girlfriends (and, no, I'm not gay), to be totally open and honest about my own so-called 'social network,' work, relationships with friends, parents, etc."

Tamilla Mamedova, a sophomore at Brown University who was raised in Turkey, thinks both sexes need each other and insists that that is part of human nature. But, she adds, "I also think that women are stronger than men in the sense that they can survive without men much better than men can live without women. I think the number and the success of women who live without men and raise children alone proves my point. . . . When there is divorce in a family, the woman is strong enough to survive on her own and start a new life, raise her children, etc. A man, however, needs a woman in his life and usually remarries because of such a need."

With the female's need for the male of the species increasingly tied to biological function rather than the provision of food, shelter, protection, or even comfort, modern man had better hope his procreational and sexual offerings aren't made obsolete anytime soon. The bad news: As the next chapter will show, his reliance on certain biological "truths" may be misplaced.

WHAT TO REMEMBER

1. Seismic social-psychological shifts are taking place between the sexes. These shifts are driven to a very large extent by the dynamic interaction of science, technology, and economics, and are magnified by the increasingly dominant media. In one way or another, most major societies today have to come to grips with big changes in the behavior of men and women.

2. The female's need for the male of the species is increasingly tied to biological function—to modern man's procreational and sexual offerings. Today men can feel belittled as sperm factories or sex objects, since so many of the other "advantages" of being male have been marginalized.

ME TARZAN, YOU JANE

THE BIOLOGY OF GENDER

Man is coarse and Man is plain;
Man is more or less insane;
Man's a ribald;
Man's a rake;
Man is Nature's sole mistake.

—Gilbert and Sullivan, *Princess Ida*

One of the must-see movies of summer 2004 was a giddy remake of the 1970s camp classic *The Stepford Wives*. Once a thriller that trumpeted the suffocating domestic masochism of the American housewife, the film had—three decades later—been remade for a different audience. This time, the whole affair was a comedy. And this time, it turned out that the brains behind Stepford's model village of submissive womanhood was none other than a disappointed wife. Bored with her unmanly, good-for-nothing husband, this enterprising woman had reassembled her mate as a perfect specimen of the alpha male. For some men watching, it must have seemed the final straw. Not only were they no longer in control; they weren't even up to the challenge of taking the reins and had to be biologically tampered with to make them resemble a real man.

But what would a "real man" consist of at the beginning of the twenty-first century? That's a question people have a lot of difficulty answering. They have a clear notion of what a "real man" was in the centuries and decades leading up to the 1950s, but after that point the image becomes fuzzier and more open to debate. Part of that comes down to the fact that men increasingly are being defined in relation to women, rather than vice versa. They know what women do and don't want them to be, to say, to do, but there's no real sense of their own agenda—or, at least, not of an agenda that doesn't take into account their desire to have sex with women, marry women, coexist peacefully with women, or simply escape attacks by women in today's politically correct culture.

NURTURE VS. NATURE

Not too long ago, man had a clearly defined role and was expected to act as he did because to do so was in his nature. He was born the hunter, the aggressor. It was his biological destiny to defend what was his and to control all he could. Then came the women's movement of the twentieth century, which, among many other consequences, had the effect of plunging modern societies into the debate over Nature vs. Nurture. What really set little Johnnie and Susie apart? people asked. Was he more likely to get into playground tussles and come home caked in mud because that's what nature intended—or was that a product of urgings, by his father and others, that he "be a man," that he take risks and not take nothin' off no one? And what about Susie? Did she spend her days sweetly rocking her dolls and enjoying pretend tea parties because that's what society expected of her—or were such behaviors hardwired into her brain?

For a while, it seemed as though proponents of the Nurture theory were winning the argument. Many of society's problems and inequities, they asserted, could be solved if we were to socialize our children differently. Get girls involved in competitive sports and encourage boys to explore their "gentler sides," they said, and the world would be a better place. And, while we're at it, let's get fathers to communicate their feelings and become fully invested in the nurturing and care of children, and let's get mothers to derive their sense of worth from career rather than family. This worked for some people, but for others the pressure to conform to new and, in the view of some, "unnatural" expectations led to alienation and dissatisfaction.

So now we're seeing the pendulum swing the other way.

Where once ideologues and professionals tried to persuade us that there was no essential difference between the male and female of the species, the last few years have seen the resurgence of certain biological "truths" and the reemergence of the idea that gender differences are innate, not learned. Where once the so-called thinking classes dismissed masculinity and femininity as a mirage of social construction, now we demand a genetic explanation for everything.

Genes, it is now argued, explain why certain people are prone to violence, why Johnny prefers Scott to Susie, why J. Lo can't seem to stay married, and maybe even why women are more apt to be religious than men.

And don't even think of blaming the guy next door for breaking his girlfriend's heart. It's not his fault; it's in his genes. A recent study conducted by Rutgers University in New Jersey suggests that even the drive for romance has biological roots. Falling in love, according to Rutgers anthropologist Helen Fisher, involves three phases, each of which entails different hormones. The first stage of love is lust, driven by the sex hormones testosterone and estrogen. Then comes attraction, the love-struck phase when people lose their appetites and their sleep, and spend hours staring out the window. This stage involves a group of neurotransmitters called monoamines: dopamine (which is also activated by cocaine and nicotine) and norepinephrine, a crucial love chemical and often the cause of temporary insanity. (That explains a whole lot.) The final stage, attachment, is vital for any relationship to last. Commitment-phobes, apparently, get stuck on stage two.[1]

So, once again, we get to pin our differences, foibles, and fabulousness on our genetic blueprints—meaning we get to blame Mom *and* Dad for all our problems, rather than just Mom. Only now, there's a difference. **Whereas earlier attempts to reduce the genders to their biological drives used to be used primarily to rationalize male superiority—centered on how nature favors the go-getting, hunter-gathering man over his meek, loyal homemaker of a wife—this new biological determinism does not come down quite so clearly on the side of man.**

WHY BIGGER ISN'T ALWAYS BETTER

It would be difficult to refute the notion that there are some things the male animal does better. Think football, for example, or tennis, where the sexes rarely play against one another because the guys would almost invariably win hands down. After all, man's genetic inheritance as a powerful hunter-gatherer took millions of years to evolve. Even though girls reach physical maturity earlier, after puberty boys have larger hearts, skeletal muscles, and lung capacity, have lower resting heart rates, and are capable of longer bouts of physical exertion than are girls.[2]

The renowned anthropologist Desmond Morris traces many of the differences between the modern male and female to their different roles within the primeval division of labor. While the guys were out hunting for food, women were left looking after the young. As a result, males became more muscular. On average, they were 30 percent stronger, 10 percent heavier, and 7 percent taller than the typical female. They had better visual acuity and a more highly developed urge to take risks and to engage in prolonged, single-minded activities. Coming down firmly on the side of Nature, Morris theorizes, "Evolution has ensured we have a slightly different outlook on life and this difference starts early. It can be seen in kindergarten and it is not due to the way we treat our offspring, but to what is in their genes."[3]

Many of those skills developed in the primeval world still translate in modern-day society. Take map-reading, for instance: According to recent research from the Gestalt Institute in Paris, men make better map readers because as hunter-gatherers they needed to be able to find their way home. The problem for men is that evolution has moved more slowly than culture and the modern world. Man's physical prowess and his facility for backbreaking manual labor, say his scientific critics, might be excellently suited to a world that depended on brute force. But in a society where weapons make physical strength irrelevant and the office makes interpersonal skills more important, men are simply ill equipped for the modern age.

The female human, on the other hand, is finding that her genetic inheritance equips her better for modern life than her predecessors could ever have imagined. While the guys were out attempting to spear the family dinner, the primeval female was sitting at home being caring and nurturing, learning to prioritize her workload and practicing verbal communication. "We know that females are much more fluent verbally," says Morris. "This is not a vague observation—it is a conclusion based on studies of brain scans when males and females are given the same verbal tasks. When trying to solve verbal problems, females employ a much more extensive region of the brain than do men. There is a fundamental, biological difference in the way in which women tackle verbal communications. If this inherent skill is combined with another inborn quality—a more-caring, nurturing temperament—it is obvious that certain key areas of social life should be dominated not by men, as in the past, but by women."[4]

Sense of hearing is one area in which women are more advanced, likely because of their role as nurturer. Women's hearing is more than twice as acute as men's; they're 2.3 times better at identifying faint sounds and six times more likely to sing in tune than men.[5]

Women's sense of touch, too, is more developed. A woman has ten times more skin receptors, sensitive to contact, and oxytocin and prolactin, the hormones of attachment, increase her need to touch and to be touched.[6] Not only do men have fewer touch receptors, they also take in less visual information and their sense of smell is less well developed. It turns out that they really may not notice the horrid odors emanating from the kitchen trash. Because of male biological programming, a man is also more likely to focus on the large space outside rather than on such minutiae (and causes of marital discord) as socks left on the stairs.[7]

Granted, the average male's brain is slightly bigger than the average female's. The reality is that brain size isn't as important as what you do with it. (Sound familiar?) For complex tasks, males tend to use the left hemisphere of the cerebrum. Females, on the other hand, use both sides more often. The two hemispheres of the brain are more symmetrical in females than in males, a symmetry that may improve communication between the sides of the brain and lead to enhanced verbal expressiveness.[8] Moreover, men have fewer electrical connections between the brain's left and right hemispheres, so the flow of information between the two sides is restricted. Because the thought process for emotion is in the right hemisphere while the brain's speech center is on the left, it is harder for men to articulate emotion. Even at preschool age, studies have shown that small girls talk more than three times as long as do boys. The instinct endures into adulthood. Women talk on average for twenty minutes per phone call, while men only last for six.[9]

The fact that women are so handy to have around may explain why they live so long after they become unable to procreate—when a strictly evolutionary approach would seem to suggest they have outlived their usefulness. Since females of most other species continue to reproduce into old age, yesterday's biologists dismissed the contributions of barren postmenopausal women. Once again, however, the new biological determinists are looking at the evidence in a new light. Older women, according to an emerging consensus among researchers, increase their fitness more effectively through care of grandchildren than through their own direct reproduction. Women, in other words, do not stop being useful to the survival of the species in their old age; rather, menopause frees them from their own childbearing to care for grandchildren.[10]

In spring 2004, some Finnish researchers published a paper in *Nature* that showed evidence of a relationship between the survival of a grandparent and good child-rearing. By examining the family histories of 3,000 women in Finland and Canada during the eighteenth and nineteenth centuries, the researchers were able to discover that older grannies tended to have more and longer-lived grandchildren. Evolution, it seems, favors families with grandmothers.[11] So women aren't irreplaceable just as mothers but also as grandmothers. And what of men? Biologically speaking, grandfathers are worth zip. Though that "pull my finger" trick can be a real gas.

BLURRING BOUNDARIES

If the new biological determinism denigrates the modern man at the expense of his more sensitive other half, even worse for men is the slow deconstruction of the entire biological basis of his masculinity. Consider a newly sexy subject, brain research: Much more important

ANIMALS GONE WILD,
OR, WOULD SOMEONE PLEASE GET
THAT MOLE OFF MY ANKLE?

People looking to win an argument involving Nature vs. Nurture oftentimes look to the animal kingdom for backup. "Men aren't meant to have sex with men," they bluster, "you never see homosexuality in the wild!" Or "The female of the species tends her nest, while the male sows his seed. It's just plain Nature!" Turns out, things aren't quite so clear-cut. Here are some examples that might win you a few arguments—or get you into a few bar fights.

- Female blue fairy wrens are highly promiscuous; they sneak off regularly at night to have sex with passing lovers.[12]
- About 8 percent of domestic rams are gay, according to a new study published in *Endocrinology*. The study found not only that certain groups of cells differ between the sexes in a part of the sheep brain controlling sexual behavior, but also that brain anatomy and hormone production may decide whether adult rams prefer other rams over ewes.[13]
- Male gerbils are among the most devoted fathers in the animal kingdom, but only after they get their libidinous energy out of their systems. Research from McMaster University in Canada reveals that, since gerbil couples only have a small amount of time after the births of their offspring in which to mate, the males are driven to mount their partners as many as 500 times.[14]
- In the animal kingdom, it is not uncommon for the female to be in control of sex, while avoiding the responsibilities of rearing the offspring.
- Giant Australian cuttlefish enjoy threesomes, even orgies, with the females choosing which male or males to copulate with.[15]
- In some reptile species, such as the two varieties of Australian lizard, the Bynoe's gecko and the Grey's skink, there are no males.[16]

than the old binary opposition between masculinity and femininity, say many of the new researchers, is the distinction between two different kinds of brains. In his recent book, *The Essential Difference: Men, Women, and the Extreme Male Brain*, Dr. Simon Baron-Cohen of the University of Cambridge focuses on two general varieties of brain: the systematizing kind and the empathizing kind.[17]

Systematizing brains, according to Baron-Cohen, have the ability to organize data and use it in different ways; empathizing brains, on the other hand, are better at being sensitive to other people's feelings and needs, and at responding appropriately. Some lucky people have both. Baron-Cohen labels people with autism, who can't relate well to others emotionally, as having an oversystematized, "extreme male" brain. But here is the rub: While it is entirely valid to talk about "male" and "female" brains, Baron-Cohen concludes, those are simply labels for different personality types that can attach to either sex—a female can perfectly well be judged to have a "male" brain, and vice versa.[18]

Another example of the new biological blurring: Contrary to popular belief, testosterone is not the exclusive province of men and (artificially enhanced) butch East German female athletes from the 1980s. What do we know about testosterone? That this hormone was first isolated relatively late, in 1935. That it is the ultimate biological foundation of reproductive behavior. That testosterone, and hence sperm production and fertility, increases during sex in men who want to become dads.[19] That it also serves to make men more attractive to mosquitoes.[20] And that testosterone levels decrease in men in response to sounds of an infant's cries or when men hold or comfort their own child.[21]

We also now know that the lives of many women, as well as men, are ruled by testosterone. The hormonal disorder that makes women bearded or mustachioed is more common than among ambitious athletes, having been found to occur in almost 7 percent of women. Women with the syndrome tend to produce about twice as much testosterone as other women.[22] Moreover, scientists are increasingly discovering connections between women's testosterone levels and their behavior. According to research from the University of Auckland, for example, behaviorally dominant women simply have more testosterone than average, and they produce more sons as a result.[23]

University of Auckland researcher Valerie Grant speculates that high testosterone levels somehow prime developing eggs to be receptive to fertilization by Y sperm, and low testosterone primes them for X sperm. Instead of the old view that it is the father who is responsible for determining the sex of the offspring, Grant argues that she can tell on the basis of a woman's personality whether she is more likely to have a boy or a girl. These theories have been supported to some extent by work carried out by John Manning at Liverpool University in the United Kingdom, whose researchers reported in 2002 that both women and men have more sons if they have a long ring finger compared with their index finger. What can the connection possibly be with finger length? Manning's argument is that a long ring finger is linked to high testosterone levels in the womb.[24]

As further evidence that women may play a greater role than previously thought in determining their offspring's sex, recent research in Europe and the United States has shown that more girls than boys are born to single mothers, a phenomenon also cited by Charles Darwin in *The Descent of Man*. The reason for this phenomenon is not yet known, though some posit that noncohabitating women are most likely to have sex on the day of ovulation, which has been shown to be more likely to produce girls.[25]

But what about sperm competition? Surely, this is the most distinctive and elementary kind of male go-getting: the race to the top. The problem is that new research suggests otherwise. Rather than waiting meekly for the men to fight it out, it turns out, women might have been actively egging on sperm competition all along. The research has discovered millions of tiny crypts within women's vaginal walls, designed to facilitate the contest. Sperm from multiple partners may be stored for up to seven days before being released in a competitive swim-off for the egg.[26] Even that staple of testosterone-fueled male aggression, the idea that men are programmed by their genes to be more competitive than women, has come under assault. Evolutionary psychologists, for example, are now arguing that anorexia might be a dysfunctional form of competition among women for the attentions of men.[27]

SOMETIMES IT'S HARD TO BE A MAN

At the beginning of the twenty-first century, then, the biological superiority of the male of the human species is being called into question. Worse, much of what's considered unique to man's essential biology is being blamed for making men innately violent, promiscuous, and aggressively competitive—not necessarily the traits that go over best in civilized society, and certainly not the traits that lead to a long and healthy life. Consider the following evidence:

- Women on average live eight to ten years longer than men, and the gap is still growing.[28]
- Testicular cancer increased 50 percent between 1970 and 1993 throughout the industrialized world, and the incidence of deformities such as undescended testicles, split penises, and ambiguous genitalia appears to be increasing. Testicular volume may also be declining.[29]
- At the age of thirty, the modern male is fifteen times more accident prone than the modern female.[30]
- Men are three to four times more likely than women to become hyperactive, autistic, or dyslexic, to develop Tourette's syndrome, and to be klutzy. Alcoholism, diabetes, lung cancer, and suicide also are far more prevalent among men.[31]
- Men are ten times more likely than women to commit murder.[32]

Neither, when it comes to healthy living, are men a model of good sense. Far from the stereotype of the gym-going, health-supplement-popping New Man, a report published in the *American Journal of Public Health* in 2003 found that American males of every age have poorer health and a higher risk of mortality than do women. The modern American man, it turns out, is more likely to smoke cigarettes and twice as likely to consume five or more alcoholic drinks in one day.[33]

And then there's the question of sperm—or, more specifically, what the heck is happening to it. Over the previous half century, scientists have reported severe declines in sperm counts in the United States and Europe.[34] In the early 1990s, Danish researchers who analyzed the medical records of 15,000 European men reported a 42 percent decline in sperm counts between 1938 and 1990.[35] This was corroborated by a study at a Parisian sperm bank in 1995. In 1997, Finnish scientists at Helsinki University concluded that the proportion of men producing "normal" sperm had decreased from 56.4 percent in 1981 to only 26.9 percent in 1991.[36]

Why does this matter? After all, every time a man has sex, he produces enough sperm to impregnate every woman in Europe.[37] It only takes one sperm that makes the journey unscathed to fertilize a female's egg. But a gradual decline in volume and sperm quality pushes some men who were hovering on the margins into infertility. Some scientists blame the decline on pesticides and other chemicals in the environment. Others blame the same lifestyle factors that contribute to male ill health: obesity, lack of exercise, or too much driving.[38] And don't forget the ever popular "tighty whities" theory: According to some, men's underwear are the culprits behind reduced sperm counts. And that theory would seem to be bolstered by an article in the British medical journal *The Lancet*, which reports on a Dutch study that concluded that men who wear tight-fitting underwear produce 50 percent less sperm than do men who wear loose-fitting underwear.[39] Which is not to say that it's necessarily a bad thing if the guys who wear ultra-tight black thongs to the beach don't reproduce.

WHY CAN'T A MAN BE MORE LIKE A WOMAN?

> Why can't a woman be more like a man?
> Men are so honest, so thoroughly square;
> Eternally noble, historically fair.
>
> —Professor Henry Higgins, *My Fair Lady*

The biological equivalent of the tale of the birds and the bees has now been written, and it doesn't have a happy ending for the male of the species: "Once upon a time, there was an XX chromosome, the default state of all human beings. Everything was sweetness and light, until the parasitical Y chromosome decided to go its own way. Y caused trouble for a while, before it burned itself out and made itself redundant."

Males, it turns out, are the real "second sex," while females are the "standard issue" human beings. Sperm carry either a Y or an X chromosome, and female eggs only carry an X. XX combinations become females; XYs become males. When an X sperm meets the egg, twenty-three pairs of chromosomes merge and swap genes. If a Y sperm fertilizes the egg, the twenty-third chromosome becomes an awkward XY union, with the Y fobbing off most of its tasks onto the female's X.[40] To an age jaded by machismo and its effects, the fact is that human embryos seem to be female by default, with the Y chromosome a mere genetic malfunction that happens to make the default female body develop into a specialized male one.[41]

Biology often reflects the prejudices of the age. **But myth-making aside, the problem for men is that the Y chromosome is far from enjoying robust health. In the first place, Y is now considered an ineffectual chromosome because it carries very few genes—only a few dozen, compared with the approximately 1,500 carried by the X. Worse, since the Y started evolving away from the X some 300 million years ago, it has left more and more of its former duties to its partner. In plain language, the Y chromosome got lazy sponging off the more industrious X, and is now in danger of being given its marching orders.[42]**

In his book *Adam's Curse: A Future Without Men*, the science writer Brian Sykes hypothesizes that the Y chromosome—the biological anvil of manhood—is progressively being destroyed, and that, within a few thousand generations, men will disappear altogether. "The human Y chromosome," he warns, "is crumbling before our very eyes." Sykes argues that because the Y chromosome is wearing out, soon there will be no genetic instructional manual left to tell boys how to be boys. When that happens, he claims, the girls will inherit the earth.[43] (Presumably, meek girls will be able to double dip.)

In a similar vein, the British geneticist Steve Jones begins his book *Y: The Descent of Men*, with the following abject epitaph to the idea of male superiority: "Ejaculate," he begins, "if you are so minded and equipped, into a glass of chilled Perrier. There you will see a formless object, but look hard enough—or at least so eighteenth-century biologists believed—and a baby appears: the male's gift to the female, whose only job is to incubate the child produced with so much labor by her mate. So central seemed a husband's role that his wife was a mere seedbed, a step below him in society, in the household, and, most of all, in herself. Foolish of course, and quite wrong, for biology proves that man, and not woman, is the second sex."[44]

"Manhood," Jones gloomily informs his readers, "is in full retreat." The Y chromosome is the "most decayed, redundant and parasitic" of genetic structures, a mere interloper that inveigles its way into the female genetic line and forces egg cells to produce Y-infused offspring. Adding injury to insult, a recent edition of the *British Med-*

ical Journal even went as far as to identify the Y chromosome in colorful terms as no less than "a biological injury."[45]

But the most ominous trend lies deep within the science departments of our best universities, where teams of experts are conspiring to put men out of their evolutionary job. Some of the most striking work has been done in the field of parthenogenesis, a form of reproduction that takes place without the help of a male and is common elsewhere in the natural world. In April 2004, in the first-ever demonstration of how a mammal might produce without a male, a team of scientists from Tokyo University of Agriculture published a paper in *Nature* announcing the birth of a mouse with two mothers—achieved by mixing two sets of female genes inside an egg, with no need for either sperm or male chromosomes. As yet, the procedure is much too finicky to be used in human reproduction: about 600 mouse eggs were used in the experiment, and only two live mice were born. Nevertheless, the Japanese work is a landmark in reproductive biology, and might be the first portent of the coming virgin birth among humans. Eggs, for example, might simply be taken from two women and united in the laboratory before being implanted back into one of the women. The genetic inheritance of each female would contribute to the genetic makeup of the child, and the absence of Y would result in a world full of daughters. As yet, it is worth noting, there are no legal prohibitions against the practice.[46]

There are, however, a few stirrings of a reproductive pushback on men's behalf. For a long time now, humble modern man has been schlepping along to prenatal classes in the hope of understanding more about the experience of childbirth. But what if he could get pregnant himself? In 2003, the science of male pregnancy became a real possibility when a thirty-year-old woman delivered a healthy baby after an ectopic pregnancy—a pregnancy in which the fetus develops outside the uterus. If a fetus does not need a womb, scientists are thinking, it eventually may not need a woman.[47]

That same year, scientists announced they might be able to develop eggs and sperm from a human male. As part of the research, conducted separately by scientists in Japan and the United States, both eggs and sperm were developed outside the body for the first time. Hailed as the next revolution in in vitro fertilization (IVF), the research, which used stem-cell embryos from mice, could conceivably be applied to humans, with huge implications for reproductive technology and regenerative medicine. The most obvious application would be to treat infertile women who cannot produce eggs suitable for IVF, or men who cannot produce sperm. But male embryonic stem cells can be turned into eggs as well as sperm, so—at least in theory—the research suggests that two men could both be biological parents of a child with the help of a surrogate mother.

RISE OF THE TOY BOY

As the biological necessity of the male in modern times begins to be called into question, we're also seeing a shift in the attributes women seek in their male partners. A commonly held notion is that what a modern woman really wants—even if she is loath to admit it—is a "real man," a man who has more in common with his ancestors' cave-dwelling days than with couture, cosmetics, or communication of feelings. For his part, modern man wants a nubile woman capable of satisfying his lusts and bearing his children. Sounds like a perfect match—in theory. The reality shows a bit more of a disconnect in terms of what he wants and she wants.

Part of the problem comes down to a simple matter of age. Whereas teenage boys rate a woman five years older than themselves as the perfect partner, by the time men reach sixty they're convinced their perfect mate is around fifteen years younger than they are.[48] All of which is a shame, really, because their prospective dates are increasingly looking in the direction of younger men. And recent scientific study suggests they might be right to do so.

New research by Dr. Narendra Singh at the University of Washington confirms what scientists have long suspected: that sperm deteriorates in both quality and quantity in men over thirty-five. So at a time when fertility treatments are extending women's reproductive lives into their fifties, and sometimes even beyond, men's reproductive longevity is beginning to look a little shaky.[49] Could it be that Madonna and Demi have their heads screwed on right, after all?

And there is another biological explanation for the rise of the toy boy. The anthropologist Desmond Morris, for example, argues that the shift toward younger men reflects women's increasing dominance in wider society. "Smooth-skinned and feminized looks are characteristics of youth," he argues. "It's possible these looks stimulate not only sexual but also maternal feelings. If women want to be more dominant, they will look for a little-boy face."[50]

The oft-quoted statistic that men reach their sexual peak at nineteen and women at thirty gives yet another clue to women's biological urge to take younger lovers. Although it's true that females, unlike males, are destined to become infertile, older women do not lose their libidos as catastrophically as do older men, who see their sexual desire take a nosedive as soon as they hit their forties.[51] Hence the thriving market for Viagra and its competitors.

The willingness of some men to step out of the gilded cage of stiff-upper-lipped masculinity and become more feminized, then, might have good cause. Recently, the Darwinian theory of sexual selection—that discerning females choose healthy, handsome, sexually aggressive mates who are most likely to succeed, and that males compete for status deemed attractive by women—has been knocked off its Victorian pedestal. Far from being biologically programmed to want a caveman, it seems, the modern woman is increasingly opting for a gentler, more effeminate man.

At the end of 2002, research psychologists from the University of St. Andrews in Scotland attempted to create the perfect male face. Volunteer men were picked from the local student population, and thirty-four female "raters" with an average age of twenty were asked to rate various aspects of the men's images. The perfect man turned out to have large, expressive eyes set in a smooth-skinned symmetrical face, a straight nose, and a rounded hair and jaw line. Although the researchers admit their perfect male looks slightly girlish, their conclusion is that modern women want caring feminine traits rather than more macho markings. Bearded men, and others with features that suggest they are unlikely to wash up or change a baby, can forget it.[52]

WHAT TO REMEMBER

1. There are some immutable laws of science that cannot be ignored, and the potential implications of the weakened Y chromosome go well beyond the metaphorical. The biological evolution of men may be an irrelevance to most people in this century, but the continued existence of men still matters to everyone.

2. Starting from the premise that seismic social-psychological shifts taking place between the sexes are driven to a very large extent by the interaction of science, technology, and economics, and are magnified by the media, if we focus exclusively on the science—as we do in this chapter—and put "sex" to one side, all of the other gender attributes seem increasingly irrelevant in a postindustrial society. This is probably why the "sexual" in "metrosexual" made the term so media worthy, and opened up much broader discussions about men and their futures.

3

WHAT IS MASCULINITY?

At about the time men started to get in touch with their feminine sides, hammer sales around the world began to drop off. At first, hardware-store owners didn't think much of it. They chalked up the downturn to the cyclical economic trends that always affect retail sales and waited for things to get better. Unfortunately, things didn't get better—they got worse. Two years turned into four and four into eight. Now, some thirty years later, hammer warehouses from Bombay to Boston hold nothing but dust and broken dreams. Men, it seems, have lost the art of swinging a hammer.

—Introduction to *How to Mow the Lawn: The Lost Art of Being a Man*[1]

While women were giggling triumphantly at the remake of *The Stepford Wives*, men were queuing up—with or without their offspring—to watch a boyish kind of superhero.

As Peter Parker in *Spider-Man 2*, Tobey Maguire not only looks like a
schoolboy, he positively oozes sweetness, good manners, and the ability to save old ladies from certain death. In short, Maguire's Spider-
Man is the perfect embodiment of what Americans have come to call
emo man—nerdy, self-critical, and constantly soul searching. America, meet the New Man!

At the beginning of the twenty-first century, biology and science
are not the only terrain on which masculinity seems to be fighting a
losing battle. Society, too, is doing its bit to topple traditional ideas of
what masculinity should be. While physiological differences between
the sexes are real, and impossible to attribute to the vagaries of cultural fashion, they cannot really explain what masculinity is and why it
changes over time. For that, we need to take the temperature of global
society: its culture, its media, and its politics.

Only relatively recently has the social construction of masculinity
become the subject of respectable academic research. Because social
scientists have historically taken men to be the "normal" subjects of
research, gender has only been taken into account when women are
the objects of inquiry. Though the word "masculine" as a synonym for
"male" is ancient (Chaucer used it in the fourteenth century), the
terms "masculinity," "masculinize," and "masculinism" came into
common parlance in English only in the last two decades of the nineteenth century.[2]

MASCULINITY AS POWER

**Once we have factored in society and culture, it becomes easier
to see how our ideas about masculinity evolve along with
changes in the social and cultural fabric. Man as a rugged piece
of powerful corporeality, it is hardly surprising, dates from a
time when brute physical labor by the mass of the population
was necessary. Nineteenth-century man, says the historian Anthony Rotundo, "was made to labour." Before the nineteenth
century, he continues, "family and community established a
man's identity, but during the nineteenth century, a man's work,
or labour, became vital to self-definition: if a man was without
'business' he was less than a man."[3]**

In his latest book, *From Chivalry to Terrorism*, Leo Braudy, a professor of English at the University of Southern California, explores

the conscious and unconscious ways in which traditional masculinity has been defined by military and warrior virtue. Beginning with codes of honor in the chivalrous Middle Ages and ending in our age of global terrorism and limited war, Braudy shows how our perceptions and images of masculinity have changed in relation to major wars, advances in military technology, and changing attitudes toward both sexuality and citizenship.[4] This is especially interesting in our current war-torn times.

As recently as 1971, affronts to masculine pride could precipitate international belligerence and even war. Gender, it is well known, was a factor in the 1971 Indo-Pakistan war, in which Indira Gandhi, India's female leader, played a key role. As president of Pakistan, Yahya Khan admitted he would have reacted less violently in the conflict with India had a male headed the Indian government. "If that woman Indira Gandhi thinks she is going to cow me down," he was quoted as saying, "I refuse to take it."[5]

If "warrior virtue" has defined traditional masculinity, how will such masculine notions be affected by the growing presence of women in the armed forces? And, indeed, how will traditional notions of masculinity and femininity be changed by the active participation of women soldiers in the stomach-turning abuse that took place at Iraq's Abu Ghraib prison in 2004? The world was repulsed by the images of Iraqi prisoners being degraded, but our revulsion was made all the more strong by the presence of women—smiling, taunting young women—in the photos. These images went against everything we had come to believe about women in the modern era. Yes, women are equal to men, we said. Yes, they can be every bit as ambitious and hard-driving and even aggressive. But, deep down, we still stuck by the notion that women at their very base are more sensitive, more nurturing, more humane. That women, even in the high-testosterone environment of the military in time of war, could be capable of such wanton abuse stunned us, sickened us—and, perhaps most of all, frightened us by providing a glimpse of what women have the capacity to become.

The political essayist and social critic Barbara Ehrenreich wrote of her heartbreak at seeing the photos of Specialist Megan Ambuhl, Private First Class Lynndie England, and Specialist Sabrina Harman at Abu Ghraib. "A certain kind of feminism, or perhaps I should say a certain kind of feminist naiveté, died in Abu Ghraib," she wrote on alternanet.org.

It was a feminism that saw men as the perpetual perpetrators, women as the perpetual victims and male sexual violence against women as the root of all injustice. Rape has repeatedly been an instrument of war and, to some feminists, it was beginning to look as if war was an extension of rape. There seemed to be at least some evidence that male sexual sadism was connected to our species' tragic propensity for violence. That was before we had seen female sexual sadism in action.

Where once women were deemed by many to be morally superior to men, now we've learned that women, when placed in the same circumstances and under the same level of peer pressure, may display every bit as much inhumanity. One of the many questions that remains from these incidents and their public exposure is to what degree, if any, the events at Abu Ghraib will cause us to adjust our notion of what is and isn't acceptable, not only on the part of women, but also on the part of men in time of war. Just as the plight of female hostages is felt more keenly by some, so, too, may we change our standards of what is appropriate in war when women are among the combatants.

For now, certainly compared with the pre-Vietnam era, we can be certain that men who go to war are taking with them far more mixed messages as to their expected role. Even in the heat of battle, society is putting limits on masculinity and how it can be expressed.

THE DEMISE OF THE MALE BREADWINNER

Given that the DNA of masculinity is in our society as well as our genes, what social explanations can we think of for its changing face? In most advanced industrial countries, the story starts not with war and conflict, but with the economics of the workplace. Households in which the man is the sole breadwinner—what used to be called the head of the household—are quickly becoming the exception rather than the norm.

Consider Australia. According to figures released by the Australian Bureau of Statistics, the labor force participation rate for married women aged fifteen to sixty-four increased from 34 percent in 1968 to 63 percent in 1998. Men, on the other hand, are leaving the world of stable, full-time employment in droves. Between 1988 and 1997, the proportion of Australian men employed on a full-time, "permanent" basis decreased from 88 to 79 percent, while the proportion of men employed on a casual basis doubled, from 11 to 21 percent.[6]

In the United Kingdom, too, household partnerships are in a state of flux. In 1980, around half of British wives and husbands agreed that a husband's job is to earn the money, whereas a wife's job is to look after the home and family. By 1994, the proportion had dropped to around a quarter.[7] Among British youth, there's a significant gender gap in this regard, with just 64 percent of boys but 82 percent of girls disagreeing with that same statement when surveyed in 2001. Similarly, 87 percent of girls and 76 percent of boys believed there was "no reason why men can't be nurses and women can't be airline pilots." On the other hand, certain behavioral traits are stubbornly immune to social change. Of the 569 eleven- to sixteen-year-olds polled about their hopes for a future career, girls were most likely to choose to become actors, designers, teachers, hairdressers, and travel industry staff, while boys opted to work in fields such as sports, music, graphic design, computing, Web design, and engineering, and in the police, fire, and armed services.[8]

The trouble is that often the line between nature, nurture, and culture is not easy to draw. Research recently published in the *Journal for the Scientific Study of Religion*, for instance, showed that women are more religious than men throughout the world. But why? Rodney Stark, the University of Washington sociologist who compiled the international research, argues that the answer is mainly biological. Men's genetic inheritance predisposes them to risky behavior, and they are less likely to embrace the religious concept of delayed gratification. Stark and Alan S. Miller of Hokkaido University in Japan say there is mounting evidence that physiological reasons may explain some of the differences. But that is not the only potential explanation. Another sociologist, Michael Kimmel of the State University of New York at Stony Brook, argues that these gender differences have less to do with genetics than with how religion is perceived in different cultures. In the United States, he believes, religious teachings to turn the other cheek and be nice do not fit with prevailing ideas about masculinity. "Real men don't rely on a crutch. Real men are men of action. Real men fight," Kimmel argues. "Church life is seen as sissifying."[9]

How men are responding to their reduced role as primary breadwinner may well have to do with to what extent that role is biological rather than learned. In either case, we can be certain that men who equate the role of breadwinner with their self-worth are likely to be dissatisfied with any role that they—or others—perceive as diminished. It doesn't take a great leap of imagination to turn Kimmel's words to the topic of men at work: "Real men don't rely on a crutch. Real men are men of action. Real men support their families. Being anything other than the primary breadwinner is seen as sissifying."

THE IRRESISTIBLE RISE OF FRAGRANT MAN

That so many men have come to not only accept but even embrace the notion of shared financial responsibility with their wives and partners suggests that today's concept of masculinity has shifted to accommodate this new reality. It has also mutated to reflect the shift from physical labor to white-collar jobs. Simply put, as increasing numbers of men began to make their livings using their heads rather than their hands, and as culture and media began to respond to the newly won independence of women, our ideas about masculinity have changed accordingly. And that has affected not only how men think and behave, but also how they look.

Very slowly, men who were previously averse to spending time and money on their appearance began to think again. In the United States, day spas and salons aimed at men began to appear, offering an extensive selection of relaxation and grooming treatments and services, and promising to give golf a run for its money as the networking hubs of the future. In a 2003 poll of American men, 89 percent agreed that grooming is essential in the business world. Nearly half—49 percent—said there is nothing wrong with a man getting a facial or manicure.[10] Quite a shift from the days of John Wayne and Steve McQueen.

The rise of fragrant man is not confined to America, by any means. Even men from the traditionally macho culture of Spain are now more interested in the health and image benefits personal care products offer. Recent surveys point out that almost 90 percent of Spanish men believe good grooming is essential to success in the business world. Health and beauty professionals are experiencing steady growth—particularly among young, urban, heterosexual men—in demand for cosmetic services, which had previously been all but confined to the gay community. Industry sources place the total market value of male-grooming products in Spain in the area of €100 million.[11] The Germans are even more enthusiastic: Total turnover in the men's cosmetics market in that country in 2003 was €648 million.[12]

This is not to say that the "feminization" of men has implications only for the health and beauty industry. Far from it. Many of those men who are beginning to realize it's okay to step outside once-rigid gender boundaries are looking around to see what else they've been missing. Some are even beginning to rethink their roles in that most feminine of bastions: the wedding. Traditional man was not a great wedding planner, seeing it as his sole responsibility to turn up, preferably sober, on the big day. Modern man, in contrast, isn't just having input on menus and flowers, he's also beginning to demand his fair share of the gift registry. And retailers are responding. In Canada, for example, the tableware giant Waterford-Wedgwood recently introduced a line of merchandise specifically targeted at men—and not only to cater to the market in gay marriages.[13] A recent survey by Sears, Roebuck and Co. found that 82 percent of grooms have an equal say in the registry process, and "couple showers" are beginning to replace bridal showers in many places.

BLAME IT ON DONAHUE

A pioneer of the daytime TV talk-show format, Phil Donahue brought sensitive and intelligent discussion to local airwaves (in Dayton, Ohio) as far back as 1967 and began reaching a national audience in the mid-1970s. Donahue was a self-professed feminist who didn't flinch from talking openly about such personal issues as women's health, religion, and sexuality. He is described in the St. James Encyclopedia of Popular Culture as being among the first television hosts "to treat the female television viewer as an intelligent, active, and aware participant"—a stance that "challenged programmers wedded to the conviction that women would only watch soap operas and cookery demonstrations."[14]

Beyond generating big ratings for his network (at least until he started getting clobbered by that upstart Oprah Something-or-other), Phil Donahue gave women a glimpse of the "alternative man." A man who was sensitive and emotive. Intelligent and informed. Caring, yet passionate about his politics and about making the world a fairer place. Suddenly, the notion that husbands had no choice but to be monosyllabic at the dinner table was called into question. If Phil could talk about his feelings, well, damn it, so could Stan and Larry and Joe! Well, hell, just what would be so wrong about these guys beginning to act a bit more like . . . women?

And then along came Alan Alda. On the air from 1972 till 1983, the legendary TV show *M*A*S*H* starred Alda as Benjamin Franklin "Hawkeye" Pierce, a skirt-chasing, gin-swilling comic surgeon who, over the course of the series, developed into a prototype of the sensitive New Age man. Both Alda and Pierce truly cared about women and about righting social inequities. This was reflected in Alda's other work and also in the later years of *M*A*S*H* (it didn't hurt that Alda was one of the show's executive producers). Alda was one of the first leading men to pursue work in films that challenged gender conventions. In *The Seduction of Joe Tynan*, for instance, his character grapples with such traditionally female issues as how to balance work and family. That movie also was Alda's first effort as a screenwriter.

Phil Donahue and Alan Alda marked a real shift in the notion of who men are and what women should expect of them. While they each had legions of fans, they were also loathed and resented by many men—and women—for turning men into sensitive creatures who required special handling. Throwing fuel on the fire, they were both married to strong-willed, feminist women, Arlene Alda and *That Girl*'s Marlo Thomas; Thomas, in particular, took flak as the Hillary Clinton of her day—outspoken, unapologetically liberal, and utterly unafraid of taking on male opponents with conviction and gusto. Together, these men marked the beginning of the end of the "real men don't cry" ethos. Next thing you knew, average Joes were ordering quiche at the local diner.

GIRLIE MAN, GO HOME!

With all the money modern man has begun to spend on pampering and coiffing himself, and with all the talk about men "finding themselves" and "exploring their feminine sides" (or, even worse, their "inner child"), we might be forgiven for thinking that traditional masculinity has entirely given way.

Not quite.

In a speech in July 2004, the former Terminator and now governor of California Arnold Schwarzenegger energized a gathering of his supporters by calling his political opponents "girlie men" because of their alleged inability to stand up to special-interest groups and trade unions.[15] The American presidential campaign of 2004 was an exercise in macho posturing, with John Kerry constantly reprising his war heroism and George W. Bush exhorting his foes to "bring it on"— whatever *it* might be.

American election battles fought on the terrain of masculinity are nothing new. Some of his critics even dared to suggest that Thomas Jefferson was "womanish." In 1840, President Martin Van Buren, who had been accused of wearing a corset and taking too many baths, lost to the relatively unwashed William Henry Harrison. In the 1950s, Adlai E. Stevenson found himself humiliated as "Adelaide" in two unsuccessful confrontations with the war hero Dwight D. Eisenhower. Today, the persistence of slurs against the manhood of political opponents suggests that traditional masculinity might have plenty of life left in it after all.[16]

In the UK, the arrival of the New Man (in touch with his feminine side) was followed in the 1990s by the phenomenon of the more-macho New Lad. Paul Fraser, a British writer based in the Netherlands, considers the New Man nothing more than "a fad . . . a mask men put on to attract more intelligent women." "Like the New Man," Fraser explains, "the New Lad understood woman was his equal. He understood he could cry, he could let his feelings out. But he also acknowledged that his primary interest in women was sexual. He liked tits. He liked drinking beer. He liked football. He liked cars. He liked hanging out with his mates." Fraser insists that, deep down, men never really change. "We might start using facial scrub and moisturizer," he says, "but men's masculinity will still break out at some point."

In New Zealand, the backlash against girlie men is reaching a crescendo. In a speech during the summer of 2004, the nation's youth affairs minister, John Tamihere, argued that the "pendulum of political correctness" had swung too far away from men. Mr. Tamihere's *cri de coeur* over the embattled state of Kiwi masculinity evidently struck a chord—it elicited, according to his office, the largest flood of mail he has ever received from ordinary New Zealanders in response to a speech.[17] The backlash extends even to advertising, where the philistine bloke is defiantly back. "Men want to feel like men," says Gabrielle Zerafa, an account director for the New Zealand research agency Colmar Brunton. "There's a strong shift back to gender stereotypes. Men are trying to reclaim their masculinity. Men are actually wanting to go back to more male roles, and have that role in the family not of protector, but hands-on doing things around the house." At one extreme are the "hard man" ads of Lion Red billboards, which mock notions of men sharing the domestic load. "Offer to do the dishes," says one billboard, underneath a picture of a pile of dirty takeaway cartons.[18]

James Cullinane, a nineteen-year-old student at the University of Auckland, shared with us a school paper in which he laid out his perspective on the Kiwi situation: "Boys' grades have seen a spectacular plummet. Girls receive twice as many 'excellences.' Minister of Education Trevor Mallard acknowledges the problem, but places the blame strictly with boys' attitudes to education. But marginalization of men is not strictly an educational problem."

Citing the research of Ilene Philipson, author of *On the Shoulders of Women*, Cullinane also notes, "the 'vanishing male therapist' is soon to be extinct. What was once an overwhelmingly male-dominated profession also once had an overwhelmingly male-dominated doctrine. Women were thought to be emotional adolescents, hysterical and incapable of reaching emotional maturity."

The criteria for emotional maturity have changed. "A mature adult nowadays is someone who is comfortable talking about their inner conflicts," writes Cullinane, "someone who values personal relationships above abstract goals, someone who isn't afraid to cry. In other words: a mature adult is a woman."

Cullinane sees the emasculation of men, in the form of metrosexuality, as an "attempt to 'catch up' to women emotionally—a cultural, if somewhat belated apology to the Feminist movement."

He concludes, "It's understandable that men might feel guilty in a feminized society where, according to academic, author, and feminist Christina Sommers, many young women are combining two dangerous things: moral fervor with misinformation. 'Feminists are so carried away with victimology and the rhetoric of male-bashing that [the Feminist movement] is full of female chauvinists.'"

To address what some see as society increasingly being skewed in women's favor, some people are calling for the male's return to traditional masculinity—and it's not just men. Some women, too, are clamoring for a return to traditional gender roles. Brenda-lee Paul, a thirty-five-year-old massage and beauty therapist living in Rijsenhout, the Netherlands, would be happy to return to prefeminist relationships. "I still feel my man must be the 'man' in the house," she says, "taking care of the manly things, fixing, building, main decision-making—basically being the head of the household." Paul thinks the biggest problem facing men in relationships today is women's increased independence. "I think the basic instincts of men, to be the 'hunter' and responsible for his family, are having to take a step back now as the woman is very independent and doesn't seem to 'need' a man. The modern woman doesn't want to be seen as unable to 'do it herself.' I, personally, like the man to be in control and do all the manly things . . . as this makes me feel like a woman."

The success of such books as *The Rules* and *The Surrendered Wife* attest to the fact that Paul is far from the only woman unhappy with the modern-day version of the husband-wife relationship. Laura Doyle, the author of *The Surrendered Wife*, calls upon the modern-day woman to restore intimacy in her marriage by ceding control and much of the decision-making to her spouse. On her website, she outlines the basic principles of a surrendered wife as follows:

- Relinquishes inappropriate control of her husband
- Respects her husband's thinking
- Receives his gifts graciously and expresses gratitude for him
- Expresses what she wants without trying to control him
- Relies on him to handle household finances
- Focuses on her own self-care and fulfillment

A surrendered wife:

- Is vulnerable where she used to be a nag
- Is trusting where she used to be controlling
- Is respectful where she used to be demeaning
- Is grateful where she used to be dissatisfied
- Has faith where she once had doubt

While a lot of women would have trouble getting their mouths around such suggested phrases as "Whatever you say" and "I'm sorry I was disrespectful," others are drawn by the fact that Doyle's advice is intended primarily to improve the life of the "surrendered wife," freeing her from the negativity and sense of responsibility that can be so overwhelming. She notes that her method is only appropriate in marriages to "good men," and advises women in abusive marriages to leave.

For many women who grew up in a time when women were expected to "do it all," surrendering a certain amount of responsibility to one's partner can be liberating.

THE RETURN OF WARRIOR MASCULINITY

[President] Bush's walking style sends a very clear signal of masculinity to the electorate. It can also unnerve people who meet him. This happened when Prime Minister Tony Blair met President Bush at Camp David in 2002. The television news footage showed the two leaders walking together, Bush casually dressed in a leather bomber jacket and Blair in an open-necked shirt. Bush is striding presidentially, with his arms pronated and extended away from his body, and his hands relaxed and facing backwards—just like a body-builder. Not to be outdone, but not wanting to mimic his host, Blair strolls along with his hands casually tucked into his trouser pockets—something he never does in public! Here Bush has clearly upped the ante in the masculinity stakes and Blair has tried to match him. By tucking his hands into his pockets Blair is trying to show that he's also tough and relaxed, but that he's not prepared to play Tonto to Bush's Lone Ranger.

—Peter Collett, *The Book of Tells* (2004)[19]

In her recent book, *Fighting for American Manhood*, Kristin Hoganson chronicled how, in the late nineteenth century, American politicians used concepts of "manhood" and "masculinity" to justify the Spanish-American War. When President William McKinley vacillated over declaring war on Spain, she noted, he met with heavy criticism and a barrage of questions about his manhood. One newspaper described him as a "goody-goody man," another declared there was a "great need of a man in the White House," and still another said it was time for a "declaration of American virility." The *New York Journal* searched for "any signs, however faint, of manhood in the White House," saying that McKinley was acting in "unmanly and irresolute ways."[20]

When war breaks out, traditional masculinity has a tendency to rear its head, and so it was with the war on terror in the wake of September 11, 2001. All of a sudden, old-fashioned macho was back in business. Jim Frank, a fifty-year-old magazine editor in the United States, contends that what is perceived as "macho" is changing, and says President George W. Bush is a prime example of the new definition. "Once upon a time," says Frank, "I'd offer that being macho meant standing for something virtuous or noble (excepting the occasional bar fight, often to impress a woman), an Old West mentality, a form of chivalry. Now it's just about the big swinging dick, who's the toughest guy regardless of the consequences to anyone else (such as the environment, Iraq, the poor . . . you get the idea). Maybe that's why the so-called liberals haven't been able to counter the loud-mouthedness success of the right. It's easier to be macho taking away food stamps than giving them, I guess."

In the post-9/11 American presidential election, the verbal and visual sparring often seemed like a fight over masculinity. At least initially, for example, the antiwar contender for Democratic presidential candidate, Howard Dean, was thought of as a butch alternative to George Bush. Until, that is, he admitted, to a crowd of his supporters in Colorado, to being a metrosexual.[21] It was shortly after this admission that Dean fell humiliatingly out of the race. The candidate the Democratic party eventually arrived at, John Kerry, took to arriving on TV shows on a Harley-Davidson. But his alleged familiarity with Botox and a Christophe hairdresser, when they were dredged up by the online smearmonger Matt Drudge, did him few favors. Meanwhile, his running mate, John Edwards, was labeled "the Breck girl," and Dick Cheney began mocking Kerry's attempts to fight a "sensitive" war on terror, ignoring the fact that one day after Kerry's comments to the UNITY 2004 Conference in Washington, D.C., Cheney's boss, George W., had used the exact same term in the same context at the Journalists of Color conference.[22]

Despite not having fought in Vietnam, George W. Bush—the reformed drinker, the anti-intellectual, the Texan cowboy—had the advantage of fitting in perfectly with the new macho. Even his gait seemed to symbolize the tough, uncompromising rancher. And his supporters knew it. Big Men, opined one right-wing think-tanker who likes his men in capital letters, "have the 'situational awareness' that the Air Force prizes in fighter pilots; Big Men tend to focus broadly but shallowly. Nerds, in contrast, concentrate narrowly but deeply. Big Men are at their best when they are improvising in the flow of a discussion, hunt, battle, or basketball game. Bush is at his most impressive in fairly small meetings."[23]

But how did the return of warrior masculinity play itself out on the international stage? A good case study can be found in Tony Blair. When he was elected back in 1997, Blair seemed a metrosexual par excellence, the archetype of a new, kindly, caring form of masculinity. Early in his premiership, he was even teased by the British press for his preference for Chardonnay over beer, as if white wine were an unsuitable drink for a real man.[24] But a strange thing overcame the British prime minister in the years after 9/11. Very slowly, during the war in Afghanistan and then in Iraq, this former SNAG (sensitive new-age guy) morphed into a classic RAMM (resurgent angry macho man). Take this revealing anecdote from Bob Woodward's book *Plan of Attack:* After the famous press conference between Bush and Blair on September 7, 2002, during which the prime minister gave full support to the U.S. president's policy of toppling Saddam Hussein, Woodward records, Bush approached Blair's then communications director, the notoriously aggressive Alastair Campbell, and said admiringly: "Your man's got *cojones.*"[25]

World leaders everywhere, haunted by the fear of looking unmanly in the face of terrorist catastrophe, went frantically searching for their *cojones.* The Australian premier, John Howard, who had carefully honed his machismo with an uncompromising stance on asylum-seekers back in 2001, now applied himself with ease to the war on terror.[26] President Vladimir Putin's über-macho approach to Chechnya, sustained in the face of a mounting and horrific body count, continued to win him the respect of voters still half in love with the idea of the Russian strongman.

But what of the role played by "old Europe"? In America, conservative commentators, enraged by the French unwillingness to support the war in Iraq, began referring to the French with such disdainful appellations as "cheese-eating surrender monkeys" (a slam taken from a 1995 episode of *The Simpsons*). But maybe, in the end, the difference between Continental Europe and the United States was simply about competing versions of masculinity. In the July 2004 issue of *Foreign Policy*, Parag Khanna went so far as to argue that Europe is the world's first metrosexual superpower. "By cleverly deploying both its hard power and its sensitive side," he argued, "the European Union has become more effective—and more attractive—than the United States on the catwalk of diplomatic clout. Meet the real New Europe: the world's first metrosexual superpower."

Khanna went on to articulate the European approach to the exercise of "soft power." "Metrosexuals," he argued, "always know how to dress for the occasion (or mission). Spreading peace across Eurasia serves U.S. interests, but it's best done by donning Armani pinstripes rather than U.S. Army fatigues. . . . Just as metrosexuals are redefining masculinity, Europe is redefining old notions of power and influence."[27]

Maybe. But playing into the rules of old-fashioned macho, it is worth remembering, sometimes does the trick. Just before the first Gulf war, it was recently revealed, Western governments responded to Saddam Hussein's taking Western hostages in Kuwait by putting it around on Arab media that true Arab warriors would not hide behind the skirts of women. The insult to Saddam's masculinity worked. Within days, he had released all the women and children he was holding hostage.[28]

GLOBAL MASCULINITIES:
ONE SIZE TOOL BELT DOESN'T FIT ALL

At home, my husband does more work. Being a Shanghainese, he is expected to do everything, such as cooking, cleaning, laundry, and shopping. I usually go shopping with him . . .

—Interviewee in academic study
on housework and expatriate Shanghai men[29]

For people in the Western world, in particular, it's easy to forget that what we would consider "macho" behaviors aren't necessarily in synch with definitions of masculinity in other societies. In reality, the Western version of masculinity is fairly modern and geographically limited. A recent international study of Chinese emigrants to Australia, for instance, has discovered that Shanghai men are intensively and voluntarily involved in housework. The tradition of men's participation in housework, apparently, goes back to the migrants' roots and can be explained by prevailing gender ideologies found in modern China. This is but one of various forms of masculinity in global society.[30]

Much of what we think of as "butch" masculinity, then, is hardly universal. Several cultures around the world even embrace individuals who do not identify as one gender or the other. In India, a *hijra* is a full-time female impersonator who is part of a traditional social organization (half cult and half caste) and worships the goddess Bahuchara Mata. And in Polynesia, each village has a *Mahu*, a male transvestite who serves as a casual sexual partner to some of the heterosexual men in the village.[31]

In a recent academic study, college men in the United States and Europe were presented with a computerized test; they were shown a male image on a computer screen and were asked to manipulate the levels of fat and muscularity to the point at which the image would represent what women would consider the "ideal male body." The men typically chose a male body with twenty or thirty pounds more muscle than that of an average man. But when the same academics gave the test to college women, the female students chose a perfectly ordinary male body without all the added muscle. When the academics gave the same test to Taiwanese students and to nomads on the plains of Kenya, those groups of men had no difficulty in judging the male body that women would prefer. In other words, young Western men seem to have developed a uniquely dysfunctional idea of what they are supposed to look like.[32]

Reinforcing the theory that machismo is rooted in society and culture rather than nature is a recent study conducted in Brazil, Colombia, Costa Rica, El Salvador, Guatemala, Honduras, Jamaica, Mexico, and Nicaragua. That study suggests that Latin "machista" is alive and well. No half days at the spa for those guys! Men in Latin America and the Caribbean, the study concluded, feel unrelenting pressure to demonstrate a macho masculinity in all spheres of their lives. The identity of men, says one of the authors of the study, the Chilean psychiatrist Rodrigo Aguirre, "is built on a relationship of 'opposition' to women, and they must prove themselves to be men in the eyes of their peers."

Machismo [the researchers found], is generally equated with such traits as bravado, sexual prowess, protecting one's honor, and a willingness to face danger. . . . Cultural norms indicate—with variations, depending on the country—that men must "never say no" to temptations on the street, which exposes male adolescents to damage from tobacco, alcohol, and drugs. [Those codes of behavior also justify] the use of violence—even against women—as a masculine form of channeling emotions or frustrations.[33]

Even within Europe, regional differences exist. One academic study of men's parenting and fatherhood in Sweden and England found clear evidence that the modern discourse on fatherhood is more established and coherent in Sweden than it is in England, regardless of socioeconomic status. "A large number of the English sample," the academics concluded, "express a wish to maintain the traditional gender role patterns. However, this discourse on fixed gender roles is very unusual in the Swedish sample, probably because there is no room for it within the framework of the predominant normative conceptions about involved fathering."[34]

MEDIATING MASCULINITY

On top of the influence of culture and economy, the mass media have become an increasingly powerful influence on the construction of masculinity. A recent study of *Playboy*, for example, concluded that the magazine was important in shaping modern ideas about sexuality. The choice of a white rabbit as the symbol of *Playboy* and the prototypical playboy, the researchers concluded, further helped to refine the meaning of masculinity. A rabbit is prey, rather than a predator, and has a number of attributes that might be considered stereotypically feminine. "Rather than reify gender stereotypes," the study concluded, "*Playboy*'s editorial direction advanced an alternative conceptualization that contradicted conventional definitions of masculinity."[35]

In other words, the media not only reflect but also help to create popular ideas about what it is to be masculine. **Once upon a time, leading men in American movies came with an imposing physique and a square jaw: John Wayne, Humphrey Bogart, Robert Mitchum, Lee Marvin, and William Holden, among them. As soon as they passed their sell-by dates, they were replaced by a new batch of masculine role models, including Marlon Brando, Steve McQueen, Clint Eastwood, and Robert De Niro. The characterization of the male hero became a little murkier in the 1970s, with the birth of such Hollywood antiheroes as Dirty Harry. How times have changed. Nowadays, for every Russell Crowe there is a baby-faced, effeminate Tobey Maguire, Orlando Bloom, Keanu Reeves, or Ben Affleck. Our role models have changed, it seems, and so has modern man.**

"In 1950, a real man was the breadwinner," says the British writer Paul Fraser, age thirty-three. "He didn't cry. He didn't complain. He got on with things. He had a toolkit and could fix anything that was broken. He was loved and feared by his children. They wouldn't talk back to him. He was loved and feared by his wife. She wouldn't talk back either. He was master of his domain. He left the childrearing and the housekeeping up to the wife." Fraser's notion of what constitutes a "real man" in 2005 leaves no doubt that perceptions have changed radically in the interceding years. "In 2005," he says, "a real man has a six-pack stomach. A real man has at least one shirt that needs cufflinks. He keeps his calm in a business meeting. He is successful. He is single, with a succession of long-term model girlfriends. He is George Clooney. He is a media invention."

EMASCULATED MASCULINITY

As we'll discuss in greater detail in chapter 7, the media (including advertising) have an enormous influence on how men are perceived, even by themselves. And real damage can result when the images men see are almost wholly negative. Paul Nathanson and Katherine Young, authors of *Spreading Misandry: The Teaching of Contempt for Men in Popular Culture*, say advertising merely holds up a mirror. "We do see a statistical picture that tells us men are in trouble," Young says. "Their suicide rates are higher, their alcoholism rates are higher, they die earlier than women, and boys are dropping out of high school at much higher rates than girls are. The more negative imaging you get, the more it reinforces this. Boys can say, 'If this is the way society is going to look at us, we'll just act that way.'"[36]

Society's changing notions of who men should be, combined with media images that deride who they currently are, leave many men bewildered as to whether they can do anything right. It's reached the point at which embattled masculinity might even be a powder keg waiting to explode. Wesley Wark, a University of Toronto history professor and terrorism specialist, notes that most adolescent males go through a phase during which rebellion and even fantasies of violence hold appeal. "It shouldn't surprise us that there might be a connection between the universal phenomenon of teenage rebelliousness and a sudden receptivity to the very violent and very simplified and conspiratorial message of jihad," he says.[37]

For some young men, particularly those who feel inadequate or alienated, membership in a terrorist group connects them with like-minded people who reassure them that others, not themselves, are to blame for their problems. Terrorist groups emphasize such manly virtues as courage, prowess, and sacrifice, which are likely to resonate with marginalized young men in advanced industrial societies. "American white supremacists," says the sociologist Michael Kimmel, "offer American men the restoration of their masculinity—a manhood in which individual white men control the fruits of their own labor and are not subject to emasculation by Jewish-owned finance capital or a black- and feminist-controlled welfare state."[38] In his book about the history of masculinity, Leo Braudy argues that a renewed warrior masculinity is at the heart of the propaganda of Islamic terrorists in Middle Eastern countries. The enemy is the West and the blurring of traditional gender boundaries that characterizes most modern, secular democracies.[39]

IS IT ALL JUST AN ACT?

You could argue that all gender is "done." The question is, how consciously? That's the definition of what we go through as adolescents, a time when, through trial and error, we're doing not only gender but our whole character. Trying on our whole persona, finding which songs, fashions, and interests feel comfortable, what creates the effect we desire. We call ourselves adults when all that stuff becomes less conscious. I would say that at some point most of our behaviour is performative.

—Jennifer Finney Boylan, author and transgendrist[40]

In spring 2004, the fashion designer Nicole Farhi, working with Gucci, decided to revive "cowboy chic" with shop-window displays featuring cacti and Stetsons. **Caught between the old and the new, and threatened by emasculation, a growing number of men at the beginning of the twenty-first century are turning to such things as body-building, chest-thumping, and Stetson-wearing in an attempt to recapture the essence of their masculinity.** But that kind of masculinity was a product of a particular historical period—a period, we would argue, whose time has now passed. And man's efforts to reverse the tide are beset by a troubling question: Do corral chic and other things of that ilk revive a simpler age of pioneers and honest masculinity? Or are they just plain camp?

Perhaps, in the end, masculinity has not changed as fast as we think, and there exists a worrying disjunction between media representations of modern man and the real thing. Perhaps, too, what we are witnessing at the beginning of the twenty-first century is not the fabled "crisis of masculinity" but its slow redefinition into something more appropriate.

Recently, some theorists of gender have begun to argue that masculinity does not simply consist of a set of static roles and ascribed identities; it is also an active performance on the part of the man, a performance that allows for innovation and change over time. But if masculinity is a performance rooted in society and culture, then perhaps it is time that men spent more time working on their act.

WHAT TO REMEMBER

1. Much of what we think of as butch masculinity is not universal. As we evolve toward a more global society, the differences in what's masculine become better known, culture to culture.

2. In the name of progress in Western society, the stereotypical markers of a man—physical strength and a hunter-and-warrior psyche—have become less relevant; in fact, contemporary examples that try to invoke this imagery more often than not end up as caricatures. Witness President George W. Bush challenging the forces of evil to "bring it on," Austrian actor-turned-American-elected-official Arnold Schwarzenegger defining his opponents as "girlie men," and U.S. presidential candidate John Kerry attempting to overcome his reliance on botox and a multimillionaire wife by invoking his wartime experience in Vietnam.

3. Perhaps not surprisingly, the media stereotype of the contemporary male looks a lot less like John Wayne than like Orlando Bloom, whose beauty and desirability seem to transcend his maleness. (No one would ever have accused John Wayne, Steve McQueen, and their ilk of being "pretty," but that's a term often associated with Bloom and other young, desirable actors.)

4. Masculinity is clearly in transition, with new expressions of maleness emerging as men struggle to reclaim their place—any place, be it cowboy macho man or power lifter or Zen master.

4

BEYOND METROSEXUALMANIA

THE ÜBERSEXUAL

I t all started with one cultural critic's visit to a fashion expo in London.

Mark Simpson, originator of the term "metrosexual," was covering the "It's a Man's World" style exhibition, organized by *GQ*, when he noticed something curious going on in Man World. Simpson, whose own website proudly describes him as the "Skinhead Oscar Wilde" and the "Gay Anti-Christ" (epithets applied by the British writer Philip Hensher and *Vogue* magazine, respectively), gave this definition for the new breed of man he discovered that day:

> The typical metrosexual is a young man with money to spend, living in or within easy reach of a metropolis—because that's where all the best shops, clubs, gyms and hairdressers are. He might be officially

gay, straight or bisexual, but this is utterly immaterial because he has clearly taken himself as his own love object and pleasure as his sexual preference. Particular professions, such as modeling, waiting tables, media, pop music and, nowadays, sport, seem to attract them but, truth be told, like male vanity products and herpes, they're pretty much everywhere.[1]

Simpson saw these men as dupes of consumerism, calling the metrosexual a "commodity fetishist, a collector of fantasies about the male sold to him by advertising." And from word one, he was openly derisive and dismissive of the creature he'd discovered.

But that was 1994—years before *Queer Eye for the Straight Guy*, years before U.S. presidential candidate Howard Dean quipped about his own metrosexual tendencies before admitting he didn't actually know what the word meant. And years before the release of a study that would pull the term into the limelight. That study was "The Future of Men," conducted by the authors of this book on behalf of the communications agency Euro RSCG Worldwide.

Simpson's term had languished for nearly a decade before we picked it up and put our own spin on it to describe a segment of men we were seeing in our online studies. (We're always on the lookout for new insights and trends that may be of value to our advertising clients.) A press release we wrote to publicize our study (and our book on buzz marketing) hit the right editors' desks, and the rest is history.

By the time we got through with it, the term "metrosexual" was in common parlance. In fact, within six months of the release of our study, the American Dialect Society had named it "Word of the Year."[2] That was in 2003, and, in the time since then, reaction to the word has moved from recognition to debate to backlash. Now you can hear Simpson himself singing with a chorus of journalists and stylemakers about the death of macho; you can even hear Dr. Laura Schlessinger bemoan the loss of the "real man."

Metrosexuals, as we've defined them, have existed for centuries. But metrosexuality didn't become a phenomenon until enough people were in on it and until it had been publicly identified and plastered with a catchy moniker. Once we spread the word, the term was quickly monetized. Such men as David Beckham, Adrien Brody, and Sting made metrosexuality interesting and, for some, desirable. Is it working as a marketing tool? Ask Gillette; even after Beckham was involved in a sex scandal, they paid him millions as a global spokesperson. And the phenomenon has moved well beyond that. Consider the episodes of *South Park* and *Law & Order* and the 101 books that have the word "metrosexual" in their titles or subtitles. During its fifteen-plus minutes, metrosexuality served as the "sell line" of these times.

But is the metrosexual phenomenon more than just Man *du jour?* Is he just a yuppie with six-pack abs and concealer? Or is he a harbinger of even bigger changes in the way men and women interact in the world?

Before we go jumping to conclusions, it makes sense to spend some time with our subject. Our study "The Future of Men" explored the spending habits and aesthetic beliefs of a newly developing class of men unafraid to devote time and money to their own appearances. "Now we're seeing an emerging wave of men who chafe against the restrictions of traditional male boundaries," we wrote. "They want to do what they want, buy what they want, enjoy what they want—regardless of whether some people might consider these things unmanly."[3]

The study, initially drawing on a survey of 1,058 American men and women, looked not only at changes in men's attitudes toward cosmetic and aesthetic practices usually associated with women, but also at men's attitudes toward themselves. For example, asked to choose from a list of self-descriptors, a full 74 percent of male respondents described themselves as "caring," while "assertive" only came in at 39 percent, and "authoritative" fared even more poorly, at 32 percent.

"One of the telltale signs of metrosexuals is their willingness to indulge themselves, whether by springing for a Prada suit or spending a couple of hours at a spa to get a massage and facial," we wrote. "Among our survey respondents, there's cautious acceptance overall of various procedures to enhance a man's appearance. . . . All except those for male cosmetic surgery are on the 'agree' side of neutral."[4]

While we adopted and adapted the term "metrosexual" from Mark Simpson, our view of who metrosexuals are and why they have come to exist is quite different from his. Whereas Simpson looks at metrosexuality as "male vanity's finally coming out of the closet," we see metrosexual behaviors and attitudes as being less about vanity and pretense and more about having the strength to be true to oneself.[5] Metrosexuals, in our view, are sufficiently confident in their masculinity to be willing to embrace their feminine sides—and to do so

publicly. Rather than adhere to the strictures of their fathers' generation, they are willing to move beyond rigid gender roles and pursue
their interests and fancies regardless of societal pressures against
them. (Which is not to say they don't enjoy catching sight of themselves as they pass by store windows.)

Rather than seeing it as overly feminine, narcissistic behavior, we
view metrosexuality as a welcome evolution in man's adaptation to the
modern world. The metrosexual's interest in life beyond his apartment, his willingness to go against macho norms, and his desire to live
more fully—these fit right in with the theory that Jim Frank, a U.S.
magazine editor, has of modern man:

> I think men are "evolving" as people, parents, and partners. Becom-
> ing more aware of what's happening, involving themselves in the
> home life by choice rather than force, genuinely taking interest in
> their children's development, sharing the good and the bad. I've re-
> ferred to it, stereotypically, as men being in touch with their femi-
> nine sides because, unfortunately, we have no other way of
> describing it—and everyone gets it when you say that. It's definitely
> the right direction as long as women don't feel they have to assume
> the worst traits of men in return. I even see some men talking for the
> sake of making a connection, and not simply to convey information;
> to say nothing of men who "shop" rather than just "buy."

Once we released our findings to the media in the United States
and Europe, the resulting firestorm of publicity and articles pushed
metrosexuality into the public consciousness; scores of people rushed
to put their stamp on the story—and even to create their own subsets.
While we define metrosexuals as straight men who "are just gay
enough," Simpson and some others use the term to refer to both
straights and gays who have adopted the characteristic behaviors and
attitudes of the metrosexual. As a New York–based headhunter told
us, "I know you use the word to describe straight men, but it is now
being used in the gay community, and by boomers, in reference to gay
men who act straight, even gay men who are occasionally bisexual and
who get off on 'straight walking' (accompanying single women to
glam events) as part of their metro lives." Others are using the terms
MetroHetero and MetroGay to distinguish between straights who are
"just gay enough," and gays who are "straight enough" to be highly
desirable as dates for single women.

In this chapter, we'll examine some of the theories and opinions that have cropped up about metrosexuality in the year and a half since we brought it to the world's attention, as well as our own take on the matter.

METROSEXUAL:
JUST ANOTHER WORD FOR
"CULTURED AND AESTHETIC MAN"?

As usual with lifestyle stories that set off media maelstroms, the release of our findings on metrosexuality touched off a race to be the first to codify the phenomenon in a book. One of the first to appear in print was Michael Flocker's *The Metrosexual Guide to Style: A Handbook for the Modern Man*, which covers everything from the proper pronunciation of the word "espresso" to body type ("the pumped-up, steroid injecting muscleman is out," Flocker asserts).[6]

Flocker's guide also provides numerous lists, including the essentials of any self-respecting metrosexual's CD collection (heavy on such proto-metrosexuals as David Bowie, Lou Reed, Chet Baker, and Serge Gainsbourg), "must watch" movies, and "must read" books. And, of course, no guidebook to metrosexuality would be complete without a list of "must wear" wardrobe items. Among the absolute necessities: flattering underwear, two different pairs of flattering jeans, quality sunglasses, and two rollneck or crewneck cable-knit sweaters.

But, apart from the new imperative that underwear be flattering, is the metrosexual so different from the cultured and aesthetic man of any generation? Is a metrosexual just a yuppie in high-thread-count boxer briefs? Mark Simpson would say no, at least when it comes to wardrobe: "Unlike a yuppie," he avers, "a metrosexual would not wear padded shoulders. He'd be wearing a sleeveless shirt to show off his deliciously developed deltoids and designer tattoo."[7] On this point, our definition of the metrosexual diverges from Simpson's. The typical metrosexual, in our view, has far more interest in Balenciaga and Burberry than in body art.

We would also argue that metrosexuality goes much deeper than many people seem to believe. Our studies have shown that, rather than just having distinct tastes in fashion and style (and a predilection for shopping), metrosexuals, and men in general, are moving away from such traditional male aspirations as wealth and power and toward what once would have been considered "female" aspirations. As we commented in our report "The Future of Men": "While fame, wealth, and desirability still appeal to the American man, his most highly prized aspirations are friendship, growing old with the woman he loves, and having happy, healthy children."[8]

We interviewed a number of self-described metrosexuals (and their female partners) for our study. Here's what some of them had to say:

> In my mind, *metrosexual* is just a term for an "evolved" man who is comfortable in his own skin and sexuality, and not encumbered by cultural baggage that says a man has to be strong, silent, and self-sacrificing. He can be emotional, indulgent, gossipy, enjoy the company of women as friends and lovers, appreciate beauty wherever he finds it, and is completely comfortable using the word *fabulous*.

> To me, a metrosexual is a man who is a gentleman and has manners . . . is accepting of the differences between people and the sexes; dresses "well," which really only means "with care," whether it is expensively or inexpensively . . .

> I am self-indulgent but not selfish. I enjoy expensive meals at fine restaurants. I prefer the pampering of a salon to the barbershop, etc. But at the same time, the responsibilities of my family will always come first.

> I'm not hedonistic, and I don't obsess over my looks, but I do demand certain things from life, as I believe any person must, to be happy.[9]

WOMEN AND METROSEXUALITY

Metrosexuality didn't form in a vacuum. It very much has to do with the social evolution of the last century and, in particular, with the evolving relationship between men and women. Some people talk of the interplay of the sexes as a zero-sum battle: if women take one step forward, men are pushed one step back. That might make sense if we were talking about competitor corporations or troops on the front line, but we're not: we're talking about actual or potential partners with numerous shared objectives, including love, fun, fulfillment, sex, family, and happiness.

With certain exceptions, heterosexual men and women still need each other, at least to some degree. But women are playing by a whole new set of rules. What they want for themselves has changed, what they can do for themselves has changed, and what they want from men has changed. As women have gained more power, including the power to stay single, they no longer have to put up with the standard-issue male. And that gives men who want to land a woman more incentive to rethink themselves and shape up.

When women had little control over their lives, they had to accept whatever was on offer from the available pool of mates and breadwinners, even if the pool was shallow and scummy. A woman who was too picky risked being "left on the shelf" and becoming a spinster. In Japan, unmarried women over age twenty-five have traditionally been nicknamed "Christmas cake" because no one wants to eat Christmas cake after the twenty-fifth of December. But now that women can get by on their own, they can afford to be choosier. What's more, if Prince Charming turns out to be less so, many women feel much less compulsion to stick it out.

It seems to us that this is particularly the case in urban areas, where women in general feel less pressure to "settle" for the first man who's willing to slip a ring on their finger. Among other factors, women in major cities are likely to have a network of supportive single friends, and certainly have plenty of role models of older women who have built nice lives for themselves without benefit of a permanent mate. Madeline Park, a thirty-something working mom who's an executive at an advertising agency, points out that such women "can now take care of themselves and don't need a man anymore." As a result, she says, "men need to accept that a relationship is based on a lot more now than just basic need."

So what's a man to do? Where can he turn to pick up the cues and clues he needs to rethink himself and adapt to the changing marketplace?

Hint: he's not going to get them from other men.

While it would be nice to have a *Book of Rules* that actually proved reliable, modern man has to make do by monitoring the female's reaction to the existing array of male behaviors, looks, and attitudes. When red-blooded "real men" had the lion's share of power in business, media, politics, religion, and entertainment, they also got to define what was "manly" and what wasn't; they set the standards to which ordinary men aspired. Gay men who held positions of power and influence stayed resolutely in their closets, and there were too few women in positions of power to make a difference. The details of standard-issue manliness varied from country to country, but within countries it was pretty clear: men were men, women were women, and both knew what was expected.

Now, in business, media, politics, religion, and entertainment, women and homosexuals have leavened the mix and championed their own visions and versions of masculinity—and of femininity, too. The granite-jawed types of simpler times don't interest today's tastemakers, or the women who are an increasingly influential part of their audience. **The new balance of power calls for lighter versions of masculinity that take more account of what used to be "female" values.**

It's a complex world, but ultimately our take on the sexes is simple: women are increasingly able to get out and earn money, have real careers, kick ass, have fun, and do all the other things that men used to regard as their preserve. And men who want to attract these women are realizing that they need to learn some new tricks. Among them: being more careful about their appearance and grooming, and being more comfortable with gossip and feelings and design—it's a whole new way for men to think about exterior and interior. And who's to say that those things don't fit with being a "real man"? They may not fit with old notions of "real manhood," and they may overlap with some aspects of gay culture, but who cares? Times change. As it has throughout history, being a "real man" today means knowing and doing what it takes to get what you want, when you want it. That may include an attractive partner (male or female), it may include power and wealth, it may include health and physical prowess. Whatever. After all, we're living in an era of infinite choice.

"My guess is that a 'real man' in 1950 had some, if not a lot more, of the machismo that still exists in many of the Latin-American cultures today," says Julius van Heek, age forty, a homosexual designer living in Chicago. "They were pumped full with predetermined expectations from previous generations and religious teachings. They were expected to provide for family and, I'm guessing, had an innate yearning for this, as well, post World War II. In 2004, a 'real man' should be the definition of flexible, understanding, and an equal contributor to the family dynamic. He ought to give his partner equal consideration and be more emotionally expressive."

One of the consistent themes to emerge in our conversations about the changing definition of the Real Man is that in today's culture, he is expected to be flawed, or at least to show some kind of vulnerability. Women are no longer quite so interested in the perfectly chiseled, ultraconfident man who sees the world—and his role in it—in black and white. They may well be drawn to an outwardly macho, muscular type, but they want him to come with such softer qualities as a sense of humor, a passion for culture, or an ability to chitchat.

We spoke at length about this with our friend and former colleague Jimmy Szczepanek, thirty-four, who works in public relations in New York City. Judging from the examples he gave us, Jimmy thinks Real Men today are typically those who exude self-confidence, clear-cut convictions, and a get-ahead attitude; often, they sport larger-than-life personas. In his words, "I think that maybe Arnold Schwarzenegger is a prime example, as gross as he is. People tend to need that macho quality, but tempered with a funny accent and a wife who's a Democrat. Also, having a ton of money doesn't hurt. Another good example would be Donald Trump. The quality that the two share is that they were both basically underdogs. The Donald continues to pull himself out of bankruptcy and land on top with a different gorgeous wife each time, and Arnold is an immigrant who became an action star and, ultimately, the governor of California."

In looking at those two figures with an eye to metrosexuality, we'd say Arnold fits the bill (after all, he's admitted to high-priced haircuts and a shoe fetish), while the Donald could be excluded solely on the basis of his atrocious hair. Honestly, would a true metrosexual leave his penthouse looking like that? We think not.

Beyond appearance and shopping habits, there's also a big difference in terms of how these two well-known and powerful men treat the women in their lives. Despite his alleged history of sexual harassment, Arnold makes it clear that his marriage is a partnership—one that includes plenty of disagreements and even fights, but also a mutual respect and admiration. There's no sense that the Schwarzenegger household is a patriarchy; if anything, Maria Shriver gives the impression of controlling much of what goes on at home, while also strongly influencing her husband's political career (even if she couldn't talk him out of stumping for W.). The Donald, by contrast, is a throwback to an era in which men brooked no backtalk from their women. This is the man, after all, who is reputed to have said he had no problem with Wife Number Two (Marla Maples Trump) having a career on Broadway, provided she was back in time to have his dinner on the table by the time he returned home. A decidedly unmetrosexual attitude—and not what we would consider indicative of today's Real Man.

THE ROLE OF MEDIA

Like any trend or movement, metrosexuality has both been trumpeted by and influenced by the media. Some would argue that it is a media construct, fueled by advertising and the media's corporate masters. In Simpson's view, "You can't have metrosexuals without the media. Metrosexuality is one of the most flagrant symptoms of a media-tized world: The male body was the last frontier and it's now being thoroughly explored and mapped."[10]

Whether one agrees with that position or not, it's hard to deny that the last couple of years have ushered in an explosion of media discussion about men, image, and gender, all through article after article discussing, analyzing, mocking, celebrating, and debating metrosexuality.

Part of the fun for many commentators has been playing the "Is he or isn't he a metrosexual?" game. Of course, some public figures obviously fall into one camp or the other. The European football/soccer standout David Beckham was an obvious early choice for metrosexual poster boy. His attention to hair, fashion, and grooming were signs enough, but then he went so far as to wrap himself in a sarong and dabble with eyeliner, placing himself firmly at the outer reaches of the phenomenon. P. Diddy, with his attention to fashion and the finer things in life, is another sure bet. More subtle are such public figures as the aforementioned Arnold Schwarzenegger and the ever sensitive Bill Clinton.

Metrosexual spotters have even given some men retroactive admittance into the club. One inductee is the legendary dancer Fred Astaire, nominated by Australia's *Sunday Telegraph*:

> A memorable addition to the annals of "ladies' men," Astaire's sartorial style recalled that of original 19th-century dandy George "Beau" Brummell. Astaire made every other man on earth look left-footed

in an era when it mattered. Way back when dancing was the closest thing you'd get to sex on screen, Astaire was the consummate smooth mover with an off-hand suaveness, billowing trousers and a twinkle in his eye. His report card from his first screen test read: "Can't sing. Can't act. Slightly balding. Can dance a little." He probably never changed a nappy, nor knew how to drizzle extra-virgin olive oil just so. But that scene in *Royal Wedding* when he waltzed with a hat rack and danced on the ceiling dispels any doubts as to his metrosexuality.[11]

All the media attention to the phenomenon probably hasn't changed the behavior of such hardcore metrosexuals as David Beckham, but it has convinced more men on the cusp of metrosexuality that it's okay to head for a salon over a barbershop or indulge in cashmere. (As Paul Fraser told us, "If dressing and looking after yourself gets you a better standard of arm candy, pass me the exfoliating cream.")

Metrosexuality has also awakened some men to the reality that deodorant and shampoo are no longer all it takes to succeed in business—or with the ladies. More and more men are paying attention to such things as skin care, fragrance, and the cut of their clothing. Even their mouths are no longer safe: "Men are coming out of the closet," jokes Stephen L. Olitsky, a Pennsylvania dentist who concentrates on cosmetic reconstruction. "From clothes to teeth, men want designer everything."[12]

Of course, men have been changing the look of their teeth for ages. But formerly, change was usually accomplished by means of a shoulder, an elbow, or a fist. The same goes for noses. Men whose only "cosmetic adjustments" took place on the backfield are now thinking about getting their noses broken by the pros. As Stephen Goldstein, a specialist in facial reconstructive surgery at Graduate Hospital in Philadelphia, told the *Philadelphia Enquirer*, referring to young "'bruisers' with smashed noses who want to get them back in joint": "More men are seeking to look professional. Now that they're not in college wrestling around, being stupid, they no longer want to have their nose on the side of their face."[13] This focus on looks travels down the chain all the way to secondary school, where boys are getting their parents to fork over big bucks for highlights and designer cuts. Not too long ago, that would have given most parents serious cause for concern.

THE PLASTIC PRESIDENT?

In the United States, as in other countries, many "advances" in masculinity get the official stamp of approval only after public figures adopt them. And the boost is even greater when that public figure happens to hold the highest office in the land. John F. Kennedy, America's first telegenic president, proved the influence of image on political success. Ronald Reagan, who refined image consciousness to a scientific edge that only Hollywood could have generated, kept his locks jet black well into his nineties. William Jefferson Clinton made crying—an act that derailed at least one previous politician's career—a sign of strength and security.

Today, one more male taboo—plastic surgery—is on the chopping block. During the 2004 presidential race, the Democratic nominee, John F. Kerry, was rumored to have undergone Botox treatment at his wife's urging—though it's possible Kerry's face did more harm than good for the reputation of such injections. The camera lens is nowhere near as kind to this JFK as it was to the previous one.

Now a rumor started by a humble blog—but that has made the rounds through badplasticsurgery.com, MSNBC, Associated Press, and *The Washington Post*, and that even garnered a joke on the David Letterman show—suggests that plastic surgery may be a bipartisan trend. On February 9, 2004, a little-known blog known simply as "Brian Flemming's Weblog" published a series of "before and after" shots of President George W. Bush's nose that do seem to show it changing from a slight hook to a cute button. The rumor is completely unsubstantiated and relies on press photos of Bush, but it does make for good late-night TV. Here's what David Letterman had to say about it on his show just five days later: "Here now is my favorite story of the week: a rumor that President George Bush had a nose job, that he had some kind of plastic surgery, he actually had a nose job. And I was thinking, well, if this is true it would be the first new job he's created since taking office."[14]

IS IT IN THEIR GENES—
OR IS IT BECAUSE WOMEN ARE WEARING
THE JEANS IN THE FAMILY?

Playing "Spot the Cosmetic Procedure" with world celebrities and gossiping over such newfound male practices as the hideously painful-sounding "back, crack, and sack" wax seemed to be the first and most common media reaction to metrosexuality, but it was followed closely by speculation as to where the whole thing came from. One British newspaper featured the views of a geneticist who contends that men's gradually increasing comfort with traditionally feminine pursuits is evidence that the Y chromosome is mutating into a genetic junkyard. Yes, it's Nature vs. Nurture yet again.

"Prof. [Bryan] Sykes cites the increase in male infertility and the increasing feminization of men, who are evolving over time into androgynous figures such as David Beckham. Speaking of David Beckham, it's men like him who are responsible for a trend that ties in nicely with Prof. Sykes' theory," reported the *Bristol Evening News.* "Because it's not just scientists who have noticed a change in men, but social commentators have spotted it too—and it has led to the coining of the phrase 'metrosexuality.'"[15]

By Dr. Sykes's own admission, the expiration date on the Y chromosome is not due to come up for another hundred thousand years or so. So you'd be excused for thinking that a genetic argument for metrosexuality is a bit premature, to say the least. But that's okay, because there are plenty of other ideas floating around.

"Blame the feminists," says the *Los Angeles Times,* "or the idea that women don't need men anymore. Oh, they still want them, but the days when a woman's survival was intrinsically wrapped up in a man's attentions are long gone."[16] According to this theory, as noted earlier in this chapter, men are paying more attention to their appearance and their behavior out of desire for survival; because they've been moved from standard equipment to optional package, they need to work on their salability. Other sources seem to agree that the emergence of the metrosexual comes from shifts in the relationship between the sexes: "Something has happened to modern man," says Sydney's *Sunday Telegraph.* "After several decades of being marginalized by feminism, portrayed as a useless plonker in beer ads, and forced to apologize for not being able to find the butter in the fridge, he has hit back with a new, emboldened image. Or at least a band of marketers have done so for him. The resulting Metrosexual Man is family-focused, caring and narcissistic."[17]

It's interesting that this source describes metrosexuals as both caring *and* narcissistic. Paradoxical as it seems, increased care for family might go hand in hand with increased time in front of shiny surfaces. And, among the other telltale signs of metrosexuality, you might be able to list comfort with the gradual ascent of women.

Articles decrying the fall of man often go hand-in-hand with descriptions of the rise of metrosexuality, and the backlash against it. Aidan Smith of *The Scotsman* had this doom-and-gloom take on the power shift between the sexes: "Women run just about everything, or they will soon. Hardly a week goes by without some shock-horror revelation about how they now wear the metaphorical trousers." He then lays the "shock-horror" out, item-by-item: "On just one day recently, a newspaper delivered this devastating triple-whammy: women would eventually be able to run faster than men; women's bodies were better equipped for space travel, should we ever get to play in that future state (and wasn't it supposed to be here by now?); and men wouldn't just be left to look after the baby, they would soon be able to have the thing as well."[18]

As evidence of "good news" for the modern man, Smith delved into the world of men's magazines. Specifically, he mentioned *Loaded* and *Maxim* as proof that old-fashioned men are on their way back into style. But even though men's magazines oriented to guy's guys (replete with electronic gadgets and exposed or nearly exposed breasts)—not only *Maxim* and *Loaded*, but also *XXL*, not to mention such classics as *Playboy*—have definitely gained prominence, that's hardly the end of the story. *Maxim* has its own brand of hair coloring for men—its website gives instructions for "highlights, tips, or all over color." It even gives this word of confidence to men afraid to venture into the world of colorizing: "Carmen Electra is giving her stamp of approval to guys all over the country. So make sure you check out Maxim Haircolor in the men's grooming section, so you too can get approved."[19]

What's so interesting about *Maxim* is the extent of its double-speak. Even while hawking its own brand of hair colorant, its publishers have gone out of their way to denigrate the rise of metrosexuality. As part of an ad campaign geared toward print advertisers, *Maxim* has produced a brochure called "Are You Dying Inside?," which warns of a serious disorder, "mantropy," a spiritual degeneration marked by frequent manicures and seaweed wraps and even excessive smoothie consumption. The magazine is meant to serve as a refuge for those men who thus far have avoided the mantropy trap.[20]

Cargo also targets the modern male with an approach that combines rugged masculinity with metrosexual self-indulgence. Almost textless, *Cargo* is to the modern man what Candyland was to the boy: all the sweetness, without any of those big words to get in the way. And the image of man *Cargo* presents is indeed a carefully constructed one—tough, almost Neanderthal, but not about women or sports, but about *shopping*. Consider this copy from an advertisement for the first issue: "Shop like a man. Read it. Club it. Drag it home."[21]

The eye of a seasoned connoisseur, the cudgel of a caveman. One journalist had this to say about *Cargo*'s slogan: "Actually, as ad copy, it's pretty effective, borrowing from Rob Becker's play *Defending the Caveman* to tap in to the male antipathy toward shopping, and suggesting that *Cargo* offers a real man's guide to bagging the good stuff. But would a cave man want snippets on male bikini waxing, collagen injections and buying high heels for his girlfriend shuffled among bits on power tools, fast cars and shoot-'em-up video games?"

As an indicator of metrosexuality, *Cargo* obviously leans much more on the side of narcissism than caring. It "touts a 'collegiate' look that costs slightly less than a college tuition payment," according to *The Washington Post*.[22] "And 'cowboy shirts' that cost slightly less than a cowboy's monthly salary. . . . There's also a gallery of hip new T-shirts, including one produced especially for *Cargo*. That one says 'SELF ESTEEM.' Which pretty much sums up the magazine's philosophy."[23]

LET'S GO, BOYFRIEND!

Beyond the caring/narcissism split, there's another side to metrosexuality's effect on culture that hasn't really been touched on yet: it's been a real boon to social tolerance of lesbians, gays, bisexuals, and transgendered people. And, to a limited extent, it has actually allowed straight men the freedom to discuss their own intimacy with one another.

Men have always bonded with other men. There's nothing new about two or three guys getting together for a few beers, a pickup game of basketball, or a trip to the local sports arena. What metrosexuality—or at least men's increased openness to traditionally feminine behaviors—has brought to the table is a willingness to move beyond sports talk and jokes with the guys and actually have discussions about things like child rearing, marital relationships, and, dare we say it, feelings.

For the most part, the male bonding we're seeing continues to revolve around sports—basketball, touch football, and other competitive games for the younger guys, gradually replaced by such "grown-up" sports as golf and tennis, as well as noncompetitive athletics (e.g., Rollerblading, running, biking). Stuart Hazlewood, an account planner at an agency in New York who has three daughters between the ages of ten and seventeen, says sports are an important factor in men's friendships because "guys need a sense of a commonweal in order to bond. It might be a hard sporting endeavor (hammering on your bike for 100 miles till you can't feel your limbs) or pulling an all-nighter at work."

The other constant elements are drinks and women (whether being with them, chasing them, or talking about them). These rituals of male bonding may evolve with age, and their frequency and intensity are likely to moderate over time, but they are well-imprinted behaviors. What's different now is that men, particularly fathers, seem more inclined to pursue relationships with men in more meaningful ways.

Brent Kaiser is someone we would consider fairly typical of a new breed of young, professional dads in big cities these days. In his mid-thirties, Brent is married, has two children under the age of three, and works as an advertising/marketing executive. He gets together with his guy friends to do the usual stuff (e.g., play racquetball, watch sports, have a beer), but he also does things with these pals that once upon a time would have been anathema to most men. One is meeting at playgrounds for playdates with the kids before work. Another is talking with his buddies via cell phone between meetings and on the commute to and from work. Brent notes that his male friends have broken into two camps: those he knew before parenthood (high school, college, postgraduation) and those he's met at the playground, in playgroups, or at the children's preschool. "My family's and my core friendship base now revolves mostly around parents with children in the same age group as mine," he says. "Others without kids or with kids much older than ours remain friends, of course, but are more difficult to connect with, both in meeting up as well as in point-of-life discussions. . . . These types of friends are difficult to coordinate with as we often are going in two different directions (both physically and mentally)."

The extent to which Brent's friendships revolve around his children and their needs and activities marks a real change from thirty or forty years ago, when fathers would have been an uncomfortable presence at the local playground. Today's dad, in contrast, is expected to be hands-on. And by sharing in the day-to-day duties associated with child care, he's also being thrust into a world in which such topics as breast-feeding, children's digestive systems, and how to deal with a bully in kindergarten are par for the course. These modern-day dads know their kids, they know their friends' kids, and they're less hesitant to discuss their frustrations, insecurities, and joys with their fellow dads. That has the potential to lead to the sorts of deeper, more meaningful friendships women have for so long enjoyed with their sisters and female friends.

And then there's the dancing.

A men's magazine called *Stuff* recently reported more frequent sightings of straight men dancing together when they go out to clubs in Manhattan.[24] This is not something you'll be likely to see around a jukebox near you anytime soon, but it is indicative of men's easing up on the strictures of behavior that were once so tightly drawn. Flirting with even the appearance of homosexuality still raises eyebrows in most places today, but it's now less likely to raise a person's ire, much less his fists.

For the most part, though, we're seeing less of men opening up sexually than we are of them opening up emotionally. And that hasn't escaped the notice of social observers who bother to look behind headlines about eyeliner and shopping sprees and attempt to dig a bit deeper into the phenomenon of metrosexuality and the trends and shifts that have given birth to it.

Kim Campbell, writing in *The Christian Science Monitor*, is one of the few journalists who seems to understand that the metrosexual phenomenon is more than just skin (or outfit) deep: "The arrival of metrosexuals prompts more discussion of men expressing themselves not only by wearing Prada, but through their emotions as well. For some advocates, especially in the feminist community, showing their emotions benefits men by letting them become 'whole' people."[25]

The magazine editor Jim Frank agrees that metrosexuality has more to do with how one feels on the inside than how one looks on the outside, and he's quick to dismiss the notion that the phenomenon is indicative of a merging of the sexes. "For years," he says, "we'd automatically brand anyone interested in his looks and clothes as gay. I guess 'metrosexual' is just a way of saying all that but not necessarily gay. . . . It really just means that instead of looking good to attract women, men are doing it to feel better about themselves, for themselves. It follows economic success. It is not, as some have postulated, the beginning of a middle gender, falling somewhere between men and women."

A GLOBAL PHENOMENON

Though much of the talk about metrosexuality has taken place in the U.S., British, and Australian media, metrosexuality has become a topic of conversation—and a reality—in numerous other countries, as well, from Pakistan to Brazil to Korea.

A survey of Indonesian men similar to the one conducted by Euro RSCG Worldwide in the U.S., U.K., and Netherlands found similar results: not only a strong emphasis on the importance of men's grooming, but also increased focus on family, fitness, and love over more traditionally "male" pursuits. Indonesian men in general are now more eager to grow old with the women they love, have happy and healthy children, and remain fit for the rest of their lives. Each of those things beat out the other options given, including having a "wherever/whenever affair with their dream woman."[26]

India, too, has seen a real explosion in the discussion of metrosexuality over the past year and a half. Here's an excerpt from a dialogue between the Metrosexual and the Retrosexual written in response to *The P Dialogues*, which was itself a response to Eve Ensler's *The Vagina Monologues*. Printed in *The Tribune* (of India), it's meant to remind readers that the battle of the sexes has become much more complicated than just boys versus girls. According to its author, "With jargon jugglers pushing metrosexuality to the center stage of public discussion, the masculinity vs. femininity debate has a whole new face to it."[27]

> M: Hey, look at my black net shirt. Just the right thing to flaunt my
>   newly waxed chest in. What do you say?

R: Ugh. Isn't it painful to have all that hair peeled off? Why bear so
much to bare so little? Anyways, that leaves you neither hair nor
there.

M: Oh boy. What do you know of the pleasures of flaunting silky
smooth skin. Time you added new spice and juice to your beauty
regimen. How long will you stick to Old Spice? Learn to savor
the fruits of the beauticians' labor. Here, try this strawberry
peel-off mask.

Kshama Singhania, a second-year college student in Mumbai, tells
us that in India, she's seeing a real flip-flop from women trying to be
more like men, to men now trying to be more like women. "Three or
four decades back," she explains, "women wanted to look tough, to be
the decision makers, to be like men . . . But now the scene is completely different. Keeping in mind the changing trends and attitudes,
men have started to behave like women; they are more aware of fashion, more conscious of their looks, more apprehensive of what they
are wearing, more sensitive, etc. In one word, the trend of 'metrosexuality' is growing."

Across the globe, a chorus of muffled yelps can be heard as the
wax strips come off. According to Kim Kwang-jin, manager of the
Green Turtle Total Beauty and Massage Salon in Itaewon, Korea, requests from men for waxing increase as the summer weather approaches. "We're getting a lot of requests. Men want their backs,
chests, arms, legs, and eyebrows waxed—especially with the hotter
temperatures, they think that it helps them to stay cool."

With his male waxing clientele consisting of a cross-section of for-
eigners, including bodybuilders, American soldiers, and businesspeo-
ple, Kim believes vanity and a desire to please their partners are the
main reasons men are using the salon's services. "A lot of men do it for
their wives or girlfriends. These days men are waxing because they
want a clean look and are trying to appear younger. Smooth male bodies really appeal to foreign and Korean women," he said.[28]

Korean men, far less likely than Europeans to need to suffer
through a back wax, are nevertheless coming in in increased numbers
for eyebrow-waxing services—and, for the daring, the Brazilian
bikini wax.[29]

This is not to say that metrosexuals have garnered such a rosy re-
ception in all corners of the world. Indeed, the backlash in England,

the United States, and Australia was at times as loud and plentiful as the hype.

"Think about it," demanded an article in the *San Jose Mercury News*. "If you were a woman, would you want a boyfriend who goes to the same salon as you to get his hair streaked? Or who has more—and more expensive—shoes? Or who spends 45 minutes before bedtime applying exfoliators, astringents, anti-aging ointments and moisturizing creams, while you wait in bed staring slack-jawed at 'SportsCenter' highlights?"[30] No doubt about it, many men decry the sight of some of their own exfoliated, plucked, and moisturized.

Women, too, are drawing their own personal lines in terms of how far they want the metrosexual men in their lives to go. Rebecca Frank, eighteen, a student at Tufts University, thinks men's greater emphasis on grooming and fashion is a good thing, up to a point. "If he spends more time on grooming than I do," she says, "it's a huge turnoff. Also, some of it is excessive, just as it would be for women. For example, no one needs to be completely hairless from head to toe." If she could shout one message from the mountaintop to the men of the world, she said, it would be this: "STOP WAXING!"

Cathy Lasowski, a baby-boomer American living in Paris, has a different pet peeve: "Men are welcome to the world of grooming," she says. "Now they, too, can know the joy of waxing. I must say I draw the line at makeup. Most women don't apply makeup that well. I can't stand the ten-year learning curve we will need to go through as men learn to apply blush."

For some, this intensified focus on appearance is nothing more than another way for men to express their egotism. "Metrosexuality doesn't surprise me," Jimmy Szczepanek says, "because it is just another form of vanity, and most men are egocentric. It makes perfect sense that they would care about their looks."

Others see men's interest in grooming as a sort of narcissism and self-involvement that is taking society ever further from the more important issues people should be facing. Julius van Heek is one of those people. Though he appreciates the upside of men being more open about expressing their feelings, he fears that the negatives outweigh the positives: "In some ways, metrosexuality is great for the overall population. The positive side I see is that men are more honest with themselves, and it certainly provides for a large market boom for businesses in the grooming/fashion world. In other ways, however, it is disheartening. Is it necessary for all of this time and money to be spent on these 'artificial' and 'temporary' products? Are we so concerned about our appearance that these product lines are so important to men all of a sudden? Where does the push come from: the men themselves or society around them? And does it continue the particularly American phenomenon of an obsession with youth?"

Unsurprisingly, one of the first to criticize the marketing of metrosexuality was the Metro-Daddy himself, Mark Simpson. Simpson, given his strong position on the role of media and commodification in culture, had none too kind words for the idea of using metrosexuality to open new markets. "'Salzman and Co. are trying to persuade as many straight men as possible to relax their sphincter muscles. They coo in their ears that there's nothing gay about being f***ed by corporate consumerism,' he says, no-holds barred."[31] Interestingly, Simpson uses the language of homophobia and "gay panic"—the same sort of panic seen by the straight men who lashed out against metrosexuality because of its open acceptance of behavior that has traditionally been considered gay—to try to make his point. In doing so, he reinforces the idea that being gay is equivalent to being powerless, a position he strongly resists in his other writing.

Though Simpson's arguments concentrate on the role consumerism plays in metrosexuality, most of the backlash comes from men—and women—not willing to see their beloved machismo sacrificed. "'The celebration of the feminine side of the guy has sort of careened out of control into this three-headed monster, the metrosexual, that needs to be slain,' says John Henson. He's doing his darnedest to beat back the beast as the star of the new Spike TV show *The John Henson Project*, where each week he spotlights what is happening 'in the world of men.'"[32]

And men who embody the trend have, according to some, fallen out of favor. "[Justin] Timberlake had bottles thrown at him at a concert in Toronto and needed to be saved by the staunchly non-metrosexual Keith Richards. Beckham was banished to Spain," reports Australia's *Sunday Herald Sun*.[33] In the same article, Adam Zwar described the "Death of the Metrosexual," and continued his obituary thus: "Some commentators suggest he was tortured to death by gangs of men in AC/DC T-shirts and army fatigue pants. Others say he died of a broken heart when he noticed many of his followers had grown bored of shopping, coloring, exfoliating and waxing. There will be no

memorial service for the Metrosexual Man as most of us are embarrassed he lived at all. He will be buried in a plot next to his perverse
ancestor, the Men's Movement. May they rest in peace."[34]

INTRODUCING THE EMO BOY
AND NEW BLOKE

The backlash against metrosexuality has come not only from men
fearing the wax; women, too, have sounded their protests, saying they
don't want to date men who are in touch with their feminine side at
the expense of their masculinity. They complain about the men who
have made an art of processing their feelings, their anxieties, their
weakness, their wounds. The men who are dwelling in their hurt and
claiming their fears, but less to grow through them than to obsess over
them.

Some of these men might correctly fall within the metrosexual
category, but certainly not all. Instead, we'd identify them as "emo
boys," a label taken from an especially sappy, emotional, "sincere"
branch of indie music. These are men who have learned some very
positive lessons from their feminine sides, but at the expense of their
backbones.

Bonnie, a poster on urbandictionary.com, defines emo boys this
way: "Boys who listen to pretentious 'you've probably never heard of
them' bands, dress with more care and style than most girls, and read
in-depth books, while sipping on low-fat lattes before they take their
Vespa home. Their hair, a special point of interest, is usually styled to
look unkempt, jet black, wooshed over to the side. They are generally
tall and thin. They appreciate the arts. They KNOW just how much
cooler than the rest of us they are."

"Forlorn poet," posting on the same site, has a somewhat different
take on emo boys, describing them as an "XY chromosome-based
apology for the sinful excesses of a patriarchal society, achieved chiefly
through the adoption of more stereotypically feminine traits while
outwardly denying identification with the more stereotypically bad
male attributes and behaviours. Nonmuscular, distant, quietly vain,
sensitive, nice, cultured, apologetic, and intimately dark, the emo boy
chooses to correlate as closely as possible to the label of 'deep'
through careful censorship and grooming, rather than by way of eru-
dition and direct illumination (which could be viewed as adversarial or

condescending) even though the average emo boy displays a higher capacity for intellect than most other male fashion–identifiable cliques."

"I think emo boys are part of a post-feminist scenario, but it's not making women very happy," Rachel Elder, a freelance writer who gained notoriety for posting an online rant against what she calls "whimpsters," told the *New York Observer*.[35]

The complaints against emo boys are not that dissimilar from those against metrosexuals, but they center on a neediness that few metrosexuals display: "It's not that he's femme-y or secretly gay," says Elder. "He's straight, all right. But this new breed of sensitive straight guy is tricky. He looks masculine enough, in a scruffy, tending-toward-boyish way. But he's vulnerable, emotional, subject to mood swings and fits of self-searching. He talks about his feelings. A lot. His fears and secret aspirations, his family pressures, his anxiety about whether he'll ever make partner, or get that book contract, or head that nonprofit organization—all are comfortable topics for emo boy. He'll sound sensitive. He is sensitive—but often more sensitive to his own emotions than to those of the woman sitting across from him at dinner. She may very well be sipping her pinot noir and wondering why her emo boy is droning on at such length about himself. Could it be that what she thought at first blush was sensitivity turns out to be good old-fashioned self-absorption?"[36]

One aspect of femininity most men don't seem to have opened themselves up to yet is paying attention to others. At least, this is what Dr. Anna Fels, author of *Necessary Dreams: Ambition in Women's Changing Lives*, believes: "I would say that historically, and right up through the present, one of the things that defined femininity—especially in the white, middle-class culture—is women listening to men and being their audience, their support system, and really asking for relatively little of that in return," she said. "There's been a really disproportionate share of attention of all kinds that men demand and assume as their due."[37]

Some critics of metrosexuality argue that, though the outside speaks of femininity and connection to a more whole self, underneath that femininity still beats the self-centered heart of the 1950s husband.

For those dissatisfied with the touchy-feely aspects of the emo boy and the chauvinism of such classes of men as the "neolad," Hugh

Mackay, an Australian social researcher, has come up with what he thinks is a happy medium: the New Bloke. "He's Blokey, but sensitive. He loves his mates, but counts women among his best friends. He's no wimp, but no macho chauvinist either."[38] Mackay says New Blokes, usually in their twenties, are "enlightened, liberated and comfortable with their own masculinity. But more importantly, the New Bloke . . . knows women are equal to men. He wants us to accept that the pathway to good relationships between the sexes lies in an acceptance of genuine equality. Any other way of operating strikes him as being unfair, unsustainable and just plain silly."[39]

In his unveiling of the New Bloke, Mackay tries to make quick work of the models of maleness that have come before him in order to distinguish his own brand as unique: "Forget the mawkish SNAG (Sensitive New Age Guy) and the marketing tool that was metrosexuality," he proclaims, "the New Bloke is the real deal." Mackay describes the SNAG as "a pathetic creature created by feminists and almost immediately despised by them," but says that the New Bloke is a creation of the more long-lasting effects of the women's movement.[40]

ENTER THE ÜBERSEXUAL

At the risk of throwing gasoline onto the fires of social debate, the authors of this book have identified yet another outcropping of man: the übersexual. This is a man whose defining qualities are passion and style. He is passionate about his interests, passionate in his relationships, passionate about feeding his senses through color, taste, scent, and feel. And passionate about doing and being what comes naturally, what feels right, rather than what others believe he should do or be.

We chose *über* as our descriptor because of its connotations of being the greatest, the best. In our view, these men are the most attractive (not just physically), most dynamic, and most compelling men of their generations. They are supremely confident (without being obnoxious), masculine, stylish, and committed to uncompromising quality in all areas of life.

How is the übersexual different from the metrosexual? The distinctions can be subtle, but they're important: Compared with the metrosexual, the übersexual is more into relationships than self. He's more sensual and not at all self-conscious. He dresses for himself more than others (choosing a consistent personal style over fashion fads). Like the metrosexual, the übersexual enjoys shopping, but his approach is more focused; he shops for particular items that enhance his collection rather than shopping as entertainment (he has better things to do than hang out at the mall). As important, his best friends are male; he doesn't consider the women in his life his "buddies."

Where metrosexuals have been called "just gay enough," the appearance and behaviors of übersexuals don't invite questions about their sexuality. They are men like George Clooney and, in a twisted way, Donald Trump. Men who are certain about what they want and who set out to get it, no holds barred.

In some ways, the übersexual is man's best response to the women's movement—at least, so far. The category is different from the others we've described, because the men in it have defined themselves, their goals and their needs, with very little reference to women. Rather than responding to feminism, they are making choices based on what opportunities are available to them today without all the analysis and second-guessing that can prove so paralyzing. They think positively of women and typically have good relationships with them, but do not go out of their way to seek women's acceptance or approval (though they almost always get it). In many ways, they mark a return to the positive characteristics of the Real Man of yesteryear (strong, resolute, fair) without having acquired too much of the self-doubt and insecurity that plagues so many of today's men. Even if they've never heard the term, they are by their very essence believers in their own M-ness.

The question that remains is whether übersexuality is simply an ideal beyond the reach of most modern men or whether these men represent an evolutionary alternative to the sad sacks who seem incapable of retaining their sense of manhood in postfeminist times. It may well be that übersexuality will soon be held up by men's media and others as the archetype to which the modern male should aspire.

A NEW WORLD ORDER?

Even in the backlash to metrosexuality, analysts are acknowledging that something very fundamental in the world of men has changed. The neolads and the New Blokes (and even the übersexuals) cannot simply return to times when men held all the cards and women put their lives on hold as they waited for an engagement ring to be slipped on their finger. They would be fools if they did. More important, they would be bachelor fools. Instead, men, whether they fall under the umbrella of one of these catchy labels or not, must recognize that a fundamental shift has taken place in the way men and women interact. In recent decades, the spotlight has been on women's social change, to the virtual exclusion of men's—a problem this book seeks to address. After all, as we see in the development of the metrosexual, the women's movement has arguably had at least as big an impact on men as on women.

In many respects, recent social thinking has cast men as villains whose insensitive, aggressive, domineering attitudes are to blame for everything from global violence to environmental destruction. Their performance relative to women is declining, and reproductive science is threatening to make them obsolete. It's now possible to ask, "What's the point of men? What do they bring to the party?"

WHAT TO REMEMBER

1. The new balance of power calls for lighter versions of masculinity that take more account of what used to be "female" values.

2. Our take on the sexes is simple: Women are increasingly able to get out and earn money, have real careers, kick ass, have fun, and do all the other things that men used to regard as their preserve. And men who want to attract them are realizing that they need to learn some new tricks. Among them: being more careful about their appearance and grooming, and being more comfortable with gossip and feelings and design—it's a whole new way for men to think about exterior and interior. These things fit with being a Real Man in 2005, even if they did not fit with old notions of Real Manhood. They may overlap with some aspects of gay culture, but who cares?

3. Being a Real Man today means knowing and doing what it takes to get what you want, when you want it. That may include an attractive partner (male or female); it may include power and wealth; it may include health and physical prowess. After all, we're living in an era of infinite choice; this is the "Dawning of the Age of M-ness."

5

MAN AS KING OF THE CASTLE

The female of the genus homo is economically dependent on
the male. He is her food supply.

— Charlotte Perkins Gillman (1860–1935),
American feminist and writer

Until the first half of the twentieth century, Western societies
still assumed that men and women both had marriage as their
eventual goal. Traditionally, women were seen as fantasizing
about it, while men were said to dread it. Regardless, a married couple
was the fundamental societal unit: the breadwinner and the homemaker, the provider and the nurturer. Men who bucked the system
were romanticized (provided they were assumed to be heterosexual):
they became the mysterious strangers, the dangerous Casanovas.

Women who did not marry, past a certain age, merely became spin-sters. People to be pitied and perhaps even scorned.

What is interesting about this division is the implicit implication: that **marriage somehow limits a man, whereas in the same mystic way it completes a woman, who is taught to feel partial or un-whole until she has performed her vows. Indeed, that sense of both limitation and completion can be traced directly back to the cultural history of marriage.** In *Marriage in Men's Lives*, Steven L. Nock writes,

> A marriage is much more than the sum of two spouses. It is also a re-lationship defined by legal, moral, and conventional assumptions. While one can imagine a variety of close personal affiliations uniting two adults, the variety of marriage affiliations is much narrower be-cause marriage is an *institution*, culturally patterned and integrated into other basic social institutions, such as education, the economy, and politics. Marriage has rules that originate outside any particular union of two spouses and that establish *soft boundaries* around the re-lationship that influence the partners in many ways. The boundaries around marriages are the commonly understood allowable limits of behavior that distinguish marriage from all other kinds of relation-ships. The social norms that define the institution of marriage iden-tify married spouses in ways that distinguish them from others. Married couples have something that other couples lack: they are heirs to a vast system of understood principles that help organize and sustain their lives.[1]

In other words, the traditional limits on marriage, those "soft boundaries," give a husband and wife access to an organizing system that helps them to define their lives and their relationship. In this way, the limits of marriage, some would argue, actually lead to greater ful-fillment for both parties.

Nock also points to other, much more fundamental benefits of marriage, including "lower rates of suicide, fatal accidents, acute and chronic illnesses, alcoholism, and depression."[2] And even though it was traditionally women who set their sights on a trip to the altar, it was men who stood to gain the most:

> Men reap greater gains than women for virtually every outcome af-fected by marriage. When women benefit from marriage, it is be-

cause they are in a satisfying relationship; but men appear much less sensitive to the quality of their marriages and gain by simply *being married*. . . . Marriage itself improves men's lives; the quality of the marriage affects women's lives.[3]

Beyond the advantages marriage inherently afforded men, the cultural models of much of the twentieth century (and, really, we're only talking forty-odd years ago) declared that Father definitely knew best. In his "castle," he was head of household, chief decision maker, and unquestioned authority. Not to mention being a focus of fear for all those children who were told again and again, "Just wait till your father gets home!" No doubt about it, the husband was cast in marriage's leading role, regardless of his suitablility for the part. And society—including the media—relentlessly reinforced that notion.

THE GOLDEN AGE OF TELEVISION (FOR MEN)

Television helped to defend men's leadership role within the household. Case in point: from October 1954 to September 1960, for a total of 203 episodes, Robert Young played Jim Anderson on *Father Knows Best*. According to www.tvtome.com, the Anderson family resided in Springfield, a prototypical Midwestern community, where Jim A. worked as an agent for the General Insurance Company. The Andersons' life was one of routine: "Every evening he would come home from work, take off his sport jacket, put on his comfortable sweater, and deal with the everyday problems of a growing family," which included Betty, Bud, and dear little Kathy. Compared with many of the family comedies of that time, in which at least one of the parents was a "bumbler" (think *The Honeymooners* and *I Love Lucy*), both Andersons were portrayed as thoughtful, responsible adults. Nevertheless, when family crises arose, Father typically did know best, taking charge, with a warm smile, sensible advice, and the authority bestowed (presumably by God and nature) upon the man of the homestead.

Margaret Anderson was played by none other than Jane Wyatt, the first wife of another actor who did a great deal for the image of the American family. Of course, most of Ronald Reagan's more famous familial troubles arose during his subsequent marriage to Nancy Davis. True, Nancy was three months pregnant with Patti when they finally got around to swapping rings, but Reagan presented in all of his roles, whether dramatic or political, a model of the strong father and the moral man. Even though conception outside marriage could have been seen as part of the revolution of his times, Reagan was always clear about which side of the culture wars he fought for. Remember that in his famous quip, the hippies not only had a haircut like Tarzan and smelled like Cheetah, but walked like Jane.[4]

The Reagans had some rough patches, but, as tvtome.com reminds us, "the Andersons were truly an idealized family, the sort that viewers could relate to and wish to emulate. The children went through the normal problems of growing up, including those concerning school, friends, and members of the opposite sex. They didn't always agree with their parents and occasionally succeeded in asserting their independence. . . . But the bickering was minimal, and everything seemed to work out by the end of the half-hour."

What better marriage model could Dad ask for? Not only were his sweaters always comfortable and his children always agreeable (even in the midst of conflict), but his wife was always sensible and his insurance job was oh so general.

A number of the most popular TV shows of the 1950s portrayed an unambiguous model of marital perfection. Those who were old enough to know, knew they wanted their families to be like the Andersons, like the Nelsons of Sycamore Road in Hillsdale: happy, ordered, "perfect." No one ever raised his or her voice, all problems were resolved before the commercial break, and Mom always cooked dinner in her pearls. Those were the days . . .

WOMEN GET A SNIFF OF FREEDOM: THE WAR YEARS

Marriage, as it existed in the first half of the twentieth century, offered all sorts of bonuses for men, including longer life, greater prosperity, decreased incidence of disease and alcoholism, greater social status, and honor and obeisance from wife and child alike. On the other hand, women's chances of benefiting from marriage depended almost wholly on snagging the right man. Nevertheless, the alternative (to the extent that it was even considered a viable alternative)—the life of the bachelorette or spinster—

TIPS FOR THE 1950s HOUSEWIFE

HOW TO BE A GOOD WIFE

Have dinner ready. Plan ahead, even the night before, to have a delicious meal, on time. This is a way of letting him know that you have been thinking about him and are concerned about his needs. Most men are hungry when they come home and the prospect of a good meal is part of the warm welcome needed.

Prepare yourself. Take 15 minutes to rest so that you'll be refreshed when he arrives. Touch up your makeup, put a ribbon in your hair and be fresh-looking. He has just been with a lot of work-weary people. Be a little gay and a little more interesting. His boring day may need a lift.

Clear away the clutter. Make one last trip through the main part of the home just before your husband arrives, gather up schoolbooks, toys, paper, etc. Then run a dust cloth over the tables. Your husband will feel he has reached a haven of rest and order, and it will give you a lift, too.

Prepare the children. Take a few minutes to wash the children's hands and faces (if they are small), comb their hair, and, if necessary, change their clothes. They are little treasures and he would like to see them playing the part.

Minimize all noise. At the time of his arrival, eliminate all noise of the washer, dryer, dishwasher, or vacuum. Try to encourage the children to be quiet. Be happy to see him. Greet him with a warm smile and be glad he is home.

Some don'ts: Don't greet him with problems or complaints. Don't complain if he is late for dinner. Count this as minor compared with what he might have gone through that day. Make him comfortable. Have him lean back in a comfortable chair or suggest he lie down in the bedroom. Have a cool or warm drink ready for him. Arrange his pillow and offer to take off his shoes. Speak in a low, soft, soothing and pleasant voice. Allow him to relax and unwind.

Listen to him. You may have a dozen things to tell him, but the moment of his arrival is not the time. Let him talk first.

Make the evening his. Never complain if he does not take you out to dinner or to other places of entertainment. Instead, try to understand his world of strain and pressure, his need to be home and relax.

The Goal: Try to make your home a place of peace and order where your husband can renew himself in body and spirit.

The preceding instructions are from a popular e-mail, purportedly taken from a home economics textbook published in 1954.[5] Though some dismiss these tips as urban legend, the e-mail's points are echoed in the following do's and don'ts from Helen Andelin's *Fascinating Womanhood* (first published in 1965 and updated in 1992).

Dos	*Dont's*
Accept him at face value.	Don't try to change him.
Admire the manly things about him.	Don't show indifference, contempt, or ridicule towards his masculine abilities, achievements or ideas.
Recognize his superior strength and ability.	Don't try to excel him in anything which requires masculine ability.
Be a Domestic Goddess.	Don't let the outside world crowd you for time to do your homemaking tasks well.
Work for inner happiness and seek to understand its rules.	Don't have a lot of preconceived ideas of what you want out of life.
Revere your husband and honor his right to rule you and your children.	Don't stand in the way of his decisions, or his law.[6]

was hardly appealing, socially or economically. Indeed, both before and after World War II, the era seen as a turning point for women's entrance into the workforce, women navigated unknown and dangerous waters when they sought economic independence.

World War II, as has been amply documented, was a time when patriotic women were called to take the place of the many able-bodied young men who were called overseas, primarily to Europe and to Asia Pacific. In addition to jobs in factories and offices, women played a vital role in the military, most visibly as nurses. A Women's Army Auxiliary Corps was established just four days after the Japanese attacked Pearl Harbor, with the wife of a former governor of the state of Texas named as its director.

Women's newfound sense of freedom was evident not just among the working classes, but also among the bluebloods who helped set fashions and styles—and raised more than a few eyebrows along the way. Among the better known was Kathleen "Kick" Kennedy, sister of JFK, who was described by the Inquirer News Service as "the most vivacious of the Kennedy sisters, and her father's favorite." After her first husband (of just five weeks), Lord Hartington, heir to the duchy of Devonshire, was killed in action, Kick risked scandal and family censure by falling in love with a married man (and Protestant), the handsome, party-loving Peter Fitzwilliam. While on their way to persuade Kick's father, Joe Kennedy, to accept their union, the couple was killed in a plane crash in the south of France.

Then there was the famous—and certainly notorious—Pamela Harriman, who kept herself busy indeed during and after the war. Born Pamela Digby, daughter of an English lord, she married a succession of wealthy and well-connected men: first Randolph Churchill, son of Winston Churchill; then Broadway producer Leland Hayward; and, finally, Averell Harriman, with whom she had had an affair while he was U.S. ambassador to Britain during World War II. Along the way, she had dalliances with such luminaries as famed broadcaster Edward R. Murrow; Bill Paley, owner of CBS (and Murrow's boss); HRH Prince Aly Khan; Gianni Agnelli, the (married) heir to the Fiat car empire; the Greek shipping magnate Stavros Niarchos; and the international banker Baron Elie de Rothschild, among others. Though some dismissed her as nothing but a courtesan, Pamela Digby Churchill Hayward Harriman, as she called herself, enjoyed much political influence in the United States and was ambassador to France when she died in 1997.

Other women garnered far less ink for their adventures during the war, but in their own way they, too, began to assert control and break free of the gender roles that had bound them. **As the war dragged on, more and more women became factory workers, nurses, writers and journalists, drivers, farmers, mail carriers, garbage collectors, mechanics—you name it, they did it. What had been male was suddenly, if temporarily, unisex.**

And with paying work, life changed—fast. Women not only earned their own money, they were more free to spend it as they pleased; independence was a given: the men in their lives were largely overseas and unreachable. This was an era that, at least for a time, transformed women from shrinking violets to capable, competent proponents of equality. With some major obstacles—most important, tradition and their husbands—out of the way, women took wartime and its horrors and turned them into an opportunity to prove they were up to the challenge of holding their own in a man's world.

TOWARD TRUE EQUALITY

When the war ended, so, too, did the dramatic burst of female power, replaced by a slow, steady climb toward genuine equality, still a work in progress in many industries, places, households, and lives.

Men actively resisted the entry of women into most jobs, the few exceptions including such "caring" and child-centered services as nursing and teaching. Immediately after World War II, men returning home from military service expected women to vacate their positions and get back to the business of being housewives or single women in search of husbands. Any woman who persisted in working was badly viewed on the grounds that she was depriving a breadwinner (and hence his family) of his livelihood. In fact, as late as the 1970s, American schoolgirls were trained in (mandatory) home economics, where they learned cooking and sewing while their male counterparts were in wood shop or metal shop. Make no mistake, even twenty-five or thirty years ago teenage girls were in obligatory training to become the keepers of home and hearth, to produce for baby and husband,

10 THINGS YOU MIGHT NOT KNOW:
WOMEN'S "RIGHTS" IN THE 20TH CENTURY

- In the United States, women weren't permitted to serve as jurors on an equal basis with men until 1968. As late as 1965, women were completely excluded from juries in Alabama, Mississippi, and South Carolina. In 1966, the Supreme Court of Mississippi ruled that "the legislature has the right to exclude women so that they may continue their service as mothers, wives and homemakers, and also to protect them . . . from the filth, obscenity and noxious atmosphere that so often pervades a courtroom during a jury trial."[7]
- In 1970, the Ohio Supreme Court held that a wife was "at most a superior servant to her husband . . . only chattel with no personality, no property, and no legally recognized feelings or rights."[8]
- The 1974 Georgia legislature approved a statute that defined the husband as "head of the family," with the "wife . . . subject to him; her legal existence . . . merged in the husband, except as so far as the law recognizes her separately, either for her own protection, her own benefit, or for the preservation of the public order."[9]
- Until 1979, Louisiana's "head and master" law permitted a husband the unilateral right to dispose of jointly owned community property without his wife's knowledge or consent.[10]
- As of the mid-1980s, the average divorced woman and the minor children in her household experienced a 73 percent decline in their standard of living in the first year of divorce. Her former husband, in contrast, experienced a 42 percent rise in his standard of living.[11]
- Prior to 1976, when the first marital rape law was enacted, it was legal in all fifty U.S. states for a husband to rape his wife.[12]
- In 1907, the United States adopted a policy of automatically severing the U.S. citizenship of any woman who married a foreign national, regardless of where the couple lived or whether the husband intended to become a U.S. citizen.[13]

- In 1919, all federal civil-service examinations were finally opened to women, but up until 1962, each department head could specify the sex of those he wished to hire for any particular position.[14]
- In 1948, the U.S. Supreme Court upheld a Michigan law that prohibited women from working in bars unless they were the wives or daughters of a male owner.[15]
- Until a court ruling in 1974, pregnant teachers in Virginia and Ohio were required to take unpaid maternity leaves beginning several months before birth and continuing for several months afterward.[16]

while teenage boys were in training for trades that would lead to paid employment.

In some cases, women had even less opportunity on the work front compared with before the world war. In journalism, for example, the ranks of newswomen thinned out once the men returned from their tours of duty, and even those who had proved their excellence were demoted or replaced; by 1968, as the situation in Vietnam heated up, and as America began to rumble with all kinds of domestic strife about what was to come, there were fewer female correspondents than there had been in the prewar years.

This is not to say that no permanent gains were made. Certainly, World War II and its aftermath were the time when the seeds of permanent and lasting change were planted. The following timeline provides a glimpse of just how much changed in the second half of the twentieth century—changes that have affected not just the role of women at school, work, and home, but also the role of the men who were and are their classmates, co-workers and competitors, and partners. In just over fifty years, the life of the average male was turned upside down. Not only did he face increased competition from women and new rules for interacting with them, he also had to face very different expectations regarding not just his behavior, but also his attitudes and even his persona. Like it or not, the rules had changed—

and this time, in the view of many, it was men who were getting the short end of the stick.

A CHANGING WORLD: 1950-2004

- 1950: The median age for first marriage in the U.S. is 22.8 years for men and 20.3 years for women.
- 1950: The Mattachine Society, the first national gay rights organization, is formed by Harry Hay.
- 1953: Hugh Hefner introduces *Playboy*. The first issue is an immediate sensation and sells out within a matter of weeks.
- 1953: Launch of *ONE Magazine*, the first widely circulated gay periodical in North America.
- 1954: The average heterosexual man in Britain first has sex at age twenty.
- 1956: The phrase "angry young man" enters the English language on publication of John Osborne's *Look Back in Anger.*
- 1957: *Gentlemen's Quarterly* is launched.
- 1958: In the UK, civil servant Irene Ferguson, having undergone a sex-change operation, is awarded the civil service's higher salary for men.
- 1959: According to the U.S. census, the median male income in the United States is $3,997; the median female income is less than a third of that: $1,223.
- 1960s: The unisex hair salon makes its first appearance in the United States.
- 1960: Every state in the United States has an antisodomy law.
- 1960: The U.S. Food and Drug Administration approves birth control pills.
- 1963: The U.S. Congress passes the Equal Pay Act, making it illegal for employers to pay a woman less than what a man would receive for the same job.
- 1964: Because of the market success of the Barbie doll, Hasbro releases the GI Joe doll for boys.
- 1964: The Beatles appear on *The Ed Sullivan Show*, creating a revolution in men's hairstyles with their "mop tops"; long hair becomes fashionable among men for the first time since the eighteenth century.

- 1965: In *Griswold v. Connecticut*, the U.S. Supreme Court strikes down a law prohibiting the use of contraceptives by married couples.
- 1966: President Lyndon Johnson proclaims Father's Day an official national holiday.
- 1969: *GAY*, the first weekly newspaper for gays in the United States, is launched.
- 1969: The Rolling Stones' Mick Jagger wears a dress onstage.
- 1969: Yale University admits women for the first time in its 268-year history.
- 1969: California becomes the first state to adopt a "no fault" divorce law, which allows couples to divorce by mutual consent. (By 1985, every state has adopted a similar law.)
- 1972: Gloria Steinem and a group of feminist activists launch *Ms.* magazine.
- 1973: The American Psychiatric Association removes homosexuality from its official list of mental disorders.
- 1976: Clinique is the first cosmetics company to enter the male skincare market.
- 1976: Nebraska enacts the first marital rape law in the United States, making it illegal for a man to rape his wife.
- 1977: The film documentary *Pumping Iron* introduces the world to bodybuilders and gym culture (and marks the beginning of Arnold Schwarzenegger's rise to fame).
- 1978: AIDS cases begin to appear in the United States; the disease goes unnamed until 1982 and HIV isn't identified until 1983.
- 1980: The U.S. Census Bureau eliminates the category of "household head," replacing it with "householder" (defined as the homeowner or leaseholder of the home).
- 1981: From London's club scene emerge the New Romantics, who make it fashionable for men to wear eyeliner and lipstick, and to dress in frilly shirts.
- 1981: The National Congress for Fathers and Children, a coalition of several hundred fathers'- and men's-rights groups, is founded in the United States.
- 1982: Calvin Klein introduces his new underwear line, making men's undergarments sexy.

- 1985: The hunky actor Rock Hudson reveals his AIDS diagnosis and, to the shock of legions of fans, is "outed" as a homosexual.
- 1989: Denmark becomes the first country to legalize same-sex unions.
- 1990: The life expectancy of the average male born in 1990 is 71.8, up from 65.6 in 1950. The life expectancy of the average female born in 1990 is 78.8, up from 71.1 in 1950.
- 1990: Men account for 5.4 percent of professional nurses, up from 3.8 percent a decade earlier.
- 1992: Colorado becomes the first state to nullify existing civil-rights protections for homosexuals by amending its constitution; the provision is struck down by the U.S. Supreme Court in 1996.
- 1993: President Bill Clinton signs off on the military's "Don't ask, don't tell" policy, allowing gays to serve in the military as long as they keep their homosexuality under wraps.
- 1993: U.S. federal law requires that all companies with fifty or more employees offer up to twelve weeks of unpaid leave to new mothers and fathers.
- 1994: The rate of death from homicide for teens aged fifteen to nineteen reaches 20.3 per 100,000, more than double the rate of 8.1 per 100,000 in 1970. Among youth aged twelve to seventeen, 141 boys per 1,000 were victims of violent crimes, compared with 95 per 1,000 girls.
- 1995: The median age at first marriage in the U.S. reaches 26.9 years for men and 24.5 years for women.
- 1995: Ten percent of all U.S. males aged twenty to twenty-nine are either in jail, in prison, on probation, or on parole. (The number of incarcerated men under age twenty-five doubled between 1986 and 1995.)[17]
- 1996: The World Health Organization announces a contraceptive breakthrough: the male pill.
- 1996: According to the U.S. Census Bureau, 35 percent of men aged forty to fifty-nine have been divorced.
- 1997: The Durex Global Sex Survey finds that the average age of first sexual intercourse is 17.3 years for men and 17.8 years for women. Americans have sex earlier than any of the other populations studied, at an average age of 16.2 years.

- **1997: A *Psychology Today* study finds that 43 percent of men are unhappy with their appearance, up from approximately 14 percent thirty years earlier.**
- 1998: Viagra becomes the fastest-selling new drug on the U.S. market.
- 1999: The Vermont Supreme Court declares the state must grant same-sex couples the same rights and protections accorded to married heterosexuals; in 2000, the state legislature backs "civil unions" for same-sex couples.
- 1999: The National Center for Health Statistics finds that approximately 35 percent of women and 31 percent of men age twenty and older are obese, up from 30 percent and 25 percent, respectively, in 1980.
- **2000: According to the Census Bureau, married-couple households make up just 50.7 percent of the U.S. population, down from nearly 80 percent in the 1950s. Fifty-nine percent of the population is married, down from 62 percent in 1990 and 72 percent in 1970.**
- 2000: A U.S. version of the British TV show *Queer as Folk* debuts on the Showtime network; it followed the lives of five gay men in Pittsburgh.
- 2001: Suicide rates among men aged twenty-five to thirty-four are double those of the early 1980s. Young men aged twenty to twenty-four are seven times more likely than young women to take their own lives.
- 2001: The leading cause of death for American men aged twenty-five to thirty-four is accidents (resulting in 31.6 percent of deaths), followed by suicide (14.6 percent), homicide (14.5 percent), heart disease (7.2 percent), and cancer (6.5 percent). In comparison, the leading causes of death for U.S. women that year are accidents (21.3 percent), malignant neoplasms (16.5), heart disease (8.4 percent), homicide (8.1 percent), and suicide (6.7 percent).
- 2001: 13.2 per 100,000 men die from chronic liver disease or cirrhosis in the United States, compared with 6.2 per 100,000 women.[18]
- 2001: According to the National Center for Women and Policing, the representation of women in large police agencies across

the United States reached 12.7 percent, up from 9 percent in 1990.

- 2001: *The American Journal of Psychiatry* reports that for every four females with anorexia, there is one male; for every eight to eleven females with bulimia, there is one male. Twenty years prior, it was believed that for every ten to fifteen females with anorexia or bulimia, there was one male.

- **2002: The percentage of U.S. females aged thirty to thirty-four who had never married reached 23 percent, up from just 9 percent in 1970. The percentage of never-married males in that age range increased to 54 percent, from just 6 percent in 1970.**

- 2003: In the United States, men undergo nearly 1.1 million cosmetic procedures this year, 13 percent of the total. The number of cosmetic procedures undertaken by men increases 31 percent from the year prior.

- 2003: According to the Census Bureau, there are 2 million single fathers in the U.S., up from 393,000 in 1970. One in every six single parents is now a man, compared with one in ten in 1970.

- 2003: The U.S. Census Bureau reports that an estimated 105,000 men are "stay at home" dads, defined as married men who have children under age fifteen and who are not in the labor force primarily so they can care for the family while their wives work outside the home.

- 2003: In the United States, women's earnings as a percentage of men's (for year-round, full-time work) are 75.5 percent, up from 59.4 percent in 1970. Earning parity is even higher in many European countries, including 91 percent in Italy and 95 percent in Portugal.[19]

- 2003: The U.S. Supreme Court rules in *Lawrence v. Texas* that sodomy laws are unconstitutional.

- 2003: In the United States, one in every 109 men is in prison, compared with one woman out of every 1,613. (The female prison population is growing more rapidly than the male, however: the U.S. Justice Department reports that the number of women in prison grew 48 percent between 1995 and 2003, whereas the male prison population increased 29 percent over that period.)

- 2004: The average American man is 5'9" and weighs 180 pounds; in 1980, the average man was also 5'9" but weighed seven pounds less.

In this timeline, we see an evolution not only of what is "male" and what is "female," but also of what is important and what is trivial, what is public and what is private.

SCALING THE IVORY TOWER

Once World War II had given women a taste of independence, there was growing awareness that equal access to job opportunities would only come about if females first gained equal access to education. Ironically, the G.I. Bill instituted after the war led to a surge in male college enrollment, to the detriment of women. Whereas women had made up 41 percent of college students in 1940 (it should be remembered that college enrollment was far less common then than it is today), by 1950 they made up just 24 percent of enrollment. It wasn't until the 1970s that women's enrollment returned to prewar levels.

One of the most important barriers to education women faced was the fact that most of the world's prestigious universities, in the United States and elsewhere, were male-only until well into the second half of the twentieth century. Arguments to keep women away from the ivory tower ranged from a desire to "protect" the weaker sex to a fear that educated women would spell the ruin of society.

Dr. Edward Clarke, a retired Harvard medical school professor, warned in his 1873 treatise, *Sex in Education*, that if women were to use their "limited energy" on studying, they would endanger their "female apparatus." Collegiate studies, he asserted, would lead to such health problems in women as neuralgia, uterine disease, and, of course, hysteria and other "derangements of the nervous system."[20]

Others argued that giving women access to higher education would lead to a reduction in the number of marriages and in family size, both of which were seen as fundamental to the welfare of society as a whole. There was even concern that educated women would weaken the family line. As one historian noted: "Women were thought to be frail . . . overstudy would surely give them brain fever! And should they manage to survive college, their children would be sickly, if they were able to have children at all."[21]

Nevertheless, barriers to female education fell one by one in the twentieth century, to the point at which women's college enrollment actually exceeded that of men in the U.S. by 1979. Harvard University offers a good example of how higher institutions of learning gradually went coed, often with much kicking and dragging of feet from traditionalists. Harvard was actually among the more progressive schools, first opening up an "annex" for women in the late 1870s. To "annex," as dictionary.com reminds us, means "to append or attach, especially to a larger or more significant thing." Not the most auspicious beginning, but a beginning nonetheless. In 1894, the Annex was chartered by the Commonwealth of Massachusetts as Radcliffe College. **Today, Harvard is fully coed, as evidenced by the fact that the class of 2007 is 48 percent female.** Moreover, the *Harvard Gazette* reports that a majority of applicants admitted to the class of 2008 under the Early Action program were female—a first in the college's history.[22]

To a large extent, male-only colleges are a thing of the past. A scan of colleges and universities in the United States reveals more than fifty prestigious women's colleges—ranging from Barnard and Bryn Mawr to Mount Holyoke and Smith—but just a handful of lesser-known men's colleges, most notably Morehouse, in Atlanta, a historically black college that was the alma mater of Martin Luther King, Jr. The balance of men's colleges are almost all religious in orientation and curriculum, typically Orthodox Jewish and intended to train future rabbis. The numbers give credence to a new catchphrase many men have begun to mumble (or mutter, depending on their frame of mind): "What's mine is mine, what's his is mine" might be something most women say in jest, but it also speaks to the new reality that women have, to a large extent, managed to claw their way into men's territory, without having to give up much acreage of their own.

FIGHTING FOR A SEAT AT THE TABLE

There are a multitude of women-only gyms and clubs in the United States, and none seem to have raised the public's ire to any significant degree. Contrast that with the furor over the men-only policy of Augusta National, the private golf club that hosts the Masters Tournament. Postings on golftransactions.com include a number of angry rebuttals to this Reader's Forum question: *"Should Augusta National bow to pressure from the [National Council of Women's Organizations] and admit a woman member?"*

R. G. posted: "Until all women's organizations (private clubs, private elementary and [secondary] schools, colleges & universities) in America have modified their bylaws to allow men to join their ranks, this nefarious effort by the Council of Women's Organizations will have no credibility with me or any other clear-thinking individual."

"A 'private' club is just that!" seconded D. B. "The members join to associate with people that they wish. If they elect not to associate with women, so be it. Can you see men members in the Eastern Star or Wesley Circle? How about boys joining the Girl Scouts? Why are some feminists so 'hell bent' on the joining of the sexes?"

And L. B. wrote, "Since when is it discrimination when men want to get together without women? Next thing you know, someone will file discrimination charges against the Miss America pageant."

Of course, Augusta is far from the only men-only club that has come under protest in recent decades. Single-sex social and professional clubs for men are now few and far between, though we were shocked to learn that our own industry—the supposedly enlightened and ahead-of-the-curve advertising industry—continues to have at least one men-only dining club, the Solus Club in the UK. That's a pretty big deal when you consider that about a hundred of the most senior members of our industry are meeting on a regular basis and excluding women from the (real and metaphorical) table. Nevertheless, women continue to make strides in our industry and others, as evidenced by the fact that advertising's oldest club in the UK, the Thirty Club, voted in 2000 to allow women to join. (For the most part, the marketing business has traditionally been more progressive in terms of the hiring and advancement of women compared with other businesses, and the existence of women in highly visible positions [such as Ann Shelley Lazarus, CEO of Ogilvy & Mather] suggests that continues to be the case. It seems to us that the gender divide is not as great an issue in the marketing business, either on the client or agency side, though some might make the opposite case.)

Numerous other traditionally male bastions have also admitted women willingly, albeit oftentimes prompted by the harsh reality of declining membership: New York's famed university clubs, including the Harvard Club, Yale Club, and Princeton Club, have aggressively pursued female graduates in recent years in hopes of reversing their declining fortunes. (That's quite a step for all of them, but perhaps especially for the Princeton Club, which until a few years ago had this slogan imbedded in the floor of its barroom: "Where women cease from troubling and the wicked are at rest."[23]) In 1998, the Oxford and Cambridge University Club also chose to admit women, ending a men-only tradition that had spanned two centuries.

Other institutions have bucked the trend, either refusing outright to admit women or attempting to discourage their membership by making certain rooms or amenities off-limits or restricting access to tee times and other club offerings. The owners of the Grill Bar in Aberdeen, Scotland, thought they had come up with a solid plan to quell complaints about their males-only policy, while discouraging female attendance. Their crafty plan: a simple sign hung on the front door that read, "Please note there are no ladies' toilets in this traditionally male bar." "To the disappointment of the regulars the sign was more of a challenge than a discouragement," reported *The Scotsman*, "and the number of female visitors quickly went through the roof."[24]

GIRLS GET IN THE GAME

Sports, now a big business, have traditionally been dominated by men, with females being encouraged to exercise and "take some air" rather than to get down and dirty in competitive athletics. The movie *A League of Their Own* documents one of the early strides in women's professional sports—made possible not so much by a desire to give women equal access as by the fact that the able-bodied men were off fighting World War II.

When America's Little League Baseball was formed in 1939, its mandate was clear: to teach sportsmanship, teamwork, and fair play to boys. A quarter century later, in 1964, Congress gave the organization a federal charter to run a program for the betterment of young boys. Back then, fathers were typically coaches, sons played ball, and moms and sisters signed on for auxiliary roles—working the hot dog and soda concession, cheering from the stands. Then along came Maria Pepe, of Hoboken, New Jersey, in 1972. A pitcher for the Hoboken Young Democrats' Little League team, she found herself barred because the rules said girls couldn't play on teams with boys. If her coach didn't remove her, the Hoboken Little League would lose its charter. This conflict became the basis of a legal decision that ensured girls in the state of New Jersey would no longer be excluded from Little League programs. Fast forward thirty-plus years, and an estimated 5 million to 6 million girls have played in the Little League.

**From baseball and basketball to soccer, young boys and girls
around the country now play on coed teams, with very little opposition. Once the children grow older (and the boys grow measura-
bly bigger, faster, and stronger), of course, coed competition all
but comes to a halt.** Sure, there are the Billie Jean Kings who will always beat the Bobby Riggses of the world, and there likely will be more
and more Michelle Wies who are willing and able to compete against
men in golf and other individual sports, but, by and large, it seems unlikely that very many professional sports will go coed. (Then again, a
computer modeler at England's Oxford University did announce recently that if the male-female gap in the hundred-meter race continues
to narrow at its current rate, women will outrun men by the year 2156.)

WHAT'S MINE IS MINE, WHAT'S HIS IS MINE

Girls and women have gained enormous ground in industrialized
Western nations over the past few decades. And they're not satisfied
simply to have a fairer chance of getting into a prestigious university
or job, or with having a shot at a sports scholarship. More and more
females seem to be emulating traditionally "male" behaviors—and not
just the positive ones. Female binge drinking is up significantly, according to a report by the National Organization on Fetal Alcohol
Syndrome.[25] And the old saw that, when reminiscing about weddings,
women talk about the ceremony, while men talk about the bachelor
party, is being called into question. Today, the bachelorette party is
just as likely to be a wild ride, including male strippers and more
booze than any of the attendees can hope to remember. That doesn't
mean the bride won't recall her ceremony to the minutest detail, but it
does mean she's no longer willing to forgo the fun of a night of de-
bauchery—what's hers is hers, what's his is hers.

Women are also fighting back more and more against the stereotypes that suggest any sort of deficit vis-à-vis males. It may be fine to
joke about men's unwillingness to stop and ask for directions, but
taunting women for being bad drivers is becoming taboo. A 2004
commercial for the Mercury Mountaineer SUV spoke to this shift by
featuring a woman who very skillfully evades an obviously-in-the-
wrong driver, after which her date says sotto voce, "Women
drivers . . ."—a comment that wins him an early exit from her vehicle,
and a long walk home in the rain.

WHAT TO REMEMBER

1. Historically, marriage was believed to limit a man, whereas in some mystical way it completed a woman, who was taught to feel partial or unwhole until she had performed her vows. Indeed, that sense of both limitation and completion can be traced directly back to the cultural history of marriage.

2. A number of the most popular TV shows of the 1950s portrayed a model of marital perfection. Those who were old enough to know, knew they wanted their families to be like the Andersons, or like the Nelsons of Sycamore Road in Hillsdale: happy, ordered, "perfect." No one ever raised his or her voice, all problems were resolved before the commercial break, and Mom always vacuumed in her pearls.

3. The half century from the mid-1950s to the present has seen a turbulent transition in gender relations that began when men went off to fight World War II and women rose to the challenge of "manning" the factories, businesses—and households.

4. Television in the 1950s and 1960s tried desperately to snap society back into traditional gender roles—witness *Father Knows Best*—but such renegade shows as *The Honeymooners* foreshadowed what was to come: men depicted as buffoons trying to bluster their way through life by invoking the most traditional stereotypes. (Ralph used to threaten Alice that he would send her to the moon, "Bang, zoom, up to the moon . . ."—an explicit threat of physical violence when he had no other way to counter the fact that she had accurately called him on his stupidity. In each and every segment, Alice's superiority was reinforced, even as Ralph strutted around the apartment like a rooster ruling the henhouse.)

5. In the 1950s and first half of the 1960s, individuality was discouraged for both genders. Men born in those decades and in the 1970s became pioneers as they began to search for a maleness that is personalized and comfortable.

THE TABLES TURN FOR WOMEN

If particular care and attention is not paid to the ladies, we are determined to foment a rebellion, and will not hold ourselves bound by any laws in which we have no voice or representation.

—Abigail Adams (1744–1818),
wife of U.S. president John Adams,
mother of U.S. president John Quincy Adams,
and an early supporter of women's rights[1]

There are all sorts of dates and events one could identify as fundamental turning points in the history of men and women— or, in some cases, men *versus* women. Certainly, in the latter half of the twentieth century, such things as the founding of the National Organization for Women, the attempted passage of the Equal

Rights Amendment, and the entry of women into the armed forces and other traditionally male domains stand out. More recently in the United States, we would point to the Clinton administration as a time when people truly were confronted with the notion that women might actually have a chance to assume real power. President Clinton appointed the highest number of women in history to a presidential cabinet: Madeleine Albright, ambassador to the United Nations; Carol Browner, director of the Environmental Protection Agency; Hazel O'Leary, secretary of the Department of Energy; Janet Reno, Attorney General; and Donna Shalala, secretary of Health and Human Services.

Of equal import, for many, was the role Hillary Rodham Clinton assumed upon taking up residence at 1600 Pennsylvania Avenue. Beginning with her early efforts to push through healthcare reform, Hillary was a lightning rod for controversy throughout and beyond her two terms as first lady. She had legions of ardent fans and supporters (of both sexes), but at the same time was widely reviled as "the worst kind of feminist" even as she raised a seemingly happy, well-adjusted child, gave up her career in law to support her husband's work, and, in the end, truly did "stand by her man" in the worst of times.

Today, the beleaguered couple has effectively swapped roles, with Bill giving speeches, promoting his book, and working out of his office in Harlem, while Hillary is the Esteemed Senator from New York—and is widely seen as a strong contender for the presidential race of 2008.

Which raises a question: If our next President Clinton is indeed President Rodham Clinton, what does this make Bill? He said upon his own election that he and his wife worked as a team: undoubtedly, this aspect of their relationship would still be in place. But the question of title seems to nag. Up to (and including) the current moment, we've always had a very clean division: on one hand, we had *presidents*, and on the other, *first ladies*.

American politics has already met this glitch in protocol at the state level, and those states whose governors wear the skirts in the family have for the most part let their husbands navigate these waters however they like. According to a recent report on the spouses of women in politics, to each first husband his own: Bill Shaheen joked that he was "first hunk" when his wife, Jeanne Shaheen, was governor of New Hampshire. The "y" disappeared from the door of the office of the first lady in Utah when Olene Walker became governor, making her husband, Myron Walker, the "first lad." U.S. Magistrate Gary Sebelius, husband of Kansas governor Kathleen Sebelius, likes the title "first dude." And Dan Granholm Mulhern, the husband of Michigan's governor Jennifer Mulhern Granholm, prefers "first gentleman."[2]

Inexplicably, the British monarchy eschewed "First Dude Philip" in favor of the more traditional "Prince" when they had to name their "first lad." Elizabeth even hyphenated the last name of her children (Mountbatten-Windsor) in honor of her husband, in a funny flip of the ever-widening practice of women keeping their maiden names. Here, too, Senator Rodham Clinton stands as Exhibit A. She broke ground when she became the first presidential spouse to use her own first name in her formal title. A list of the honorary chairs of the Kennedy Center's board of trustees (a traditional duty of the first lady) shows the rupture clearly: "Mrs. Lyndon B. Johnson, Mrs. Gerald R. Ford, Mrs. Jimmy Carter, Mrs. Ronald Reagan, Mrs. George Bush, Senator Hillary Rodham Clinton, Mrs. Laura Bush."[3] Whether Laura Bush asked that her first name be used for similar reasons, or just to avoid confusion with her mother-in-law, it does appear that a new precedent has been set.

NEW OPPORTUNITIES FOR WOMEN

To understand just how much has changed in terms of opportunities for women—and increased competition faced by men—in the past fifty years, one need look no further than the schoolyard. Academia is an important steppingstone to power in business and government—and one that long was outside the reach of most women. In the previous chapter, we discussed how the Ivy League and other institutions of higher learning in the United States went coed one by one. The Citadel, a military academy in South Carolina, was one of the last holdouts against coeducation, but it finally graduated its first female cadets in 1999.

Today, girls and women have moved well beyond the struggle for parity at most schools. In fact, where females are given equal access to formal education, they are leaving the guys in the dust. For example, of the 850,000 high achievers from U.S. secondary schools recognized in the 2003 edition of *Who's Who Among American High*

School Students, a full two-thirds are female.[4] Granted, *Who's Who* is a for-profit listing, but its gender skew is nonetheless indicative of a larger trend. Thomas Mortensen, a senior scholar at Washington's Pell Institute for the Study of Opportunity in Higher Education, notes, "In the past 30 years, nearly every inch of education progress has gone to [females]."[5] Now, according to a May 2003 report in *BusinessWeek,* "in every state, every income bracket, every racial and ethnic group, and most industrialized Western nations, women reign, earning an average 57 percent of all BAs and 58 percent of all master's degrees in the U.S. alone." For every 100 male college students, there are 133 females, and by 2010 the gap is projected to widen, to 142 women for each 100 men.[6]

We're also seeing movement of women into traditionally male academic majors, including economics, engineering, and the sciences. In 1999, Smith College became the first U.S. liberal arts women's college to offer a degree in engineering. This is not to say that women have succeeded in using their educations and degrees to push ahead of men on the job lines, but equal access to education does mean women have a better chance than in times past of entering lucrative and prestigious careers.

In talking with college students and recent graduates for this book, we were struck by the extent to which young men and women anticipate equal treatment in the career world. They see vestiges of gender distinctions primarily in traditionally male fields, but, even here, they consider these distinctions surmountable by qualified women. Elisabeth Cuming, a public policy student at the University of Chicago, contends that the "opportunities afforded to students graduating from college matter more on the student's concentration (or major) than on the student's gender." She notes that certain fields (e.g., biology, economics) attract more men because these disciplines are more mathematical and scientific, but, she says, "Given a man and a women with the same credentials and the same concentration, there isn't a distinct difference in the opportunities available to each."

Tamilla Mamedova, who was raised in Turkey and is now studying international relations at Brown University, has a slightly different take on postcollege gender distinctions, particularly in traditionally male fields. She explains: "I think men are taken more seriously in 'serious' fields such as business, economics, foreign service, banking, etc. Even in the movie industry, we rarely see women directors or screenwriters. So I think that, as unfair as it may be, this is still a man's world." Tamilla also notes that, though she hasn't experienced this firsthand, many of her friends who work in male-dominated fields complain that there are lots of women in their workplaces who seem to have landed the job "only because they look like supermodels and have big breasts." She adds, "This has led them to think that having an Ivy League degree is less important for certain companies than having a nice body."

The consensus among the young people we've interviewed is that there can be some disadvantages for women trying to enter and advance within male-dominated fields, including harassment and other forms of discrimination, but that, at the same time, women may benefit from being a rarer commodity. Alex Wagner, a computer and telecommunications engineering major at the University of Pennsylvania, thinks her postgraduation prospects may actually be improved by her gender: "I think that companies are so ecstatic to find female engineers (we only make up about 10 percent of the workforce, according to the Society of Women Engineers), that being a woman in my field will probably be an advantage."

THE IMPACT OF WOMEN IN THE WORKPLACE

Though some fields are more accepting of women than others, we would argue that no field could be considered entirely gender neutral. As long as jobs are filled by and with individuals with varying backgrounds, mind-sets, and agendas, we will never see a major corporation, much less an entire industry, that hires and promotes and rewards its workers in a manner that is entirely blind to gender. People are people, and, subconsciously or consciously, we tend to factor gender into our dealings with one another. That applies to all our relationships, whether we're conversing with someone in line at the grocery store or deciding who deserves a promotion.

It's also true that men and women don't necessarily go into the work world with the same goals and priorities. This statement can't be applied to all men and all women, of course, but there seems to be sufficient evidence to suggest that women continue to be more likely to look at career as just one facet of their life achievements rather than as the be-all and end-all. And that perspective may well inflect their behaviors and attitudes on the job. Cathy Lasowski, a baby-boomer

American who's currently based in Paris, says she considers educational attainment the area in which women are catching up to men most rapidly, but she also notes, "I'm just not sure if women are using their educations in the work world as consistently or purposefully as men have."

That said, the transformation we've seen in the workplace in less than half a century has been dramatic. This can partly be attributed to the legal and attitudinal changes wrought by the women's movement. Women are much more apt today to enter the workforce and remain there even after marrying and bearing children. And most employers not only fear the consequences of gender discrimination, but also have come to recognize the important contributions women play in their companies' business success. Perhaps as important has been the concurrent shift in the types of jobs our modern world is producing. All over the developed world, the sorts of jobs that called for male muscle and daring are disappearing fast and are being replaced by the type of work women can do at least as well as men. Office jobs, service jobs, jobs that involve working with people and information rather than with things and machinery are gaining in prestige and power—and in paycheck. Maybe this explains why the percentage of males in the workforce has shrunk as more and more women have come on board. The proportion of American women of working age who are economically active grew from 51 percent in 1973 to 71 percent in 2000, while the proportion of economically active men dropped from 86 percent to 84 percent. The trend is similar in Britain and France.[7] The all-women management team with a token male isn't going to be the norm anytime soon, but it's no longer unimaginable.

We're also seeing that social perceptions of women in the workforce have changed to the extent that a man who has a woman as his boss no longer excites remark—much less ridicule or pity. Can you imagine the TV show *Who's the Boss* debuting in 2005? There would be no question who the boss is: the woman paying the guy's salary. Big deal.

Also being called into question is the long-held assumption that a husband's career is the "primary" career in the family; this no longer holds true in many households. In 2000, a study of 154 companies (mostly American) by GMAC Global Relocation Services found that 13 percent of expatriate employees were women. Married women accounted for 10 percent of female expatriate employees, placing many husbands in the position of "trailing spouse." In the absence of a support network for such husbands, a group of expatriate men in Belgium founded STUDS (Spouses Trailing Under Duress Successfully) in 1994. The support group meets in person and through its website, www.gamber.net/studs/.[8]

ARE MEN STILL THE DOMINANT SEX?

A slight majority of people we surveyed in researching this book agreed that, to some extent at least, men would still qualify as the "dominant sex"—particularly if one looks beyond highly developed Western nations to the world as a whole. But the general attitude was that this is inexorably (and not necessarily slowly) changing, and that, particularly in the workplace, women are on a path toward equal opportunity, equal recognition, and, ultimately, equal power. The writer Paul Fraser, age thirty-three, commented that men's dominance is much less clear-cut today than it was in the 1950s or even the 1970s. "In those days," he says, "it was more important for a man to be seen as the king of his castle, the numero uno. These days, especially in office work, you want your boss to be the best person at the job, whatever the makeup of his or her chromosomes. More men worry less about being dominant these days (although we would like our girlfriends to question our decisions less—we just don't beat them into submission anymore)." Fraser envisions a time when power will be more evenly distributed between the sexes, but he doesn't foresee women becoming the dominant sex. "Men will still rule the world," he says, "because men are more competitive, more obsessed by power."

Certainly today, women aren't yet on equal terms with men with regard to workplace authority and salary. Just recently, in fact, the gender gap in wages has come back into the spotlight. Major lawsuits against such U.S. corporate megaliths as Boeing, Morgan Stanley, and Wal-Mart have shaken any illusions we might have had that the fight for equal pay ended in the last century. Data from the U.S. Census Bureau and the Bureau for Labor Statistics shows that median wages for women in 2002 were just 76.2 percent of men's wages. That's up from 68.5 percent in 1989, but still quite a ways off from total gender equity. In fact, research from the Institute for Women's Policy Research indicates it will be another half century before income earned by women and men is equal in the United States.[9]

Even in industries such as advertising, public relations, and publishing—supposedly bastions of creative, "enlightened" minds and certainly workforces heavily populated by women—we're still seeing very few female CEOs. Some of that can be chalked up to differences in socialization or temperament (again, depending on whether you emphasize Nature or Nurture); women, it is commonly held, are less assertive in salary negotiations and less likely to look aggressively after their own needs. Not all women, granted, but a lot of them. That doesn't explain the full extent of the disparities, however, leaving plenty of scope for good, old-fashioned gender discrimination, consciously or unconsciously applied.

On the other hand, we have also come to the conclusion, through our workplace experiences and interviews with men and women around the world, that more and more women professionals are intentionally sacrificing bigger paychecks, loftier titles, and more statusful perks in favor of establishing the style of work and life they want and/or need to lead. This has been particularly evident in the last decade or so, as the average workweek has expanded, and as working mothers have had to decide how much they are willing to sacrifice at home in order to lay claim to the coveted corner office at work. For many women, a shiny nameplate on a big office and a fatter paycheck aren't worth the loss of day-to-day involvement in their children's lives.

And that, in a nutshell, is where we see opportunities for men and women diverge. The women's movement was always positioned as being about "choice." Having the choice to work outside the home or not, having the choice to attend any college for which one is qualified, having the choice to reproduce or not, having the choice to marry or not. For a while, in the 1980s and 1990s, we saw these choices turn into virtual mandates. Women were made to feel (mostly by themselves and other women) that they *had* to do it all. Taking a break to stay home when the children were young, opting for part-time work, or straying from a hard-and-fast career path were considered somehow disloyal to the cause of women's progress. That's one reason the 1980s saw an increase in labor force participation on the part of women with infants, the only group that had resisted the move toward working outside the home in previous decades.[10] At the same time, there was enormous pressure to be the "perfect" mom and spouse, keeping the house "sparkling," preparing meals from scratch, and generally facilitating the success of the children at school and on the sports field and of the husband at work. It's a wonder more women didn't out-and-out crack from the pressure.

Instead, women began to take stock of what their lives had turned into—and what their families' lives had turned into—and decided to make unilateral changes. We began to see the push toward flex time, job sharing, and part-time employment that actually came with a bit of status and, of enormous importance, benefits. We also saw legislators get into the act, most particularly by mandating maternity leave in all but the smallest companies.

But what of men? Regardless of what official policies may state, we all know that men face tougher battles when trying to veer from career norms. And part of that simply has to do with societal expectations that say it's the mother who's supposed to be the classroom parent, the mother who's supposed to supply cut-up oranges for the soccer match, the mother who's supposed to lug the offspring to the doctor, dentist, and orthodontist, and the mother who's supposed to bring the meal home and get it on the table. Men may well be playing a greater role in child-rearing, but they're not expected to allow it to interfere with their "real" jobs—i.e., the ones that pay in cold, hard cash rather than sticky kisses and hugs.

Therein lies the rub for many men. The fact is that a lot of fathers have taken seriously women's calls for them to be more hands-on in their approach to parenting. And these dads are perfectly willing to make the work sacrifices that would entail. According to a Radcliffe Public Policy Center 2000 survey, 82 percent of American men between the ages of twenty and thirty-nine believe that a work schedule that allows for family time is more important than money, power, or prestige. Nearly three quarters (71 percent) would give up pay for more family time.[11] In Singapore, 61 percent of single men polled said they were comfortable with the idea of being "househusbands," while just 60 percent of single women were comfortable with the notion of being housewives.[12] And in Britain, a survey of men between twenty-four and thirty-four found that 60 percent would consider taking time out of their careers to look after their children.[13]

It's not just big talk, either: According to the Census Bureau, single fathers headed 2.2 million U.S. households in 2000, an increase of 62 percent from ten years earlier, whereas the number of single-mother households rose just 25 percent during that period. Similarly,

the number of single fathers in Germany increased 63 percent between 1991 and 2001 (to 332,000), while the ranks of single mothers
increased 31 percent (to 1.7 million).

As men have begun to express greater interest in child-rearing, organizations have emerged to better equip fathers to properly parent
their children. Boot Camp for New Dads was begun around a dozen
years ago in California and has since spread to more than a hundred
communities across the United States. It teaches fathers-to-be everything from diaper changing and bathing techniques to how to handle
overbearing mothers-in-law.[14] In Toronto, Canada, an eight-week
course called Focus on Fathers caters to new dads "caught in the trap
of trying to do a good job at work and at home" (sound familiar?) and
includes pointers on managing stress and anger, in addition to more
general child-rearing information.[15]

Paternity leave has also become far more common, helped along
by such high-profile men as Finnish prime minister Paavo Lipponen,
who twice took paid leave while in office. As of 2001, Finland mandated what may be the world's most generous paternity policy, forty-
two days of fully paid leave, compared with, for example, zero days in
Germany and five days in Brazil.[16]

Nevertheless, men continue to face much social pressure to not let
their personal lives interfere with their work lives. This is part of the
reason women are still more than twice as likely as men to work part-
time in the United States.[17] It also helps to explain why only 34 percent
of new fathers took some form of parental leave in 2000, compared with
68.2 percent of women who did so. The unspoken truth may be that the
modern workplace is more willing to "forgive" women for their decision to place family over work in some instances, because the people
who run the workplace continue to believe that women play a more essential role than men in their households. Until society concludes that
men play an equally valuable role in child-rearing, men who make career tradeoffs to spend time with their children will be seen as somehow
less focused, committed, and worthy than men who don't.

HAVING IT THEIR WAY:
THE CONTRASEXUAL VS. THE DOMESTIC DIVA

While men grapple with increased pressure to take on a larger share
of child care and other domestic duties, even as they're also expected

to continue to contribute the bulk of the family income, women—at least, those women who are financially comfortable—have a whole range of options. And in a real change from just twenty or thirty years ago, today's women are feeling a lot less societal pressure to follow a single prescribed life path.

The spectrum of women we're seeing today is as broad as women are diverse, but there are two types of women we find particularly intriguing, largely because their lifestyles are so different from each other's, yet both are focused on the pursuit of self: self-interest, self-gratification, and sometimes even self-aggrandizement.

At one end of the spectrum is a group of women the Future Laboratory in the UK has termed contrasexuals. The trend-research group describes these women as typically being in their late thirties and "forsaking Bridget Jones binges on chardonnay and *Sex and the City* nights out with their mates for a more measured, determined, self-fulfilling and dare we say it, adventurous approach to living, working, learning and doing in ways that leave their 'sad pad' metrosexual counterparts [looking] desperate and insecure in comparison."[18] (For the record, the Future Laboratory's bleak take on metrosexual man is far different from our own.)

Contrasexuals are, for the most part, women who have put any thoughts of marriage and children, or indeed serious romantic entanglements, on the back burner (if they haven't removed them from the stovetop entirely). They are financially independent (thanks both to their jobs and to savvy investments), and they are far more interested in making the most of the opportunities available to them now than they are in some vague future their older relatives likely are pushing them to consider. They are hungry for life experiences, happy to splurge on their every heart's desire, and disinclined to compromise their goals. A man may be part of the picture, but he is nowhere near center frame.

Contrasexuals, like singletons before them, are on marketers' radar because they're not putting off life until marriage. These are women who buy their own homes, set up investment portfolios, and enjoy adventure travel and exotic vacations with friends. Marketers have come to discover that they need to speak directly to these women rather than to the men who used to be their providers and gift givers. That's why we're seeing such things as the De Beers diamond campaign that intones: "Your left hand says we. Your right hand says me. Women of the world, raise your right hands."

Then there are the women we call domestic divas. These women include men in their lives. In fact, they're married to them. And they rely on them for their food, shelter, and all manner of luxuries. They might technically be termed homemakers since they have children and don't work outside the home, but that would be a misnomer, for domestic divas have managed to delegate the usual chores of home-making (e.g., cleaning, cooking, childcare) to household staff or paid services. Instead of the usual drudgery, they spend their days doing what they please, whether it's lunching with friends, working out at the gym, leisure shopping, or pursuing hobbies. These women don't necessarily fit the stereotype of the pampered wife, having her nails done and nibbling on bonbons all day. They may very well spend their free time doing entirely worthwhile things like heading up school fund-raisers or sitting on the board of a local art institution. What they're not doing is juggling. They have no problems finding "me time" because most of their time is spent exactly as they wish, doing what they want. The pressures most women face simply do not apply.

Domestic divas have been around for a long time. In the United States, a classic example would be Carol Brady on *The Brady Bunch*. She had Alice the housekeeper to do the cleaning and cooking, so, even with six children at home, she was free to shop and go to the beauty salon and do whatever else struck her fancy, while boring Mike stayed hunched over his architectural plans. Back in Carol Brady's day, this version of homemaking was perfectly acceptable. Live-in domes-tic help was widely available—at bargain prices—and there wasn't nearly as much pressure on both parents to do it all. But now? These days, both men and women are expected to contribute fully to the running and financial support of the household. And men are growing increasingly resentful of wives who seem to have it all without doing much at all. This is particularly the case for those husbands who feel keenly the sacrifices they're making by missing out on time with their children.

When we released our findings about domestic divas to the media, the reaction was swift—and varied. Some journalists (mostly women) decried our criticism of these nonworking mothers, saying essentially that women are damned if they do (work) and damned if they don't. Other journalists recognized our domestic diva archetype right away in some of the women they encounter in their daily lives. In London's *Independent* newspaper, a self-confessed domestic diva named Rose Lomis explained her approach to living this way: "My girlfriends nickname me the Princess and tease me for being spoilt. I just laugh it off. I loathe housework, so why bother doing it? It's boring and ruins your nails and I don't see why—as I have the money to pay someone else to do it—I need to waste my valuable time and energy. . . . Of course, I adore my children. I love reading them stories and painting with them, but I'd be bored and unhappy if I had to spend every moment with them. So, although I don't work, I'm not remotely ashamed of having a nanny."[19]

For all we know, Lomis's husband is perfectly happy with the roles he and his wife have carved out for themselves. Our conversations with other men in similar situations suggest that such acceptance is by no means universal, however. And this is particularly the case when money is an issue. When the effects of the women's movement began to be felt, it would have been natural to assume that men would be more likely than women to object to having their wives leave home and hearth for paid employment. Now that women have made such strides in the workforce, we're seeing signs of backlash. Only it's not the men who want women to return to the home, it's the women. A survey we conducted in spring 2004 found that a great majority of American moms (83 percent) agreed it's fine for a woman to be a homemaker and not do paid work.[20] And a substantial majority of non-moms said the same (71 percent). In sharp contrast, only 66 percent of dads approved of the wife-as-homemaker idea, and even fewer non-dads approved (60 percent). The reasons likely have a lot more to do with finances than social attitudes. According to Elizabeth Warren, a Harvard Law School professor, today's two-income family has, on average, 75 percent more income than the one-income family had a generation ago, but the increased costs of such basic items as mortgage, school tuition, a car, and health insurance have more than offset that difference, so dual-wage families today have less money to spend. Mortgage costs alone have increased 70 percent faster than the average man's wages.[21]

So does this all come down to money? Perhaps affluent men have no cause to resent their domestic diva wives. After all, as Rose Lomis pointed out, they can afford the nannies and other household help. And domestic divas really are no different from wealthy women of earlier ages, who wouldn't even have considered taking on household tasks themselves, much less contribute to the family income. So what's the problem?

The difference today doesn't simply have to do with the fact that society expects women to do *something* productive, whether at home, at work, or (most often) at both. It also lies in the one-sided nature of the arrangement. In times past, men got a great deal in return for their support of their nonworking wives. Today, in many instances, some would argue they get very little other than grief. Tim Lott, writing in London's *Evening Standard*, put it wonderfully. He calls domestic divas "Victorian Wives with Attitude." In his view, such women are living an ideal existence that combines all the perks of the nineteenth-century model of "middle-class femininity" with all the freedoms accorded the twenty-first-century female. And all their overworked and underappreciated husbands are asking in exchange, Lott says, is one thing—and it's not cooking or cleaning or even sex. Lott explains, "They just have to do one thing when hubby gets home. Because what men want, in contrast to what women want, is usually very simple. They want their spouses to like them—still better, to respect them. This is how things have changed. In the Victorian age, women sacrificed themselves to get the love of a man who took his status and privilege for granted. In the modern age, it's the other way around."

We'd find it difficult to deny that the average married man receives less respect—and certainly far less deference—from his wife than did his father and grandfather before him. In the ongoing battle-slash-dance of the sexes, we may well see a time when the tides turn against the blatant disrespect women are expected, even encouraged, to show toward their husbands. Until then, we'll continue to leaf through sales catalogs full of T-shirts emblazoned with such messages as "Three Wise Men? Be Serious."

MEN AT ("WOMEN'S") WORK

We hear a lot about women's incursions into traditionally male lines of work, from engineering to law, investment banking to computer technology. And most of the time, those forays are greeted with huzzahs from women's groups and not a whole lot of kicking and screaming on the part of men. There are exceptions, of course; women's entry into firefighting, police work, the military, and even construction jobs has been hard fought and slow going. But, in general, the catcalls have been reserved for the opposite trend: namely, men entering fields typically associated with women. And suddenly, there are quite a lot of them looking to do so.

Even in mucho-macho Spain, men are beginning to find work as nannies, secretaries, and even housemaids. At Telefónica's national information service, fully 20 percent of telephone operators were men at the start of this decade.[22] And speaking of macho . . . in the United States, the human resources director of the Visiting Nurse Service of New York has tried to fill nursing vacancies by recruiting active and retired firefighters and police officers to train for the jobs.[23]

In the UK, the number of male nurses is on the rise, thanks in part to high-profile recruitment campaigns. As of 2001, men accounted for just under 2 percent of nursery nurses (childcare workers), but the government was working to increase the figure to 6 percent by 2005.[24]

It is also increasingly common for men to be employed by their wives. The president of the National Association of Home Based Businesses (U.S.) estimates that the number of husbands working for their wives or becoming partners in businesses already established by their wives increased 50 percent between 1995 and 2000.[25] Experts caution that such untraditional working relationships can add strains to a marriage if both parties aren't prepared at the outset to cope with the inherent issues.

THE MASS REDUNDANCY OF MEN?

So, here's where things stand: Modern man now has to compete not just with other guys in school, but also with girls and women. When he moves into the work world, he must jockey for position with female colleagues who may well have outshone him in the classroom. And what of home? Is that still a safe haven for men, a castle in which he is king? Hardly. It would be unrealistic to think that men and women who treat each other as equals at school and at work would suddenly dismiss their notions of gender equity when they enter into a relationship. And sure enough, we've seen a dramatic shift in the behaviors and expectations of men and women in their romantic partnerships. To begin with, many women are now far less anxious to enter into a life-long commitment. Now that more women are able to complete higher education, work, earn, and do such "male" things as drive cars and install a security alarm (or at least pay to have it done), they can afford to be choosier. What's more, if a partner's initial charms fail, women are feeling freer to nix the relationship and move on.

"I suppose I will marry," Rachel Taranta, a student at Tufts University, told us, "but I'm in no rush. Ideally, I will just live with someone and be exclusive with him forever and only resort to marriage if we ever decide we want the joint ownership of property, or decide to have kids."

Elinor Mileti, a middle school student in Torrington, Connecticut, is just entering the world of dating but already considers marriage one of a number of life options, rather than a primary goal. "Whether I marry depends on if I meet Mr. Right or not," she says. "If I don't, then I will just fly solo because, if there is no reason to get married other than walking down the aisle, there is no point to it."

We've already established that marriage is good for a man. It gets him up in the morning, gives him an organizing principle, and keeps him alive longer. But, as we also have established, women on the same diet seem to get nowhere near the same dose of vitamins. And as modern times have ushered in a famously roulettelike divorce rate—put it all on the black or the red, then give it a spin—the lessening of marriage as a cultural institution is likely to take its toll.

In a piece for *The New Statesman*, Sean French relates Professor Richard Scase's scenario of the future of men in Britain—and, presumably, elsewhere in the developed world:

> Research has shown that single women really do behave in the way that single women behave in TV commercials. They sit in groups at tables on pavements in Soho and throw back their heads in laughter. They go shopping together. They go to the gym . . .
>
> By contrast, men will be more like the wino you see on a park bench with his trousers tied up with string clutching a can of Heineken at 11 in the morning. Actually, that comparison isn't entirely fair to the wino. Winos generally seem sociable and hang around in public spaces in cheery groups."[26]

Professor Scase, according to French, foresees single men of the twenty-first century in Britain as being "sad, isolated, lonely cases," sitting alone at home, eating a curry and drinking beer while watching a video.[27]

In our view, Professor Scase has laid out a worst-case scenario of the future of men—and a grossly exaggerated one, at that. Still, his analysis does bring up what we would call the greatest male fear, the castration terror embodied: the mass redundancy of men. Fear of redundancy was why those poor saps in Stepford had to reprogram their women in the first place—so that the men could keep feeling needed. The inessentialness of men was the most terrifying implication of the women's liberation movement, and it is the fear that still resonates in the words above: that without women to buy into the game of marriage, men will prove useless.

Useless, you say? How on earth could the people who share in responsibility for procreation, for the very future of our species, ever be useless? That brings us to another unhappy reality for the future of men . . .

DO-IT-HERSELF CHILDBEARING

Until recently, procreation was widely perceived as a woman's primary responsibility in life. She partnered, gave birth, and raised her children to start the cycle anew. As we mentioned in chapter 5, one of the arguments against permitting women access to higher education was that it would somehow prove harmful to her role as childbearer. Well, wouldn't ya know? Turns out they were right! All over the world where women have access to education, jobs, and birth control, they are on reproductive strike. In Japan the fertility rate is just 1.3 per woman, down from 2.0 in 1960; in Germany it's 1.4, down from 2.36; in Spain and Italy it's 1.2, down from 2.46 and 2.41, respectively, in 1960. Between 1960 and 1985, the U.S. fertility rate dropped to 1.8 births per woman.[28] (In the 1990s, possibly because of higher-than-average fertility among immigrants and the U.S. economic boom, the U.S. fertility rate rose to just below the "replacement level" of 2.1 births per woman.)[29]

And even in those cases when a woman does decide to have a baby, she doesn't necessarily have to wait for Mr. Right to show up to provide the sperm; she can just go to the sperm bank. According to Melanie Phillips, author of *The Sex Change Society: Feminised Britain and the Neutered Male*: "Instead of being seen as an integral part of the family unit, men are now permitted merely to bring—in certain circumstances defined by women—additional value to it."[30] Men are no longer the motor of the family. They're no longer even the chassis. According to Phillips, they're becoming an optional accessory package, akin to a nice racing stripe, rack-and-pinion steering, and a good set of all-weather tires.

All of this downshifting in importance can be a real blow to men's egos. And if a man is not standing tall inside, Lord knows he may need a bit of a boost every once in a while to get standing tall outside. Hence, the booming market for Viagra and its competitors. But are erectile-function enhancers a miracle of modern science or a crutch in a pill? And, most important, has the need for pharmaceutical intervention grown in response to societal changes, or has the problem always been as widespread, but simply not acknowledged?

There are all sorts of theories as to why Viagra was such a huge success. The buyers may be subject to the Hefner effect—men who are already sexually active looking to turbocharge their performance. Some sales may be due to the pill's chemical sex-toy effect, promising hours upon hours of pleasure. Some of the pill's success may even be due to the downright unnatural demands of the burgeoning adult film industry. But a lot of it comes down to the men who are desperate to perform at all. Whether you blame it on stress, on beer, on the increasingly stringent demands of women who suddenly feel it's their right to get some pleasure out of this thing, too, or on the virtual lobotomy of television, many men around the world clearly feel the need these days for pharmaceutical assistance to get and/or sustain a satisfactory erection. The prevalence of the little blue pill (and newer entrants to the erectile-dysfunction marketplace) and the tide of "grow your penis" spam e-mails confirm that doubts about virility are more than ever the lot of modern men. (We've even heard stories of men in their twenties buying Viagra online.)

In a time of increasing doubt and crisis around the role of the modern man, even around the very importance of the modern man, it makes sense that the one little act that means so much to a man's ego—and for which English has generated words faster than the Ford assembly line did cars—might get a bit more complicated. Think about the words used to describe it: "Hard." "Firm." "Erect." "Stiff." "Raging." "Intense." Are we talking about a man's ego, or about his penis? How much difference, really, can we find between them?

Earlier in this book, we noted that many researchers now believe that, at some point in the future, the Y chromosome may become so mutated that it disappears completely. Jennifer Marshall Graves, a geneticist at the Australian National University in Canberra, reminds us that the Y chromosome loses from three to six genes every million years or so to mutations. This gives the Y a lifespan of about another 10 million years.[31]

Does this mean that men will disappear, or that women will just be the dominant sex? Nature has plenty of ways of making men and women. X and Y are the preferred route that mammals tend to take, but not the only one. Still, the time-limited nature of the Y chromosome doesn't do much to dispel the creeping feeling of lost ground for men as women slowly gain power and as men adjust to a new world.

In this chapter and the previous one we've talked about the forces of social change—in education, in the workforce, in politics, in the family itself—and the impacts these changes have had on the once central role of men. We've seen how advances in some areas—and frustration with a lack of them in others—have helped to give women a voice, an authority, and a centrality that they previously were not allowed. As women have gained authority, we have seen men, in an almost mirroring response, start moving to women's margins.

Suddenly, masculinity is not made by men, but is determined by women. Women define it, women chastise it, women defend it. Men can only lay claim to old parts of their masculinity through irony, by falling right in with the joke. And men are finding new roles appearing for themselves—at the margin of the successes of women.

In the next chapter, we'll look at how men are being perceived in advertising and the media, how they're responding to it, and how it's influencing the relationships between them and the women in their lives.

WHAT TO REMEMBER

1. To understand just how much has changed in terms of opportunities for women—and increased competition faced by men—in the past fifty years, one need look no further than the schoolyard. Academia is an important stepping-stone to power in business and government—and one that long was outside the reach of most women. Now it's a sphere in which girls and women are outdoing the guys.

2. Society caught up to the waning influence of the biological imperative of male superiority; today, we live in a world of mutuality, where women see men as a preference rather than as an imperative, and where men are being forced to adjust their behaviors to be more appealing to the fairer sex.

3. Just as women were not prepared to enter the workforce before World War II made them do it, men were not prepared for a life of mutuality. And they have been suffering from the recognition that masculinity, circa 2005, is not determined by men, but by women. Women define it, women chastise it, women defend it. Men can only lay claim to old parts of their masculinity through irony, by falling right in with the joke. And men are finding new roles for themselves—at the margin of the successes of women.

7

MASS MEDIA, ADVERTISING & THE MODERN MAN

There's been much debate in recent years about media bias and to what extent audiences are receiving "unadulterated" news. **One thing on which most of us can agree is that the media—and by that, we mean everything from advertising, TV, and newspapers to blogs—wield enormous influence over not just how we think but what we think about.** It's through the media that we learn about the latest political developments, scientific advances, and economic theories. It's through the media that we know that people outside our zones of interaction exist. And it's through the media that we know the most intimate details (sometimes far too intimate) about what other people are doing and saying in their relationships. Like it or not, the media help to shape our sense of what's normal, what's possible, and what's desirable. By picking up and reporting what's happening in real time and by emphasizing those things they regard as newsworthy (or "sexy," in newsspeak), today's ubiquitous media actually amplify what they report.

This chapter looks at how the media are portraying men and their roles these days, with a focus on action films, television sitcoms, and advertising. In our view, these forms of media are among the most important in how they influence men's ideas of what they are supposed to be and how they are supposed to act. They also have a real impact on women—on how women regard men in general, and on how they measure the men in their lives.

Do media images of men really matter? Absolutely. There is a good case to be made that the influences of biology and the media on gender roles are inversely proportional: the more men and women break loose from the biological destiny of their XX and XY chromosomes, the more they come under the sway of the media. The genes that shape their biology evolve an infinitesimal amount just once every generation, whereas the memes that shape their psychology are in a constant ferment of evolution. We become what we consume, media-wise. And a lot of what men are consuming today is disparaging at best.

MODERN MAN ON THE BIG SCREEN

If Hollywood presents a model to the world of how a man should be a man, what are the rules in place now? They're certainly a far cry from the rules Hollywood stars adhered to in the middle of the last century. Consider today's hot male movie properties: Tom Cruise, Keanu Reeves, Hugh Grant, Brad Pitt, John Cusack, Leonardo DiCaprio, Ben Affleck, Jude Law, Orlando Bloom. . . . **Not one of them would pass muster among the rugged leading men of the old school. It seems clear that Hollywood is increasingly tilting toward a "lite" version of masculinity—one that emphasizes sensibility and sensuality over power and bravado.**

Johnny Messner, a little-known Hollywood actor most recently featured in the soon forgotten *Anacondas: The Hunt for the Blood Orchid*, recently quipped that "Orlando Bloom . . . is a hermaphrodite. . . . I don't want to be prettier than the woman I'm walking with."[1] Messner might aspire toward being a "real man" à la Steve McQueen, but if blockbuster success is any indicator, Bloom is a lot closer than Messner to the ideal man of the day. What we've seen is that the expectations placed upon men have radically changed over the past twenty years—and that is being expressed in the media. **In order to be seen as more human and more real, men have been forced to openly and publicly embrace their emotional sides.** Along with that, they've found greater scrutiny of their *out*sides. The ideal leading man has changed: where he once had the supersized shoulders of Arnold Schwarzenegger, he now has the sculpted abs of Brad Pitt. And in the process, the very way men have learned how to be men has changed.

Without question, Hollywood and what it expects of its leading men has gotten more complicated. "When men were men," as the saying goes, their roles in film and entertainment were clearer. Men mostly battled one another to gain the favor of their leading ladies, who sat tantalizingly out of reach until the "Boy Gets Girl" moment: the big kiss accompanied by the orchestral swell.

In some respects, not a whole lot has changed on the "macho hero" front. Even after the radical transformation of the women's movement, Hollywood beefcake was more apt to be covered in mud and blood than in exfoliant. The 1980s and 1990s took us through summer blockbuster after blockbuster featuring super-muscled, gruff, dirty, bleeding men (often with some degree of real fighting training) swimming through bullets and explosions on their way to victory and the love of their ladies-in-waiting. One of those actors is now California's most powerful celebrity, the Governator. Before Schwarzenegger delivered his speech at the Republican National Convention, he was speaking very different lines. Among the more notable: "If it bleeds, we can kill it." But Arnold was just one of a pack. We had at least a dozen of these supermen march across our screens in the last two decades of the twentieth century—Sylvester Stallone, Jean-Claude Van Damme, Bruce Willis, Dolph Lundgren, and Steven Seagal among them. Some of the films were blockbusters, many of them were awful, and the majority had a number after their titles.

Even in the new millennium, we have our pec-packing action heroes, the most famous being The Rock, a.k.a. Dwayne Johnson. Having transitioned from pro wrestling to film, he assumed the mantle of new blockbuster action hero. But his upcoming roles seem to give a new twist to the old action-hero formula; instead of becoming more of a superhero, he's under pressure to trim down to more normal proportions. His new workout regimen, as recounted in *Men's Health* magazine, focuses not on building his body, part by part, but on slimming him down and giving him more definition—on dropping fat instead of building muscle. "As he transitions into meatier roles that require him to look less superhuman—this spring's gritty remake of 'Walking Tall'; the summer 2005 flick 'Spy Hunter'; and a comic turn in 'Be Cool,' the ensemble follow-up to 'Get Shorty'—his body has needed to transition as well," explains the article. "He's lost 20 pounds and slashed his body fat from 14 percent to 7 percent."[2]

Don't get us wrong—The Rock is certainly not en route to becoming Jude Law. But as his career transitions from action flicks to comedy and drama, his body transitions, too: from a focus on power to a focus on appearance. And that transition is being seen throughout the industry, as audiences look to the likes of Jet Li, Orlando Bloom, and Will Smith rather than to overmuscled Schwarzenegger and Stallone clones.

It's important to recognize that it's not just straight men who dictate what the action hero should look like anymore. Today, women and gay men have leavened the mix and championed their own visions of masculinity—and of femininity, too. The granite-jawed types of simpler times don't appear to interest today's audiences as much as do their more sensitive, less bulky counterparts.

And when it comes to action heroes, it's not just the men who are changing. Look at the explosion of action flicks in the 1990s, and you'll find that some of the most prominent "he-men" of that era were women. When *Terminator II* came out, people were talking less about Schwarzenegger's reprogramming into a do-good cyborg than they were about that other smash-'em-up hero in the film: Linda Hamilton. In the first movie, she played the innocent-waif role. In the second, the newly buff Hamilton kicked nearly as much android butt as Schwarzenegger did.

The pattern holds for one of the other most memorable women action heroes of the eighties and nineties, Ripley, played by Sigourney Weaver. In the first *Alien* film, Ripley is the surprise hero. At the start of the film, she is surrounded by much more traditional action-hero stars, but they are knocked off one by one. In the second film, Ripley is a pure fighter. Both Weaver and Hamilton transformed their bodies for their roles with intensive workout regimens—and in both films, their bodies were on display in a decidedly macho fashion. Sure, we got a glimpse of Ripley in her panties, but the lingering shots were reserved for her buff arms and shoulders.

A few years later, we've moved beyond the "butch" women heroes of the 1990s to the vampy, sexualized Lara Croft in the *Tomb Raider* series and Uma Thurman's "Bride" in *Kill Bill*. These women aren't role models so much as they are mavericks and outlaws, which imbues them with a sense of danger as well as strength. They're also a break from tradition because they aren't sidekicks to male action stars, but heroes (or antiheroes, as the case may be) in their own right.

Our male action heroes have had a change in attitude, too, but in the opposite direction. Where once they were stoic and all but silent, now they have feelings and angst and self-doubt. And they can afford to: No one's going to call a super-powered pugilist a "girlie man." As Danny Fingeroth, author of *Superman on the Couch: What Superheroes Really Tell Us About Ourselves and Our Society*, has noted, "Spiderman's allowed to have a sensitive side because he's got the macho stuff going on. He has the costume. He swings around from buildings and punches Dr. Octopus."[3]

In other words, it's because of the bravado, the strength, and the superpowers that the men are allowed their feelings today. Compare this with Arnold, who wasn't even allowed to be human, let alone show human feelings, in the *Terminator* films. Or with killing-machine Stallone in the *Rambo* flicks. As the transformation of the Rock's film roles from two-dimensional cartoon characters to fuller, more human, more developed characters may show, we expect new levels of complexity and emotion even from our superheroes now. We're sick of kryptonite: we want our heroes to have broken hearts.

Which brings us to Superman, the ultimate action hero, a symbol of strength (mental and physical), incorruptibility, and justice for all. DC Comics has found that this twentieth-century version of Heroic Man simply doesn't fly in the twenty-first century. Translation: people aren't buying Superman comic books, because they think the super-hero is *too* perfect, *too* invulnerable, *too* self-assured. What's a super-hero to do? Jim Lee and Brian Azzarello, the new artist-writer team in charge of Superman at DC Comics, are giving our old-time hero a makeover. As Lev Grossman reported in *Time* magazine, "[Superman] debuted in the 1930s, when Americans liked their heroes like they liked their steaks: tough, thick and all-American. Nowadays we prefer

our heroes dark and flawed and tragic."[4] If Hollywood ever stops talking about getting a new Superman movie on the big screen and actually does it, we can be sure the man in blue is going to be a little bit
less of a Boy Scout and a little bit more of a basket case.

THROUGH THE PRISM OF TELEVISION: MEAT VS. VEGETABLES

The differences between movies and television have to do with a
whole lot more than screen size and stars' salaries. The men we see on
TV are an entirely different beast from those we see in darkened theaters. On the big screen, men in blockbusters face big challenges, lead
big lives, and face big risks. On the small screen, storylines are much
more likely to dwell on the day-to-day minutiae of ordinary lives. The
characters, by and large, are intended to be "like us"—and that should
give modern man pause.

In chapter 5, we looked at how man's role as head of household—
perhaps even as superior being—was promoted by TV shows. Suffice
it to say that times have changed. If *Father Knows Best* were in the
lineup today, its title would be dripping with irony, and the titular father would no doubt be inept, out of touch, and a complete buffoon.
Oh, and overweight, too. As Wendell Wittler (a pseudonym) noted in
a piece for MSNBC, the fat husband/hot wife formula has proliferated
in recent years, "starting with Kevin James and Leah Remini in *King of
Queens*, spreading across the CBS schedule to Mark Addy and Jami
Gertz in *Still Standing*, to ABC with Jim Belushi and Courtney
Thorne-Smith in *According to Jim*, to FOX with Andy Richter and Rebecca Creskoff in *Quintuplets*, and even NBC succumbing with an ani-
mated John Goodman and Cheryl Hines on *Father of the Pride*."[5]

TV sitcoms, by and large, are intended to appeal to the demographic that has the highest percentage of viewers: in other words,
women. You see the same sorts of tensions playing out a lot: tensions
about dating, about not dating, about relationships and marriage; tensions about what men think (if they think), about what men mean
when they say something, and about why they don't say what they're
supposed to say—or at least not in the way they're supposed to say it.
It seems we have an epidemic on our hands: a men-centered mania, or
*men*ia, perhaps. And in the fictional world of TV sitcoms, it's a menia
orchestrated and led by women, who somehow have emerged as the

unchallenged leaders of the domain. How do we know that men on TV are always saying the "wrong thing"? Because women (real and fictional) are constantly telling us it's the wrong thing. It's women who determine whether a man is dressed appropriately, whether he behaves appropriately, even whether he thinks appropriately. (And, for the record, we don't see the same thing happening in reverse. Women also determine whether *women* dress, act, and think appropriately. They are the rule makers and the scorekeepers for both sexes.)

In modern-day sitcoms, it's man's lot to be the butt of jokes (which is quite a step down, metaphorically and anatomically, from being the head of the household). The majority of roles men play can be divided into two categories: meat and vegetable. Where women can be negatively portrayed as crazy or ditzy or indecisive, the meat men are just plain dense. Think of Joey (compared with Phoebe) on *Friends*. If these characters are not entirely stupid, they are at least incompetent, particularly in performing household chores, picking out clothes, or dealing with women. Their wives and girlfriends, in contrast, are unfailingly witty and bright, not to mention highly competent. Raymond from *Everybody Loves Raymond* and Homer Simpson are two prime examples. At the end of each episode, usually after some act of ridiculous inconsideration, they crawl back to their wives, give schoolboy apologies, and draw on one last reflective beer. Raymond and Homer could both charitably be considered lovable lugs (okay, maybe only Raymond could), but the message is clear: **Men have somehow become the inferior sex, a lesser version of the species that couldn't possibly cope unless handed directly from the care of a mother to the care of a wife.** Raymond, at least, has a "cool" career (sportswriter), but it's a sign of how much things have changed that a man today can have a successful career but still be derided at home as virtually useless in any situation requiring savvy or tact.

And this attitude isn't confined to TV land; it has leached into other areas of society, as well. How else can one explain the fact that Urban Outfitters and other stores recently were selling shirts that read, "Boys are stupid; throw rocks at them"? The makers and sellers of the shirts defended them as harmless fun—a playful product that one shouldn't take at all seriously. Just imagine if someone had tried to sell the same shirts, but this time saying "girls" rather than "boys." The reaction would have been intense and immediate.

The same could be said for many of the plots and characterizations we're seeing on TV. **Reverse the male and female roles, and there likely would be an outcry against negative stereotypes of women.** And the outcry would be even louder if the women were overweight. One could argue that it's acceptable to mock men and exaggerate their frailties on television precisely because they have for so long had the upper hand in society, but that doesn't begin to resolve the larger issue: Namely, how are men—and boys—being affected by the seemingly relentless onslaught of negative media portrayals? And how are these negative depictions influencing society's attitudes toward males and their perceived competency and expected roles?

It might seem like a stretch to move from Homer Simpson to the U.S. presidency (or not . . .), but it's interesting to note the simultaneous decline of respect for our leaders and respect for leading men on TV (though "led men" might be a more apt description). Much has been made of the media evolving so quickly from a profession that helped mask President Franklin Roosevelt's infirmities (not to mention his wheelchair) to a profession that considered it the general public's business to know what was taking place under President Clinton's desk in the Oval Office. Where once men—and, most particularly, world leaders—were put on a pedestal, now they're fair game. Only the game doesn't actually involve playing fair. It's more like seeing how much you can get away with before people—or censors or public advocacy groups—squawk in protest.

Jim Frank, father of two, says the negative portrayal of dads, in particular, is a pet peeve of his. "Not all men, but fathers are portrayed as bumbling boobs," he complains, "totally clueless about their wives' and kids' lives, simply going to work and having nothing to do with anything substantive happening in the home (and coaching Little League doesn't count). Fathers are usually shown as being unable to talk to their families about anything important, bottling up their emotions (playing that 'macho' role), more as providers and protectors than partner and parent. . . . When the defining moment of a sitcom is Dad 'getting it,' there's something wrong." Jim's daughter, Rebecca, an eighteen-year-old student at Tufts University, also decries the media stereotypes: "As one who doesn't hate men," she says, "I find myself defending men when rabid, man-hating feminists latch onto the negative stereotypes as gospel."

Not all men on TV are portrayed as utterly daft, of course. Which brings us to the second categorization: vegetables. This depiction is more positive, if a bit idealized. The characters of Aidan and Smith on *Sex and the City* represent this group. They are manly, considerate, and sensitive; they are not threatened by a woman's power and can dish emotion when appropriate. They want families and love. That's the best-case scenario. Then there are the veggies who move beyond sensitivity and into neuroticism. These typically are not the boys who get the girl. Nuance is not in their vocabulary. Drew Carey's character on *The Drew Carey Show* is a prime example. In one episode, a woman he used to love announces she is engaged to be married. Drew, wallowing in defensiveness, announces an engagement of his own. He sets a date and starts planning the wedding—despite the fact that he hasn't actually tracked down anyone to marry him yet.

There's also the crossbreed of a vegetable disguised as meat: a veggie burger, or perhaps a Tofurkey. Tim Allen on *Home Improvement* fits here. In some ways, he seems to be a traditional male: He likes cars, babes, and fixing things. He talks about how he hates talking about things and how he loves being a man. He even hoots and grunts. He has his own show, and it's filmed in a workshop, meaning he can happily spend his days surrounded by sawdust and metal and big blocks of wood. Yet, whenever a family issue arises, he sheds his tool belt and, suddenly . . . oh, my God, he has feelings!

Rebecca Frank notes that on TV "men are either TOO 'masculine' (i.e., sports-obsessed and chauvinistic) or too 'feminine' (hugging, questionable sexuality)." She concludes that perhaps the problem is with the entertainment industry's "inability to draw complex characters." **Yet we can't help but notice that, in contrast to the (largely) one-tone male characters populating the airwaves, we're seeing some genuinely multidimensional female characters.** *Sex and the City* is a case in point. During its six-year run, the show focused on the lives of four women, each of whom was beautiful, smart, and powerful. Each woman represented a different attitude toward relationships and marriage, and each episode pitted the women against the savageries of dating in the big city. The women were in and out of relationships, in and out of beds, up and down with each other, all the while following finely honed scripts that were widely commended for exploring dating with a frankness and an honesty TV hadn't before seen. As in *Friends* before it, all of the characters on the show became so familiar that women now describe themselves in terms of the four characters—Samanthas and Mirandas of the world, unite!

WE BREAK FOR THIS IMPORTANT MESSAGE

Thank goodness for commercial breaks. At least those show men as they really are, right? Difficult as it may be to believe, **current advertising may be even worse than television sitcoms when it comes to negative portrayals of men.** The truth is, men and masculinity have become very easy targets. And now men are so used to being mocked, and to mocking themselves, that marketing directed toward them seems to snap to this mode instinctually.

"Men [in advertising] are typically defined as useless fools, sexual predators or extreme action junkies," laments an article in the *Australian Financial Review*. Mike Morrison, the chief strategy officer of the American advertising agency Young & Rubicam, voices his protest in the same article: "As a marketer and a male, I see more ads that are offensive and demeaning to men than I ever did. . . . Does every pay-off have to be at the expense of men?" Another marketer concurs: "I think there's a dearth of good strong images of masculinity, in part because we don't really know what that is any more."[6] From television to marketing, it's easier to typecast men than it is to try to dig out individuality.

The British writer Paul Fraser, thirty-three, tells us advertising is no better in Europe. "Advertising's negative portrayal of men annoys me because it's lazy," he says. "The idiot husband who doesn't know how to wash his own clothes. The dishwasher that's so simple, even a man can use it. These do not reflect most men. It's out of date." Then again, Fraser does see the silver lining: "The upside is, all the wives in these adverts are intelligent, in-control babes—so even if you're a real dummy you can still get a hot chick."

Prominent conservative women have been particularly vocal in their defense of the embattled man. *The Christian Science Monitor* reports that in the book *The Proper Care and Feeding of Husbands*, "Radio host Dr. Laura Schlessinger chronicles her efforts to get the listeners who call into her radio show to think more about appreciating the qualities of men that are traditionally male—stoicism, bravery, strength—rather than expecting them to exhibit more emotional behavior like that of their female friends."[7]

Men, too, are fighting back. Late in 2003, a forty-year-old New Hampshire engineer named Richard Smaglick launched the Society for the Prevention of Misandry in the Media—**misandry being the hatred of men** (the counterpart to *misogyny*). Among his first efforts was a call for a boycott of the clients of Saatchi & Saatchi. The Saatchi ad that so offended Mr. Smaglick featured a woman laid up in bed with a virus and her husband given charge of the house. The joke is that Dad can't cope with his own children: among other bright moves, he sends them to school in the snow wearing next to nothing.

On such websites as the Men's Activism News Network (www.mensactivism.org), disgruntled men compile lists of companies to boycott in retaliation for their men-phobic approach to ads. Imagine the consequences, posted a website administrator, if the roles were reversed and men were encouraged to "threaten women in a whole new way." Imagine "just switching the gender roles for a minute and see if it would still be funny. Imagine having a laugh track when a woman's genitals are attacked."

BOYS GONE WILD

This isn't to say the only images we see of men on TV today are of henpecked morons and clueless dads. Men actually do exist outside the sitcom and advertising environments—heck, someone's got to play the sexy gardener on *Desperate Housewives*. When we look at all the male icons out there, we see two in particular who are worth a deeper look, since they manage to embody both stereotypes of old and an entirely modern type of man. The first is the sort of man who might once have been referred to as a "hooligan"—or just a plain old "bad influence." Johnny Knoxville is a prime example. During the run of his show, MTV's *Jackass*, Knoxville and his merry men took scorpion stings to the rear. They turned themselves into human urinals. They did idiotic act after idiotic act just for the sheer thrill of being idiotic. On its face, this seems like the most childish, boorish, and ridiculous sort of masculinity imaginable; the pranks were amateurish, potentially dangerous, and usually embellished by such touches as fat men and dwarves in costume. But some have suggested that the foolhardiness and idiocy of a show like *Jackass* transcend boyhood pranks and enter the decidedly adult territory of masochism. A *Salon* column from 2002 makes the argument:

[*Jackass* star] Steve-O got his ass pierced and he bobbed for jellyfish; he snorted a live earthworm and pulled it out through his mouth in a flurry of dry heaves. . . . These, the public agrees, are acts of daring that require serious mental discipline. Knoxville commented in one interview that when he's enduring painful acts, they "get me so hot I feel just like Audrey Hepburn in 'My Fair Lady.'"[8]

Cintra Wilson, writer of the piece, compares the "har-har" tough-boy masochism of *Jackass* to a much more emotional, "dangerous," wounded, and sensitive sort of foolhardiness: the duration acts of David Blaine, the tattooed and brooding self-described "street magician" who is recently most famous for having suspended himself in a plastic box above the River Thames for forty-four days. Unlike Steve-O or Johnny Knoxville, Blaine packages himself as a sensitive and damaged artist, obsessively driven to push himself further and further, yet terrified of where his desires might lead him. In fact, upon emerging from his clear plastic box, the emaciated Blaine immediately "burst into tears . . . saying: 'I love you all forever.'"[9]

The models of men that Blaine and the Jackass crew present can't be written off as a throwback to earlier times, despite some similarities. These men and their actions are more complicated than their predecessors. Blaine and Knoxville typify, to some extent, the ideals of the metrosexual, even as their actions seem to lie somewhere between the bravery of Houdini and the sheer idiocy of Beavis and his sidekick, Butt-head. **"Both young men are *hawt*, fashionably macho, and famous through their acts of simulated crisis,"** says Wilson.[10] And regarding Blaine, she continues, "Blaine might be wearing a Mylar cummerbund and performing in Vegas with an albino ocelot if he were not (1) a photogenically seductive, tattooed, proto-geek/thug contradiction, (2) strangely Rasputin-esque and maybe *psychic*, and (3) a champion star fucker."[11] In other words, he's a well-groomed and carefully assembled mixture of *faux* street toughness and churning inner turmoil, all well dressed, curled, and perfectly performed.

Most important, though, is that both Knoxville and Blaine are honest about where their desires come from. It's less heroism, less a celebration of stupidity qua stupidity, than it is genuine pleasure. We heard it from Knoxville already—flushed as Audrey Hepburn at the pleasure of being hurt, humiliated, soiled. For his part, Blaine has admitted to *The New York Times*, "When I'm doing the stunts, it's the only time I feel alive."[12]

Blaine is the new Houdini seen through the lens of the new man, the metrosexual man—with the same brooding, the same mystery, better marketing, and more pathos. He also acknowledges something men were never supposed to openly admit to before: that it's pleasurable to cede control to others. It's pleasurable to be physically and emotionally debased, to be starved to the point of weakness and pelted with tomatoes in a little acrylic box hanging from a crane. Houdini's tricks always concentrated on his own personal power, his own ability to defy death. Blaine's seem to concentrate just as much on his own personal weakness.

With Knoxville and Steve-O, too, we get something more than just frat-boy pranks. They both really seem to love being hurt—especially in embarrassing, silly, "shameful" ways. Steve-O turns his rear end into a dartboard, then bends over and has his friends throw darts right into him. Everyone is cracking up the entire time, but the power dynamics are clear. Steve-O dresses himself in all white with a urinal suspended from the front of his costume and searches through bars, looking for men to "use" him. Again, he's asking for it, he's searching it out, he's embracing and loving the debasement of it. He's basically performing the role of the masochist in the guise of the buffoon.

Here, too, then, we see the transformation of the male roles in the media. Men have been doing stupid stuff on TV for a long, long time, but the audience was rarely privy to the mental processes of the men in question. We just called them daredevils, said they were "foolhardy," and took their stunts as evidence of bravado. We never asked Evel Knievel why he wanted to jump twenty cars. We never asked Houdini why he wanted to bury himself alive, and whether the idea excited him. Now, in the age of the new man, we want to get inside these men. We want to understand the reasons they do what they do.

It doesn't hurt that neither Steve-O and Knoxville nor Blaine is that hard on the eyes. You'd be hard pressed to find as much media interest in a middle-aged, slightly pudgy man who had turned himself into a human latrine. And many of the stunts of all three of the men involve them displaying their bodies—Blaine stripped off his shirt to sit seventy-two hours in an ice cube, and Steve-O seems to be out of his pants more often than not. But escape artists/magicians and stuntmen were always about display, weren't they? Houdini was often photographed shirtless. Knievel did himself up like Elvis on the comeback tour. That aspect of the foolhardy man has not really changed so much, but the sexualizing of Blaine, Knoxville, and Steve-O dovetails with a bigger trend toward the public appreciation of men's bodies—to a degree and a thoroughness that used to be reserved exclusively for women.

MESSAGE IN THE MEDIA

There are those who would say that television is entertainment, period. And that the characters and content therein have no real significance outside the family room or media room. The truth is that television (and, indeed, all media) both reflects and influences reality. Sitcom writers cull observations from their own lives and intertwine them with those of their characters; reality shows expose people to real-life conflicts in unreal situations. Television sends us the message that it's okay for single women to play the field (*Sex and the City*), that men and women can work together on equal terms as professionals (*Law & Order, ER*), and that homosexuality is a part of life that needn't be hidden from public view (*Will & Grace, Boy Meets Boy*).

It seems equally clear that television is also sending us the message that today's males simply aren't measuring up—except, perhaps, to their own expectations, a fact that is depicted as even greater cause for concern. When you look at comedic television, examples of male dominance are almost always heavily coated in irony. A man who tries to assert himself as head of household (always good for a laugh) typically ends his macho chest-thumping with a plaintive, "Okay, honey?"

Even *The Man Show*, a program purportedly geared toward men and their baser instincts, to a large extent mocked the audience to which it supposedly was trying to appeal. Aired in the United States from 1999 to 2003, the show was hosted by Adam Carolla and Jimmy Kimmel, and featured such entertainment as "juggy dancers" and cheerleaders on trampolines. Finally, a show by men, for men, and about men that had to do with something other than sports! But not so fast. The supposed joys of objectification came with a price. Men who watched the show knew that, to some extent (maybe even a large extent), the joke was on them: men's minds are in the gutter, men are lazy, men are pigs, the show said again and again. Those who hated the show did so for its reinforcement of gender codes that our culture has fought to rid itself of for the past fifty years. Those who enjoyed it—at least, those who weren't busy videotaping the juggy dancers— saw men cheering their own mockery.

Is it any wonder that TV viewership is declining among males aged eighteen to thirty-two (the prime demographic for advertisers)? Even if television both embodies and reinforces the currents of mainstream thought, there must be some tension between the way men view themselves and the way they see themselves portrayed on TV. In so many ways, men still dominate the airwaves. Flip on a TV at random, and you have a 90 percent chance of seeing a man. Watch the nightly news, and you'd barely know that women existed outside the co-anchor chair. But turn to a sitcom, and you likely won't see men who are much more than caricatures.

Media images have an impact on men, to be sure. Young boys, particularly, take their cues and clues from the people they admire on the small screen, just as girls try to dress like Hillary Duff and Lindsay Lohan. The number of young males admitted to burn wards as a consequence of trying to copy the Stupid Human Tricks on *Jackass* leaves that fact in no doubt. In the next chapter, we'll look at some influences that aren't always framed by a TV screen, including fathers and teachers and gay culture.

WHAT TO REMEMBER

1. If today's "real world" role models for males are not much in evidence, how about the even more pervasive and influential media? Not much good news to report here either: on the big screen, today's icons have little in common with the traditions of Bogey, Gable, and McQueen. Leo, Ben, Jude (and pretty-boy Orlando) represent a very different brand of male prototype than those of generations past. While this is no doubt in part an effect of cultural evolution, it's also at least partly attributable to the tyranny of marketing. Women, and to a lesser extent gay men, who have become a larger portion of the contemporary media audience, are demanding new definitions of the male stereotype, even as women start to look more like their most macho counterparts, witness Ripley and Lara Croft.

   And what do we see on television? Something very different from *Father Knows Best*. In fact, contemporary television could well be summed up in a fictional program called *Men Know Nothing*. That's the theme of so much of what we see on family sitcoms today.

2. Ads, which one would think would at least strive to appeal to a male audience, aren't much better at dispelling negative stereotypes of men. They certainly aren't doing a good job of creating the sorts of stereotypes of M-ness modern man might want to emulate. All too often in the marketing arena, we're seeing man as victim—of his sexual organ or his lust, of his emotional neediness, his over-inflated ego, or his sheer ineptitude. What we rarely see are positive portrayals of "balanced man," "man of the world with conscience," and so on.

8

REAL MEN AND
THEIR REAL ROLE MODELS

From higher divorce rates to the constant cultural focus on the success of women, many feel that the past three decades have left young boys behind. Is there a genuine crisis in masculine role modeling?

In this chapter, we'll look at some of the people who are changing the ways young males see themselves and their sex, from celebrities and athletes to gay men. But first we'll look at two of the more immediate and less visible influences shaping young men today: fathers and teachers.

MASCULINITY: BROUGHT TO YOU BY WOMEN

Somewhere in the march of years, the game of the genders has begun to change. Masculinity was, and still is to a large degree, defined and controlled by a culture that benefited men a lot more than it did women. The cultural system nurtured a man's masculinity and even machismo, rewarded him for their display, and set the other sex in deference to him. Along the way, masculinity became more complex. The old version of masculinity is not something one wants to think about, much less talk about or see. Nods to the old dominance that masculinity used to enjoy are only accepted when tucked inside one of two things: man-mocking sarcasm or conservative ideology. And a big part of this is because, with the exception of a few canonized professions (particularly firefighter and police officer in the years since 9/11), **the defense, mockery, or mere definition of masculinity is now largely in the domain of women.**

Men agree that defining masculinity is no longer man's prerogative. As reported in a *Christian Science Monitor* article discussing the new manly man, "Ken, a 40-something man who owns a small business in the Atlanta area (and asks that his last name not be used) says he's more of an emotional guy; he also drives a nice car and wears stylish clothes. But in his case that doesn't seem to be what women want, he says. For him, masculinity is all about women. 'Masculinity has nothing to do with men,' he says. 'The whole issue of masculinity rests entirely with women. It is not, per se, a male issue. Men spend most of their time in relationships in trying to be what the woman perceives as masculine.'"[1]

Which brings us to the question of male role models. What sorts of men are still influencing how boys and young men perceive the masculine "ideal"? So far, we've focused exclusively on the media—on cinema and TV, especially—and their role in shaping what we imagine a real man of the twenty-first century to be. But surely it's not just the job of the entertainment media. After all, before we had mass media, how in the world did anyone learn how a man was supposed to behave and think? Presumably, from the men around them. Most particularly, their fathers and other older male relatives and their teachers.

Well, like everything else, that seems to be changing. A slew of recent reports in Australia echo concerns that have been emerging in the United States and Great Britain for a while now: **young boys seem to have fewer and fewer positive male role models in their lives, and that includes teachers and dads.** Divorce rates in many postindustrial nations are edging near, or even exceeding, 50 percent. Many children are now raised in single-parent households, and the parent doing the raising is likely to be Mom. Citing the increases in gang activity among young men, especially in working-class neighborhoods, many governments—the Australian, UK, and U.S. among them—have sought new ways to bring male role models into the lives of young boys who might not have men immediately around them.

Australia has turned to teachers. The Australian government has taken steps to adjust the gender balance among teachers in an effort to bolster boys' examination scores and success rates. "The number of students from single-parent homes, almost invariably headed by mothers, is rising, and the number of male teachers is falling. The result, according to a federal parliamentary committee report, is a shortage of positive male role models in schools," said a recent article on the report.[2] "The teaching profession has long been the preserve of women, prompting the Government to launch a campaign to attract more men to the classroom."[3]

We see a similar scenario in the United States. Men make up only 21 percent of America's 3 million teachers, and among these, only 9 percent teach at the elementary level.[4] Despite the nation's hugely expanded population, there are as few men teaching today as there were in the days of schoolmarms in one-room schoolhouses; apparently, teaching is regarded as an essentially unmasculine occupation—not to mention that it pays poorly.

Does it really matter if boys are taught almost exclusively by women? The Australian parliamentary report "Boys: Getting It Right" says yes. The report's authors see the gender imbalance among teachers as an important factor in boys' being outperformed by girls in the classroom and even in their dropping out of school. Its recommendations include taking whatever steps are needed to employ more male teachers, even if that means salary increases. "The committee found the Australian education system has been so keen to ensure a fair go for girls that it has over-compensated, to the detriment of boys," reports the Australian newspaper *The Advertiser.* "The result is that boys are becoming the underclass of Australia's education system. Not only are girls outperforming boys, boys are more likely to be suspended, expelled or drop out altogether."[5]

The problem is certainly not unique to Australia; the following description comes from an article about a street pastor who attempts to interact with working-class boys in England in order to partially fill their need for positive male role models:

Think Los Angeles with shades of Dickens: a lawless underworld where seven-year-olds run drugs for addicted parents, fourteen-year-olds deal cocaine and hordes of fatherless boys find companionship in gangs but are barely able to read or write. That's the Britain Les Isaacs sees. "It's the realm of Fagin and the Artful Dodger. I often can't quite believe this is happening, but it already has," says Isaacs, a Christian pastor with the Icthus Fellowship in London.[6]

If boys see teaching as a profession only women are willing to enter, then it's not difficult to see how they might think that very little of what happens at school will make them into real men. Those boys who stay in school often get attention by playing dumb or behaving disruptively. Most of us have memories of a white-knuckled female teacher's mounting, and often impotent, rage in the face of some bad boy's antics. Experts feel a greater male presence in the classroom would not only give boys positive role models, but would also provide boys with educators who might find their behavior less trying.

The fact that so many boys are turned off by school has lasting consequences, particularly since they've fallen behind in such fundamentals as reading and writing, which somehow have been classified as "for girls." The literary arts have always suffered allegations of effeminacy. In the early twentieth century, modernists such as Ezra Pound and T. S. Eliot sought to purge poetry of the "feminine" excesses of Victorian writing, advocating "masculine" objectivity instead. They failed in their quest; succeeding generations of writers of both sexes have, in large numbers, embraced the "subjective" and even the confessional. In fact, teen memoirs of recent years have been precisely that: confessions of painful experiences such as drug and sex abuse. Teen authors Ned Vizzini, Marty Beckerman, and Nick Mc-Donnell have, like Katie Tarbox and Rebecca Ray, capitalized on a market whose appetite for the lurid appears insatiable. But these teen sensations prove an exception to the legions of ordinary boys who still adhere to what educators and therapists call the "boy code": sure, don't tell on others, but above all, don't tell others about yourself. If something womanish like shame, embarrassment, or sadness should attempt to express itself, it must be swallowed whole, leaving no traces on stiff upper lips.

The need to maintain at all times a stoic exterior dissuades boys from seeking help, at school or at home. While girls are more likely to articulate feelings of inadequacy or frustration in one way or another, boys tend to "act out" aggressively or withdraw entirely. A widespread presumption of male violence has led to what some feel is the "pathologization" of "boyish" behavior. The surge in diagnoses of attention deficit disorder in the past decade has made daily pill-poppers of thousands of schoolboys, a trend many see as a dangerously easy way out of addressing problems that may be environmental rather than biological. Attention deficit may be partly responsible for many boys' comparatively lesser interest in reading, but reading's role as a mode of expression and sharing could also be a key factor. And the general reluctance of boys to read beyond what's assigned in school often follows them into adulthood. Men make up a marginal percentage of the reading market; witness the premature fizzle of "lad lit" in 2004.

Boys' weakening performance in school is often linked to class, race, and ethnicity. Academic achievement, including SAT scores, often, and predictably, suffers where income and opportunities are low. But recently discussions of working-class underachievement have indicted "maleness" as a root cause. Pat Clarke, a former president of the British Columbia Teacher's Federation, complained of an "underclass of louts," that is, of young men who have failed to achieve academic and career goals and who make up the majority of the economically disenfranchised. In Britain, a "laddish, anti-learning" environment is blamed for boys' failure to keep pace with girls.[7] In the United States, peer pressure among boys to keep their studies low on their list of priorities is fairly intense among African Americans. An astonishing 42 percent of African American boys have failed at least one grade, and only 18 percent of black men between the ages of twenty and twenty-one are enrolled in college. Black women are twice as likely as black men to earn bachelor's or master's degrees. In one middle school in Savannah, Georgia, only 45 of 302 African American boys are enrolled in the school's magnet program. Many capable boys do not take full advantage of the competitive courses at their disposal, and some choose to drop out of the program altogether rather than be teased for being nerds or "acting white." They feel excluded by the mostly white kids in the magnet classes, as well as by the black kids in the rest of the school. On the other hand, students who find themselves in remedial courses feel humiliated by the low expectations placed on them and make little headway.[8]

Low expectations are cited as a deterrent to boys' progress generally, but the ever-decreasing number of male teachers is also considered an important factor, and perhaps one that could be more easily solved. Reformers who would like to see more men in the classroom come up against a number of problems, starting with low salaries and lack of status. In many parts of the world, teaching is no longer accorded much respect. Men who might be drawn to the profession are also discouraged by today's litigious times. As a report in *The Advertiser* commented: "How sad it is that teachers of both genders are advised not to cuddle children, even small children who have been hurt in the schoolyard or are otherwise distressed. The teachers could leave themselves open to allegations of sexual interference or child abuse. Male teachers are particularly vulnerable. . . . [The] possibility of being sued by a student, even later in life, is a constant fear."[9]

The situation described by Les Isaacs and others seems bleak, but the reaction to it also raises some questions: Obviously, it's of concern that boys are dropping out of school and sometimes falling into crime, but is it necessarily bad that girls have accelerated past boys in their courses? Is the problem for boys that they're not connecting to school because of a lack of male role models, or is it simply that they no longer want to compete in an arena in which girls are being seen as the "winners"? The Australian parliamentary report spoke of resorting to options such as increased pay incentives for male teachers in order to address the critical lack of men, but doesn't that serve simply to reinstate the gender inequalities that the women's movements of the latter half of the twentieth century spent so long trying to correct?

ISO DOTING DADS

Boys who go through the school day without seeing any men may not find one upon their return home, either. And this isn't true only of single-parent households headed by women. Very often, Dad lives in the household but doesn't spend a whole lot of time there. Restrictive working conditions have been one culprit, in Australia and presumably in other industrialized nations, as well. "Australian research," reports the *Canberra Times*, "finds that over the past decade workplaces have become less family-friendly, not more. Fathers feel pressured to choose between work and family, and they complain of inflexible working conditions and unsupportive bosses."[10]

Though the problem of "absentee dads" is nothing new, the proposed solutions show a real rethinking of the fundamental roles of men and women. Reports from Australia and Great Britain cite a lack of male tenderness as a critical flaw in children's upbringing, leading both countries to attempt not only to expand the numbers of male teachers, but also to support paternity-leave programs in order to encourage men to take a more nurturing role. **Instead of the distant breadwinner, new family models demand that men take on a more hands-on role in child-rearing.**

Some families are outsourcing the job. In such cities as Los Angeles and New York, "mannies"—male nannies—are in demand. More and more young men are taking care of children and finding themselves enjoying it. Parents of boys especially like the care a man can give: he's more likely to play rough and channel all that boyish energy. Not to mention the fact that a young man who can prepare meals and change diapers is a natural corrective for boys who fear anything that smacks of the girlish. There's a lot of media coverage of husbands failing to hold up their end in terms of child care and household chores, but it turns out this pattern is set long before marriage. When we asked teen respondents in one of our studies what they do after school, 44 percent of girls said they do chores, compared with just 32 percent of boys.[11] Some moms are hoping to reverse the trend by hiring male caregivers.

But manny care is a phenomenon pretty much restricted to urban areas. And many parents, perhaps most, continue to feel safer with a female nanny. One hurdle is stereotyping: A man willing to care for children must be a pedophile. Or the manny in question is a loser who couldn't find a "real job" elsewhere. Young men continue to struggle to find a place for themselves between the fixed poles of violence and "effeminate" weakness.

INFLUENCES

In *Bowling for Columbine*, Michael Moore asks the shock rocker Marilyn Manson whom he thought kids today were more influenced by: himself (Manson) or then President Clinton. Why, the president, of course, Mr. Manson demurred. But many people have a hard time believing that. Kids and teens respond to what's in *their* worlds—to what their friends are doing and thinking, to what they watch and listen to, to what they place on their video game consoles and PCs. And in today's environment, those sorts of activities and entertainments are often centered on violence, particularly where males are concerned.

Violence, whether it's dropping bombs, playing paintball, shooting up a school, destroying worlds in video games, or singing along to Eminem's song "Kill You," seems to hold great appeal among kids today. Many parents and commentators have decried violence in various media and worry that kids can't distinguish between the fictional and the real. What may begin as an imaginary expression of violence often becomes an all too real bid for power and glory. Wanting to fit in also encourages violence; tribal loyalty is alive and well. A New York University study found that young males are more likely to engage in violent behavior when the ratio of males between fifteen and twenty-nine rises to a level of between seventy and eighty young men for every one hundred men over age thirty. Jihadists, new military recruits, and street-gang members are all roughly the same age, each seeking ways to express courage and sacrifice, and thus live out, as the anthropologist Lionel Tiger puts it, the "authoritative drama of what they hope to do."[12]

But a culture obsessed with celebrity also motivates kids to be successful. Competitive reality TV shows like *Survivor* and *The Apprentice* teach kids to keep their eye on the prize. Teens, hungry to gain fame and fortune, are forming career and financial goals much earlier. With 80 percent of teens in the United States working after-school or summer jobs and teen purchases of goods and services rising to $170 billion in 2003 from $122 billion in 1997, financial management is already a reality for a lot of teens.

When previous generations of boys looked around for career role models, they found people like Neil Armstrong and Warren Buffett. Successful professionals focused on their particular fields of endeavor. Today, career idols are people like Sean (P. Diddy) Combs and Russell Simmons, men whose fame started around music but who have crossed over into everything from fashion labels to restaurants/bars to film and TV production. For teens, it's less about building résumés than it is about building "Brand Me."

"It's not just teens who are looking to live a mogul lifestyle as they get older," says Cory Berger, a former colleague of ours who is now a strategist with Mother, a New York creative hot shop. "Kids as young as eight idolize superstars like Jessica Simpson and Hillary Duff, who are transitioning between media outlets at an unprecedented level. They are crossing the lines from music to film to TV projects, giving fans more and more access to them. With so many young stars attaching their names to restaurants, production companies, and product lines, kids today are getting a very clear message that their idols aren't so much about the 'art' as they are about accumulating power and wealth, and creating their own brands. And that's something these kids intend to emulate."

One thing these would-be moguls are seriously into is online chat. Overall, 81 percent of American teens online use chat programs. Stereotypes would suggest that chat's bigger among girls, and that's true: 85 percent of teen girls chat online. But so do 77 percent of guys. Chat is so popular, in fact, that 75 percent overall (71 percent of boys vs. 79 percent of girls) spend at least two hours a day online.[13] Researchers have found that cell phones and text messaging may allow boys to let down their "boy-code defenses." What a guy might be unwilling to share with another guy in person might be written instead.[14]

Changes in gender roles have led to a very confusing time for teenage boys. Some suggest that women and girls, embittered by past prejudice, feel they have legitimate reason to treat boys and men badly—in other words, as they or their forebears had been treated.[15] Boys certainly are aware of the conflicting messages they're receiving. Society is asking men to become more sensitive and emotional, but only when it's convenient, and only to a certain vaguely defined point. If teenage boys open up and assume more "girlish" traits, they are going to be called gay (which even today is to be avoided); if they stay strong and silent, exhibiting traditionally masculine traits, they are accused of being antisocial or even violent.[16] In the book *What Makes a Man*, a fourteen-year-old named Brad is quoted as saying, "Guys feel ashamed to show their emotions in public. We're not supposed to show emotion. We have to be strong and tough."[17] Teen boys, like men, are torn between believing they should be able to provide a girl or woman with everything she needs and fearing being yelled at for being chauvinistic. Finding a happy medium can be difficult, particularly when they don't have role models around who might show them how to do that.

William S. Pollack, the author of *Real Boys' Voices* and director of the Centers for Men and Young Men, makes an interesting point when he says that a boy's reluctance to "grow up" (female teens are well documented to be more mature than their male counterparts) and accept responsibility may be caused not by laziness, stupidity, or lack of consideration, but instead by fear. They are unsure of what is expected of them in today's world and uncertain about how to meet the nebulous expectations they do confront.[18]

In a comic piece entitled "The End of Men," the filmmaker Michael Moore argues that men are actually becoming extinct. He starts by relaying how the Census Bureau reports that the number of male babies being born in the United States has declined every year since 1990, continues with the thesis that women don't need men anymore due to test-tube procreation, and finally concludes that "nature has a way of getting rid of its weakest links."[19] Darwin might have taken exception to Moore's thesis, but Moore is certainly correct in his assessment that modern man—and modern boy—is uncertain about his role and purpose in today's world.

Whereas some men mourn the loss of yesterday's less complex gender relations and expectations, others celebrate the birth of what they see as a new masculinity, or at least a chance for a new masculinity. Colin Mortensen, a former star on MTV's *Real World Hawaii* and author of *A New Ladies' Man: Getting the Girl*, promotes in his book the ideas that men should feel able to cry, that a man's worth should be judged by more than his muscles, and that neither gender should be sexually objectified.[20] Pretty obvious stuff, but ideas that a lot of young men haven't been hearing.

The former All-Star football player Jackson Katz is also known for his views on gender stereotypes. He addresses issues of teenage violence by traveling around the world conducting seminars to teach boys about gender role-playing. In addition to his Mentors in Violence Protection program (MVP), he has worked to combat sexism. His video *Tough Guise: Violence, Media and the Crisis in Masculinity* analyzes the images youth culture is presented. He's an unusual example of someone who has the credibility, thanks to his days with the New England Patriots, to get away with talking about emotional issues and encouraging teenagers to do the same.[21]

CRISIS OR CHANGE?

When we look at the "crisis" of today's dearth of positive male role models, we do wonder whether it may be less about destruction than about change. **As the rules of gender change across cultures, it becomes harder and harder for individual men to know how to model proper male behavior to young boys.** How much of the so-called crisis, then, is genuine crisis, and how much of it is backlash against the societal pressures pushing men toward new roles? The social and economic shifts that have taken place over the past half century have resulted in contradictory expectations regarding how men should behave. Society wants them to be both strong and gentle, daring and nurturing. As the *Canberra Times* put it, each man must face the question "Should I be a stoic breadwinner or a nurturing caretaker, a real bloke or a sensitive metrosexual?"[22] Are boys truly in trouble because of a lack of role models, or are they simply not living up to our new (and perhaps not entirely realistic) expectations? Given the sea change in the rules of masculinity in recent decades, the real problem may be less a lack of men in caring positions and more a lack of understanding about what those positions are supposed to be.

Obviously, the issue is a complicated one; no single influence can be pegged as the central force leading to the new look of masculinity and the new definition of what it is to be a man. The truth is, the way society teaches itself about itself is also changing. **The mass media play a huge role in the instruction of culture—and often provide much stronger role models than community or family can offer.** It may well be true that the deck is a bit stacked against young boys—or, at least, that it's less heavily stacked in their favor now than it was before. But sometimes the voices mourning the loss of positive male role models are the same as those mourning the loss of "real men" in the movies. (Steve McQueen, where are you?) That invites the question of whether society as a whole truly wants a return to the domination of the "real men" of old, or whether we're simply in a period of flux that will end when we've decided exactly what we want our boys to grow up to be.

We'll look now at a couple of the major influences that have helped to expand the boundaries of masculinity, giving boys and young men new parameters within which they are "permitted" to operate: "feminized" men within modern music and gay culture.

MAN IN THE MIRROR

Our overall image of modern man, how he behaves, and what he thinks is shaped by men in every high-profile field, whether it be politics or acting, sports or marketing. The industry that has made what we might call the most complicated contribution to the image of men is music. This is the industry that seems to allow men the greatest leeway to explore their own femininity—with minor keys and power ballads, with rouge and heels, even with plastic surgery.

Feminine musicians are nothing new, especially in rock and roll. Little Richard, with his sequins and his flawless pompadour, could get away with his highly mannered rendition of "Tutti Frutti" all the way back in 1955. From the 1960s to the 1980s, the number and variety of male stars working androgyny and drag into their performances continued to explode—from Jagger to Bowie, from Kiss to Culture Club, from the big hair of new wave to the big hair of metal. But one male singer whose radical transformation of his appearance continues to obsess (and appall) us stands out from the crowd: Michael Jackson. He may have far fewer fans now, but for a period, he truly was the "king of pop," and he influenced the attitudes and dress of millions of his young admirers.

Now, there's plenty that can be said about Michael Jackson; we can all draw up a long list of his eccentricities (and now, his alleged—though unproven—proclivities). He started shocking the world with his gradual physical transformation and has continued pushing that envelope of shock all the way into the court system, where he has just been acquitted of charges of child molestation and contributing to the delinquency of a minor. Before his legal troubles, though, he was already in the press for blurring his own sex and race. Back in 1987, before the more extreme surgical procedures that led to the uncovering of Jackson's crumbling nose in a U.S. courtroom, *The Los Angeles Times* was already acting spooked by his transformation:

> In the past few years, Jackson has been chiseling, cleaving and re-molding his face, forming a visage that has become both the symbol and the reality of his career as a music superstar. It's as if he wants to make himself into one of those idealized pieces of graphic art on the side of every corporate high-rise that beam out a message of power and profits.[23]

For many, the discomfort is less about what Jackson has done to his face than why he has done it. The suggestion that it's all been an effort to perfect his image as a star, and with it, his salability, seems a bit contradictory at first. If his appearance is moving further and further away from the public's comfort level, how could it help his marketing power? It would seem to carry the danger that his own freakish reputation would transfer over to the product being marketed. But at the time of his greatest media saturation (when the media were music videos and commercials, instead of court footage), his own controversy machine and his corporate sponsorships seemed to exist independently of each other. He could get that nose job, hang out with Bubbles the Chimp, and still hock Pepsi.

The *L.A. Times* journalist Bridget Byrne argues that Jackson's surgeries have actually made him more of an "everyperson"—an embodiment of many sexes and races—at the same time that they have seemed to mark him as an outsider. The fact that Jackson was somehow representative of everyone while simultaneously being so fiercely individual as to be a bit of a freak was, in Byrne's view, the main source of the energy behind his commercial success. "The corporate love for Jackson endures," she wrote in 1987. "It is a love that seems mutual. Perhaps that's why Jackson looks the way he does—neither young nor old, neither black nor white, neither male nor female. He seeks perfection, to become the perfect marketing logo."[24]

The theory that Jackson's multiple surgeries are marketing driven surely is too simplistic. (It's difficult not to wonder how much Jackson's external scars owe to the emotional scars of his turbulent and pressured childhood and young adulthood.) Yet, we see in Jackson's extreme, and presumably ongoing, makeover an acute example of the male celebrity's movement away from stereotypical "he-man" to more nuanced, more sensitive—more feminine—man.

We all know we give musicians some leeway in terms of their appearance and their eccentricities, and we always have. But we can see in Michael Jackson the same thing we see in The Rock and Spider-Man— the notion that being a fuller, more complete, more "perfect" person requires bringing female into male, letting traditionally feminine traits or characteristics in. The method is different: For The Rock, it means focusing more on appearance than strength. For Spidey, it means becoming the first mainstream "emo" superhero. And for Michael Jackson, it actually means resculpting his face. The end effect is different, too: Both The Rock and Spider-Man look more complete, well rounded, and complex. Jackson, on the other hand, seems somehow to become less of a person even as he strives to embody every person. In the eyes of many, including former fans, he is no longer a man. He is no longer black. He is no longer anything recognizable, perhaps not even quite human.

RAINBOW CULTURE
AND THE INFLUENCE OF GAYS

Michael Jackson's fame and influence reached their zenith right around the time that AIDS hysteria was taking hold and homophobia was the standard response to anything that even hinted of homosexuality. Jackson's androgyny was accepted because it was eclipsed by his talent. But rumors that he might be homosexual drew furious denials from his fans, male and female alike. Everyone was far more comfortable with the idea that he was some sort of asexual "man-child."

So much has changed in the twenty-plus years since *Thriller* became the biggest-selling album of all time. One of Jackson's chief competitors in the music store at the time was Wham!, a duo that included George Michael, who was still firmly in the closet, where he would remain until he was arrested for lewd conduct in a men's public restroom in 1998. Would George Michael have felt compelled to mask his homosexuality in 2005? It seems far less likely. It's not just that homosexuality has become more accepted; gay culture has actually become cool, something that's celebrated rather than hidden. And that's had a real impact on our notions of men and masculinity. From body to brain to boudoir, how many of the traits of the new man were nurtured and developed in the "laboratories" of the gay world?

It was in the 1990s that we saw the change begin in earnest: gradually, moment by moment, we started seeing portrayals of gay men and lesbians crop up on TV. Not just as hairdressers, serial murderers, and drag queens (though we still had plenty of those, too). We saw lesbians calling plumbers; we saw gay men in a panic over what to wear for a date. We even saw a kiss or two.

This didn't come without some remarkable growing pains: The first time a show attempted to televise an image of gay men that acknowledged both their normalcy and their sexual lives, advertisers ran scared. The show was *thirtysomething*, and the episode in question, "Strangers," featured a brief shot of two men in bed. They didn't really touch, they certainly didn't kiss—though a kiss and an embrace were originally included in the script. Their conversation revolved not around sex or romance but around a friend they'd recently lost to AIDS.[25] Despite this cautious approach, the episode, which aired in November 1989, eventually cost ABC $1 million in lost ad revenue.[26]

As tame as that scene was, it was a watershed event. "As has been well documented," says one researcher into the history of gay representation on television, "the U.S. television industry has a long history of ignoring, stereotyping, and marginalizing homosexuality."[27] As far as television families of the 1950s and 1960s were concerned, homosexuality did not exist. The faces on television were made to match the faces of the United States—or, what the conventional wisdom of the day assumed them to be. You could call it the Most Conservative Common Denominator: the image of American family life sure to match most easily with the largest majority of television viewers, but handily dismissing anyone not in that Wonder Bread majority. As in every other cultural frame, though, the next two decades brought the first taste of change to the representation of gays and lesbians on television. As Steven Capsuto notes in *Alternate Channels: The Uncensored Story of Gay and Lesbian Images on Radio and Television, 1930s to the Present*, screenwriters quickly settled on two "safe" ways to tell gay-themed stories: the coming-out script and the "queer monster" script. Then, as now, gay characters were typically played by straight actors and marketed to a straight audience.[28]

This tactic—downplaying minority characters by turning them into caricatures based on one or two dominant narratives—has been the curse of underrepresented populations since there were mass media. What to do with the scary minority whose culture is a bit more than the mainstream can take? It seemed too much at the time to have a complicated character whose sexuality was simply one aspect of a fuller psychology—no, the sexuality had to dominate. And what's more, the mainstream public needed some faith restored that, even though gays actually existed, their sexuality either made them pitiable (the coming-out narrative) or fearsome (the monster narrative). And, really, it was best if the poor gay thing didn't survive the episode.

The 1990s brought a third member to the collection of possible gay stories: the AIDS narrative. Most gay activists mark AIDS as a watershed—for organization, for acknowledgment, for strength. The AIDS crisis, paradoxically, brought mainstream visibility and recognition to the gay community even while decimating it. Just like the coming-out narrative, AIDS stories gave the mainstream a safer filter through which to approach gays. All but the most homophobic could agree that young men dying of AIDS was tragic. Hence *thirtysomething:* They couldn't show two gay men attracted to each other yet, let alone actually touching. But they *could* have gay men talk about how sad it was to have a friend die.

What a difference we've seen in ensuing years. The latter half of the 1990s brought several unprecedented gay appearances to the small screen, notably the simultaneous outing in both real life and fiction of Ellen DeGeneres. When it was announced that Ellen's character would get an onscreen kiss, the advertiser exodus—by Mazda, Chrysler, JCPenney, and Wendy's, among others—was followed by an even bigger influx of companies eager to have their names attached to the episode. In the end, NBC doubled rates for the ad slots the gay kiss had emptied.[29]

Such a marked shift in both the visibility and marketability of gay faces on television was due to a number of factors, including the new threat presented by the burgeoning cable market, which forced network TV to radically diversify its programming. Along with this, a growing activist outcry against the invisibility of gays combined with stigmatization of homophobia to force network executives to dip their toes into slightly edgier waters.

Networks track cultural trends and developments voraciously—and just as they did in the fifties and sixties, they try as hard as they can to make the world crafted on the television as similar as possible to the image in the heads of the majority of their viewers. But the makers of TV don't only track what's happening out in the world or in the news; they also mimic each other's successes. As a consequence, as small barriers were broken one by one, momentum increased. In the 1990s, there were approximately fifty network series with regular, recurring lesbian, gay, or bisexual characters—more than double the number of such characters (recurring or not) television had seen up to that point.[30]

The movement toward increased visibility of gays and lesbians didn't just happen on its own; it reflects years of activism on the part of such groups as the Mattachine Society and the Daughters of Bilitis of the 1950s and 1960s, all the way through to such groups as ACT UP, Queer Nation, OutRage!, and the Lesbian Avengers of the 1990s. One of the primary struggles of the myriad gay and lesbian movements of the twentieth century was to confront the wall of shame and silence that so long surrounded sexual orientation and to force mainstream America to at long last acknowledge the existence of the gay community.

Media in the second millennium have seen the trend toward visibility strengthen—from the ubiquitous Fab Five of *Queer Eye for the Straight Guy*, who have already littered our lingo *du jour* with such male-makeover terms as *tjuzing* and *manscaping*, to *Boy Meets Boy*, the first-ever gay dating reality show, to the ever-popular *Will & Grace*. In fact, MTV Networks launched an all-gay cable channel in February 2005, named LOGO. According to Judy McGrath, president of MTV Networks Music and Comedy Group, "LOGO is all about identity: the individual and collective identities present in the gay and lesbian community that are amazingly diverse, but are joined by similar points of view and sensibilities."[31]

If the first half of this decade has been any indicator, the media will continue embracing gay sensibilities at a breakneck pace. Even the soaps, masters of the art of escapism, have moved to addressing homosexuality in a systemic, recurring way: no tragic vanishing gays, but a character with both a past *and* a future. *All My Children* was first to break the ice, with the recent outing of young Bianca Montgomery.[32] The importance of this advance should not be overlooked—the only other gays and lesbians visible on American daytime television are those who walk onto the Jerry Springer stage to reveal yet another treacherous husband's gay love affair or secret cross-dressing double life.

TAKING THE SHACKLES OFF STRAIGHT MEN

In the context of looking at the "future of men," the explosion of gay characters and of real-life gays in the media isn't simply important because it shows a side of life too long hidden. Even more important is that these new depictions actually show straight men listening to their gay counterparts, respecting them, even deferring to them. "What's new," says one critic, "is how heterosexual male identity on television is being viewed in relation to both women and gay men—and . . . is being found wanting."[33] The result is that heterosexual protagonists on TV now are more apt to demonstrate their emotions and even weaknesses, something that at one time would have been unheard of for anyone other than female or gay characters.

Consider Tony Soprano (James Gandolfini) of HBO's *The Sopranos*—a boss who fends off debilitating panic attacks with therapy and anti-depressants. Or Adrian Monk (Tony Shalhoub), of USA Cable's *Monk*—an obsessive-compulsive detective with a slew of phobias. Or Nate Fisher (Peter Krause), a health-food salesman turned funeral director on HBO's *Six Feet Under*—who regularly talks to his late father.[34]

In fact, the inclusion of stronger gay characters and the expansion of allowable modes of masculinity often happen in the very same show. As the television critic David Zurawik noted in the *Baltimore Sun*, "The new attitude about masculinity also is reflected in contemporary gay male characters. In Six Feet Under, for example, actor Michael C. Hall plays a young gay man named David Fisher who has sexual orientation issues as well as out-of-body experiences. But he also keeps the family mortuary business running while his straight brother, Nate, flakes out on alcohol, sex and self-hatred."[35]

Increased acknowledgment of men with problems is only half the story. If the upswing in visibility for gay men has increasingly pushed straight men into deferential roles and openly flawed characters, it has also pulled straight men closer to the model presented by gay men. This has been the impact of *Queer Eye for the Straight Guy*, a program that showcases straight men who can't solve problems themselves, and watches as they turn to a team of together, confident gay men for support and advice. Over the course of the show, they rediscover their confidence and self-esteem right along with learning what to do with their new exfoliating rubs and salmon marinades.

It's clear that the sensibility, style, and unabashed sass of the Fab Five have had a dramatically positive effect on the public perception of gay men. But it's also had a positive effect on the perception of a separate, yet related, subgroup: *feminine* men. The five style gurus make no secret of their sexuality and make no attempt to turn down the brightness of their flaming. Especially prominent is Carson Kressley, the fashion maven of the team. His strong model helps to banish the stereotype of the feminine man as a tragic figure, a poor eunuch who puts on a happy, attitude-laden façade in order to cover his inner pain. This is what Michael Bronski, a journalist and cultural critic who teaches the course "Contemporary Issues in GLBT [Gay, Lesbian, Bisexual, Transgendrist] Studies" at Dartmouth College, had to say about student reaction to the Fab Five, as related in *USA Today:*

> Bronski . . . says the perception of who gay men are and what they are known for has changed dramatically, especially with the younger generation. . . . "Some said these five were the same characters in 'Boys in the Band,'" says Bronski, referring to the now-classic 1970 movie about closeted gay men at a dinner party. "But we like them now. The bitchy queens are now the saviors, rather than guys to be pitied.
>
> "Some of the students did say the show reinforced the 'good-taste' stereotypes that gay men are neater, cleaner, fussier and dressed better," he says. "But some of the students also referred to the Fab 5 'as the new Charlie's Angels,' even fairy godmothers, literally, who have the ability to transform straight men."[36]

Here, instead of a destructive negative, the femininity of the Fab Five is a positive—it's a gift, nearly a magical one, that they bring to bear in order to save poor straight men from their own chronic style deficiencies.

More and more, we're seeing strong portrayals of gay men and straight women pulling together to showcase new allegiances and relationships that used to be eclipsed when straight men stood in the center of the story. *Will & Grace* jumps to mind as a model of a brand new power dynamic: the allegiance of the previously dominated. But the bond between gay man and straight woman also shows itself among *Queer Eye* viewers, about half of whom are straight women. "Since the 1960s or so," says Ron Gregg, the programming director of the University of Chicago's Cinema and Media Studies Program, "there has been an alliance between gay men and straight women, along with lesbians, because they have been together in fighting straight white men for power."[37] Now, straight men are starting to listen to what they have to say.

GAY MARKETING

It's not only on television shows that we've seen increased acknowledgment of gays and lesbians; television advertising has seen a gradual increase in openly gay marketing with acknowledged gay representation. We've also seen a parallel increase in "gay vague" ads, advertisements that gay consumers are likely to "read" as gay, but whose gay connotations are missed by most straight consumers, thus potentially giving the ad double draw. Even an Ivory Soap ad from 1917 has been recently reclassified as "gay vague": the spot, hand-drawn by the artist J. C. Leyendecker, shows a crowd of men in a locker room, most completely nude. One man seems to have a bit of a wandering eye, and it doesn't seem to be soap that's on his mind. It's the sort of suggestion, though, that you might only notice if you were already looking for it; hence its ability to pass by the straight audience (including, in this case, World War II–era readers of *National Geographic*!) without notice.[39] More recent examples span everything from homoerotic clothing and cigarette ads to a commercial for the Volkswagen Golf, featuring two twenty-something men in the car and set to the 1980s Trio song "Da, Da, Da," which first aired during the coming-out episode of *Ellen*.[40] You'd think that such prominent placement would make the intention of the ad clear, but Volkswagen continuously denied that the two men in the car were meant to be read as a gay couple. Such is often the modus operandi of businesses using "gay vague"—they let the implication stand, hoping to draw the gay market without the potential of stigmatizing themselves in a still-homophobic straight one.

The depiction of gays and lesbians in mainstream advertising further "normalizes" homosexuality, and in so doing increases its capacity to influence the broader market. At the same time, the fact that more mainstream companies are willing to advertise in gay-oriented publications not only strengthens the publications, but also lends greater credibility to products that get their start there. This, in turn, further strengthens the role the gay community plays in establishing and popularizing brands. Some of the earliest supporters of the gay market, especially Absolut Vodka, found that the gay community's support also translated into crossover success in the mainstream market. The same goes for 2(x)ist, the men's underwear brand that was heavily marketed to gay consumers. As reported in *American Demographics:*

> Launched in 1992, the [2(x)ist] brand didn't begin to target gays through ads until 1996. Because gays help set the trends in men's fashions, the gay press was an obvious fit for the underwear brand, which became a crossover success. "It helped catapult us to the next level," says Jeff Danzer, the company's executive vice president of

marketing. Sales for the underwear have risen to more than $20 million from just $3 million in 1998.[41]

In this case, targeting gay men and gay markets was not merely a strategy to get "pink" dollars. Knowing the influence the gay community has on fashion, 2(x)ist theorized that establishing itself among gay men would act as a sort of endorsement in straight markets, and would bring greater recognition and credibility to the brand across sexualities. This, too, marks a fundamental change in the way media and marketers have approached the GLBT community: instead of skirting an association with the gay, bisexual, lesbian, and transgendrist community, many now seek it out.

The new openness of media and advertising to the GLBT communities around the industrialized world has brought understanding, interest, and curiosity about gay lives and gay culture to an extent not seen in the twentieth century. We've seen gay people move from virtual invisibility to the embodiment of stigma, to sudden, even overwhelming presence. And this one change has brought transformations to culture and gender right along with it, especially in the role played by straight men. No longer do they sit comfortably in the driver's seat of culture. Increasingly, television shows set them in relation to women and to gay men, forcing them to face their shortcomings, and to grow.

Gay culture certainly had much to do with the emergence of metrosexuality. As straight men have grown more comfortable with (or at least less panicked by) gay culture, they've picked up an amalgam of cues from the gay world in areas ranging from grooming and fashion to conversation and "open" relationships.

"All men have benefited from this phenomenon of gay culture coming out into the mainstream," says Julius van Heek, forty, a designer involved in real-estate consulting. "Men are free to express themselves in many ways not generally accepted in the U.S. in the near past."

Even men who would claim not to have any direct contact with gays are influenced by media and by other straight men who have responded to cues from the gay world. The reduction of the stigma of homosexuality has opened many doors for straight men as well as gays. With less fear of the potential consequences of being mistaken for gay, men have more options in terms of everything from how they dress to what jobs and hobbies they pursue.

BODY BEAUTIFUL

One of the more obvious influences of gay culture on males and masculinity is our changing expectations of how a man's worth and appeal should be measured. Physical attractiveness is an increasingly big part of the equation. As the global culture becomes ever more visually mediated, and more focused on looking good, men are increasingly looking at themselves and at each other, just as women have always done and have mostly always admitted doing. Menswear, grooming products, toiletries, and magazines reflect and reinforce new takes on maleness. Men's bodies are sensualized as never before, with highly groomed hair and burnished, moisturized skin suggestively lit and shot. Not so long ago, such images would have been strictly for gay men; now they're mainstream fare, and perhaps even the price of entry to seduce the male mainstream.

We've seen an international explosion of the sexualization of the male form, especially in marketing. From Calvin Klein to Abercrombie & Fitch, men's bodies are under the public eye more than ever. We saw it with The Rock, as he shifted his workout from strength to sculpting. And we certainly have seen it in the marketing domination of that metrosexual archetype David Beckham. A 2003 study from Warwick University found Beckham to be, unquestionably, the most influential man in Great Britain. The study called him an "emerging master, global phenomenon, chosen-one, sporting messiah, corporate and commercial standard bearer. Calm, considered, slight yet strong, tattooed for the cause, quintessential sporting icon."[42] We hear about his strength directly here, but before we even get to it, we have it qualified—"slight yet strong." Slender, trim. We care about the power in him—how could we not? We need him to perform, to score goals. But we idealize his body for its litheness, its more feminine characteristics.

Becks, we admit, has been old news of late, but other sporting figures have occupied a similar role. Two Olympian swimmers, especially, seem to have drawn the eyes of the media worldwide: the American Michael Phelps and the Australian Ian Thorpe. Is it any surprise that it would be swimming that offered up the new athletic ideals? After all, whose body is more on display than a swimmer's?

Thorpe also exhibits metrosexual tendencies in his involvement with fashion. He has his own self-branded line of underwear and undershirts, modeled on the toned body of none other than Thorpe himself. In this, he follows the lead of a fellow Australian, the skivvies model Travis Fimmel, whose pecs have been used to great advantage in his work for Calvin Klein.

But for David Beckham, an appealing physique and sporting prowess are just the beginning of what makes him such an icon and role model for young males worldwide. It's his perfect combination of sporting ability, telegenic style and body, and evolved, comfortable gender and demeanor that has won him such adulation—and imitation. His sporting skill acts as an influential trigger for the myriad young male fans around the world who track him and model their own development after him. "Every time Becks scores a Premier League goal he increases his influence on young men," said a paper out of Hobart, Australia, in its discussion of his sway. "They may not be able to play football the way he does—no one can—but they can be inspired by his broader example."[43]

WHAT TO REMEMBER

1. In a macro sense, the critical issue of role modeling for boys and young men is at a crisis point. With male teachers few and far between and single-mother households all too common, today's young male is increasingly likely to lack the day-to-day influence of men in his formative years. This is particularly important today because society is defining new and more complex notions of what maleness should mean: a complex mixture of physical development, good grooming, and warm sensitivity. While M-ness sounds great in theory, teaching young men and boys to be all they can be, and then some, is man's work. It requires models of positive behavior that can come only from men. And, for too many boys, those models are available neither at home nor at school.

2. Boys are getting more of their cues from gay culture, which is gaining influence via entertainment, fashion, and advertising. This isn't inherently bad; on the contrary, it arguably has given rise to the sort of men who are more appealing to modern women in the way they dress and groom themselves, and also in how they communicate with others. What strikes us, though, is the limited extent of heterosexual men's impact on shaping the next generation of men. With so many men (straight and gay) missing from the formative places, and with gay men dominating the stylish spaces, heterosexual men's influence is far weaker than it would have been even a quarter of a century ago.

9

NEW RULES
FOR THE MATING GAME

Millions of years of biology, thousands of years of mythology, hundreds of years of tradition, and decades of popular fiction, song, movies, and entertainment all around the world have given us infinite variations on the same basic theme: the Mating Game. It's the oldest game around, and one of the most compelling. Witness the relentless media interest in the love lives of the famous and even the not-so-famous; witness the surge in dating shows on TV. Witness retro advertising in which famous couples argue over butter.

Like so much else in life, mating used to be a lot simpler because there were far fewer choices to be had. A great majority of people, no matter from where they hailed, knew early on who was around for them to choose from. So playing the mating game meant making the best match possible as quickly as possible. Ideally, he would be sturdy and dependable, with good prospects; she would be nice-looking, sweet-natured, and skillful around the house; and together they would be prepared to bring up the kids, who were expected to come along quickly. The few who didn't get married were the odd ones out. Those who tried to buck the system and choose an inappropriate mate became the stuff of cautionary tales and tragic fiction. Think Romeo and Juliet, Heathcliff and Cathy, Michael and Kay Corleone.

This by-the-numbers approach to courtship and marriage was the experience of a lot of the older folks still around today. They'll tell you that people didn't ask too many questions back then; they just got on with it, the same as everybody else.

The mating game is just not that simple anymore. People have become used to choices in everything, and they've gotten into the habit of asking questions. A lot of questions. Bucking the system and even ignoring the system are as common as going along with it. Come to think of it, what is the system? As someone pointed out on a National Public Radio phone-in show about arranged marriages, once people's work is no longer handed down to them, once they don't wear their parents' clothes or use the loom that their parents used, once they have to go invent their lives for themselves, it just becomes philosophically impossible to ask them not to choose their love partners on the same grounds.[1]

It's an article of modern faith that more choice is better than less choice, but as the Dutch soccer legend and pop philosopher Johan Cruijff is widely quoted as observing, every upside has its downside.[2] And the downside of more choice is more questions to be asked. These days, absolutely everybody, without exception, faces the same sorts of questions about the mating game sooner or later: Do I want to play? With whom do I want to play? Where do I find them? Will they let me play? What are the rules, and who decided them? Do I have to keep playing if I don't like the game anymore?

There's no doubt that the urge to play the game owes a lot to basic biology (that is, "doing what comes naturally"). But hormones are only part of the story. They power the basic motivation, the underlying "why" that gets people into the game. **But the bigger issues of what the game is for and how the game is played come down to social culture, individual psychology, and the way these things are increasingly affected by science and technology.** This chapter examines these issues and how they affect the sort of questions people are asking about the mating game, as well as the sort of answers they're coming up with.

SCORING A MATE

Thinking of the whole business of mating in terms of a game in no way detracts from its seriousness; quite the reverse, in fact. The vast amounts of time, money, and energy devoted to games (sports, gambling, interactive games) show just how seriously people take them. And when it comes to the mating game, such expressions as "playing hard to get," "playing the field," "playing by the rules," "making a pass," and "scoring" all confirm that "game" is an apt and resonant metaphor for the whole business of finding and connecting with eligible others.

But "game" is not the only viable metaphor; "market" also works well. The spread of market economies and the consumer mindset that goes with them have helped to lay bare a lot of the calculations people make when they play the mating game. Consumerism and its leading edge, prosumerism, have greatly influenced thinking about relationships in general and "mating" relationships in particular. Today's widely used online matchmaking and dating services jostle for business alongside the likes of Amazon.com, eBay, countless discount merchants, and sophisticated product-comparison services. If indeed "the medium is the message" and the Internet is fast becoming the smart shopping medium, then it's no surprise that people now talk about "shopping" for a mate.

"Shopping" for a mate? How utterly romantic.

As *The Toronto Sun* has noted, "With little time to spare between career, school, kids and errands, people are burning up dating Web sites such as Lavalife.com, eHarmony.com, Friendfinder.com and Match.com like never before, shopping for other singles."[3] Notice that the article mentions "singles" but acknowledges that this doesn't preclude them from having kids. Today's singles may be "never married" singles, they may be "newly single" (as in widowed or divorced), they may be "never married and recently separated from a long-term partner" singles, or they may be "not exactly unattached but feeling in need of a change" singles. Any of these varieties of singles and any between or beyond them may have kids or not. Singles may be in the traditional age range for eligible singles—late teens through mid/late twenties—but they are increasingly likely to be well into their thirties, forties, and even beyond. That's just part of what makes the Twenty-First-Century Mating Game more complex than previous editions.

That shopping metaphor pops up on the other side of the world as well. An article in Australia's *Sunday Telegraph* outlined the experiences of Katherine Mamontoff, age twenty-six, and Anthony Robinson, thirty-five, two top-requested dates of the moment on the dating site RSVP: "'It's a way of hedging your bets,' says Katherine, talking about online dating. 'I compare it to going shopping.'"[4] Katherine clearly combines the game and market metaphors in her approach, and she's far from the only one to do so. One of the current crop of TV dating shows prompted a critic in the *Denver Post* to observe, "The messages of the 'reality' dating shows are clear: **Love relationships are essentially consumer relationships; dating is a competitive sport.**"[5]

For shopping of all kinds, the Internet is becoming the twenty-first-century successor to such catalogs as Sears & Roebuck laying out their wares with images of smiling models and alluring descriptions of the goods on offer. Writing in the *Philadelphia Daily News*, a former skeptic of online dating describes her moment of conversion as follows: "Not too long ago, I was induced by another friend who was having altogether too much fun plowing through Yahoo! personal ads. 'It's like catalogue shopping for men,' she would tell me. Being a diehard shopper, how could I resist an invitation like that?"[6]

It seems that when the dating gets tough, the tough go shopping—online.

Internet "love shopping" is likely to become the dominant force in bringing together would-be kindred spirits. In the United States, it's widely reported that at least 29 million Americans, or two out of five singles, used online dating services in 2003. And the market is expected to keep growing over the next five years.[7] Overall, more than 38 million Americans have visited online dating sites, according to web-tracker comScore Networks, which researches online behavior.[8]

In the UK, data compiled by the Office of National Statistics show that 14 million Britons live alone, with that number likely to increase in the future. Udate.co.uk claims to be the most-visited general online dating site, with more than 1.2 million members and 60,000 new members every month.[9]

A global study we conducted in 2004 of today's "prosumers" indicates that Internet dating truly is on the rise. (Prosumers are the approximately 20–30 percent of any market who wield greatest influence by virtue of their information-seeking tendencies, social natures, and technological empowerment.) A consistently higher proportion of influential prosumers agree they would consider the Internet as a source of "leads" for potential love interests if they were dating today. In the United States, 46 percent of prosumers agreed compared with 30 percent of nonprosumers; in the UK, it's 39 versus 30 percent, and similar disparities also emerged in France (39 vs. 32 percent), Germany (44 vs. 36 percent), and China (57 vs. 50 percent).[10] Typically, the fact that a behavior or attitude is more prevalent among prosumers than others indicates that it is on the upswing and will soon be embraced by even more people. This is a function of the fact that prosumers tend to be on the leading edge and also that they are more influential than others. So it's a good bet that online dating will continue to grow in these and other markets.

All over the world, new online "relationship destinations" are springing up and signing up hundreds of thousands of members in competition with leading sites such as Yahoo! Personals and Match.com. As with stock markets, the more players are in, the more "liquid" the market is, and the more people are likely to find "bids" to match their "offers."

In a sure sign of a maturing market, online entrepreneurs have moved beyond the general population to target specific subgroups. Sites such as JDate.com (for Jewish singles) have led the way in services targeting ethnic niches. And now singles can even match their love hopes to their political persuasions by signing up on such sites as RepublicanSingles.com, SingleRepublican.com, DemDates.com, and DemocraticSingles.com. (Given the sharply divided nature of the U.S. electorate today, it probably makes sense to reduce the potential for conflict prior to the first date.) Singles who are passionate about pets have an expanding range of sites on which they can find like-minded animal lovers, including DateMyPet.com, AnimalAttraction.com, and ReinsAndRomance.com.

Would-be daters who are already in a relationship but want something more can use ordinary singles sites and lie about being unattached, as around 12 percent of registered users reportedly do.[11] Or they can check out sites that cater specifically to them, such as

AshleyMadison.com and philanderers.com. And for singles who are confused about which site they should use, there are sites such as dateseeker.net that compare and rate what's on offer, from the plain-vanilla dating services through "senior dating" to "adult personals" (= close encounters of a sexual kind) and "alternative lifestyles" (= gay and beyond).

Shopping in the mating game isn't restricted to the online environment. Offline, people in search of significant others are flocking to organized speed-dating sessions: a matched number of women and men of similar ages pair up at tables in a meeting room (typically a bar or restaurant) and have a set period in which to chat. At the end of the period, a bell rings to tell the men it's time to rotate to another table for the next chat, and so it continues till everyone has had a few minutes to talk to every member of the opposite sex. Participants jot down which "speed dates" they would like to meet again, and hand in their notes to the organizers. The organizers then compare the notes and, where there's mutual interest in further contact, give out telephone numbers and e-mail addresses to the parties concerned.

Speed-dating provides all the plusses of one-stop shopping: a broad selection of potential mates, all in one place. Plus, it gives leery would-be daters a bit more security than if they were meeting privately with a blind date from a newspaper's personal ads, for instance.

Good old-fashioned matchmakers are still very much in the game for people willing to invest a bit extra in the personal touch. Their cause is helped by the trend toward private individuals hiring specialized professional services such as caterers, personal dieticians, trainers, and coaches. As one professional matchmaker argues, people hire agents to find a house for them and headhunters to find them a job, so why wouldn't they pay a professional to find a pleasant companion with romantic potential?[12] This thought is echoed by a divorced Jewish lawyer in New York talking about his personal *shadkhan* (matchmaker): "I have a personal trainer, a personal accountant, lawyer, masseur and so forth. . . . Now I have a personal *shadkhan*. I simply don't have the time to wade through zillions of on-line bios or go to parties. My *shadkhan* knows what I want."[13]

Singles with a little more time on their hands have a growing range of opportunities to get together with others in places where the mating game is an option rather than an upfront objective. The appeal of such activities as gyms, yoga classes, bowling clubs, special-interest vacations, religious gatherings, and culture clubs isn't necessarily what it seems on the surface: whatever the ostensible agenda, they all offer a great way to spend time with others and size them up in a safe environment. And for those of a more touchy-feely bent, what better place to find kindred spirits than in the burgeoning field of "personal development" seminars?

IS IT ALL TOO MODERN?

The language of the modern mating game inevitably reflects twenty-first century frames of reference with today's distinctive fusion flavors—a contemporary buffet of hard and soft technology, self-help pop psychology, management-consultancy speak, abundant all-you-can-eat consumerism, and a dash of sweet nothings. It's a mixture that previous generations would probably have found baffling and none too romantic. Take the following press release for one online dating site; it must surely be a leading candidate for inclusion in a time capsule to sum up this zeitgeist:

> PerfectMatch.com, the fastest growing online relationship destination, has attracted nearly double the number of women found on other online dating sites—largely because of its unique set of relationship tools, encouraging and promoting self-identity, inner-confidence and personal growth. In addition, thanks to Duet™, PerfectMatch.com's Total Compatibility System, women now have the opportunity to not only discover themselves, but also establish relationships with "pre-qualified" and commitment-oriented men.
>
> We're pleased to win the trust and attract a strong union of women who are committed to self-awareness and growth that leads to long, healthy and mutually beneficial relationships. We've accepted the challenge of finding more quality men . . . men who are prepared to learn more about themselves, and ultimately meet more well-balanced and self-assured women. Ultimately, this will enable them to enjoy life's sweetest reward, true love.[14]

So far, so new for the modern mating game. Speed dating seems perfectly normal these days, but it took the always-faster, increasingly time-crunched, don't-waste-my-time twenty-first century to make it happen. As for Internet dating, the technology barely existed just a decade ago, and only in the last four or five years has penetration been deep enough to make it a mainstream proposition. Even now, many people have to overcome a certain distaste at the whole idea, as if taking the mating game online were tantamount to admitting they can't make the grade in the "real world."

It's all so speedy and so modern that dyed-in-the-wool romantics may well find the modern mating game entirely too calculating, way too transactional. They may wonder whatever happened to the sepia-tinted innocence of times gone by. In truth, those "innocent" times could be every bit as calculating, if not more; what's different now is who is manning the calculator. Many traditional-style matches were (and in some places still are) highly transactional; that's what dowries are all about. **The difference between the traditional transaction and the modern transaction is that in the old-style version, the prospective partners were young and their parents made all the calculations and did all the bargaining. In the modern version, the prospective partners may be older— sometimes a lot older—and they themselves have to figure out all the angles of the transaction.**

Any relationship, modern or traditional, has risks and benefits. In old-style versions of the mating game, parents calculated the balance of risk and reward, and the partners-to-be who didn't buck the rules could count on the support of the family in times of need. Now balancing the potential risks and rewards is mostly the job of would-be partners. The fact that so many of their potential mates are unknown to them and their families is one reason so many women are turning to dating sites and systems (such as speed dating). These dating facilitators don't eliminate risk, but they do limit it somewhat, offering safeguards against everything from poor personal hygiene or Neanderthal social skills all the way through to testosterone frenzy and weirdo tendencies.

Modern daters have plenty of ways to minimize the downside and stack the odds in favor of getting a good date. Online services can screen participants and assure a relatively good level of security, although few go as far as TellCupid.com, which boasts "the safest online dating environment in the world today by providing our members the choices they deserve." The service, founded by a private investigator, offers members the option of conducting a criminal background and sexual offender/predator search on their potential dates. If that's not enough "in a world full of uncertainty," the site also offers bodyguard services for men and women who may want the extra security of knowing they are not alone on their first date. The offer of a bodyguard *for men too* may just be a sop to gender-equality advertising, but it raises an interesting question: why would a man need a bodyguard on a date? Despite the specter of unhinged single females (a la *Fatal Attraction*) and the rise of drunken "ladettes" and kickboxing girls, surely men don't feel the need for physical protection from their dates? Maybe the idea is for the bodyguard to serve as a chaperone, guaranteeing the proper conduct of both parties and thereby protecting the man from possible charges of molestation.

In the UK, the dating service Vivacity.com provides discreet security for people who are embarrassed about going on a blind date. Market research found that a third of the women quizzed in London would be too embarrassed to tell friends where they were going, while eight out of ten keep quiet because they want to be "independent." So Vivacity.com users can call in the "who, where, and when" of their dates to a personally manned secure phone service developed with the Metropolitan Police. At the end of the date, the user calls again to check in; if she doesn't check in and can't be traced after three days through her contact numbers, the police are informed.[15] (Are we the only people who think three days seems like way too long?)

OPTING OUT

Looking at the booming dating business, you would be forgiven for thinking that everyone who's not already paired up is keen to find a significant other. That's certainly the case for many people, but increasingly not the case for all.

The prosumer surveys we created asked people to rate the statement "Having a spouse/life partner is essential to my sense of fulfillment in life"; in the United States, overall 70 percent of respondents agreed, but 14 percent disagreed and 15 percent were neutral on the issue. Across the marriage gap, 58 percent of the unmarried and 80 percent of the married agreed. Most telling was the difference between the sexes: **77 percent of men think having a life partner is essential to their sense of fulfillment, compared with just 64 percent of women; only 9 percent of men disagreed, whereas the figure for women was 20 percent. In other words, in the United States the signs are that men are more likely to need women** than women are to need men. The situation is even more skewed in the UK, where 78 percent of men and 55 percent of women agreed with the statement, while 12 percent of men and 26 percent of women disagreed.[16]

In the opening chapter of this book, we quoted a number of people on the subject of whether women still need men and vice versa. The consensus appears to be that whereas women may *want* a man around to provide specific services (from sex and procreation to fixing the bathroom sink), men are more inclined to admit to an *emotional* need for women. "Men will ALWAYS need women," asserts Friso Westenberg, a married thirty-something with kids who works as a marketing executive at Heineken in Amsterdam. Madeline Park, also in her thirties, an advertising executive in New York and a mom, agrees: "I think men need to be taken care of on an emotional and nurturing level—that hasn't changed."

What we're seeing isn't just a fleeting fad of women expressing their independence. We believe we're in the midst of an important shift of power taking place in the mating game as played between men and women. For most of history, women haven't had much choice about whether they paired up with a man; if they had a choice, it was more a matter of whom they chose to play the mating game with. If they didn't settle on a mate, they were likely to be regarded as unfulfilled; they also were likely to lose out on status, protection, and access to money. Women's need for what men offered meant that sooner or later a man would find a woman to pair up with.

Now it seems that women are choosing not only with whom they want to play the mating game, but even whether to play it at all. A lot of the old reasons to play no longer apply. Women are increasingly succeeding in education and in the workplace, which gives them greater access to money and status of their own. In most of the developed world, they are protected by laws and law-enforcement officers. Pension and healthcare systems provide them with some measure of protection against poverty and ill health. What this means for men is that they can't automatically expect to find a woman willing to play the mating game with them on their terms. They're selling in a buyer's market, so they need to work out some new sales pitches—either that, or play the mating game in poorer places where the women can't afford to be so choosy. Hence, the proliferation of "mail order" brides. Back at home, these men are facing the sort of women who can confidently grouse, "I hate to have to compromise my lifestyle so much when I meet somebody,"[17] and even the sort of older woman who's going to stand her ground: "You get to this age; everybody's kind of lonely. But I'd rather be alone than settle for what I don't want."[18]

Women (and men) who are prepared to embrace singledom have a new standard bearer in Sasha Cagen, author of *Quirkyalone: A Manifesto for Uncompromising Romantics* and owner of Quirkyalone.net. In case you're wondering, a "quirkyalone" is someone who prefers to wait for the right person to come along rather than dating indiscriminately. He or she has come to appreciate singledom as a natural state, a way to live a fulfilling life. Quirkyalones would rather spend time hanging out with friends, people with whom they have a real rapport, than endure a bad date. Cagan and her fans aren't alone in their efforts to help people embrace their single status—and that of others. Among the more formal organizations that support singledom are the Alternatives to Marriage Project and the American Association of Single People.[19]

NEW STAKES, NEW CHALLENGES

The stakes in the mating game are different from what they used to be, and they're changing fast. Moreover, singles who want to play the game face different challenges at different ages.

Most people who are still in their late teens to mid/late twenties can easily meet a wide range of unattached prospective partners. They are likely to have a network of high school and college friends, plus a range of haunts where people their age hang out, so meeting others is not their problem. Their big issue is how long they can wait before committing to a long-term relationship. If they jump in young, they risk missing out on all the fun and freedom of never-married singledom. They also run the risk of buyer's remorse. On the other hand, the longer they hold back and play the field or focus on their careers, the more the pool of available partners shrinks. That makes it harder to meet others and increases the risk of growing old either without a significant other or else with one who's left over—the dating-pool dregs. Encouragingly for the "hold back" brigade, there's a steady rise in the number of people getting married later, which means more choice than in past eras.

In previous versions of the mating game for young singles, the advantage lay with men. Not only did they have better access to money, through work, they also had no physical or time limits on their ability to have children, no pressure to procreate before it was "too late." Pressure to marry could come from an unwanted pregnancy leading to a "shotgun wedding," but men theoretically had the option of leaving the mother holding the baby. And if, after years of fun and frolics, they decided they wanted to have children, they could go ahead and do it at more or less any age. Contrast that with women, who were at a distinct disadvantage in the mating game because they were under intense social pressure to have children and needed a man to father those children and provide for them. And it all had to happen before the dreaded "biological clock" started ticking too loudly.

In the twenty-first-century mating game for young singles, men are still free to love 'em and leave 'em as before, but some of the pressure is off women—if they choose that it be. The more their education equals men's, the more they have access to work opportunities, the more they can take care of themselves, and the less social pressure there is on them to "fulfill themselves" through motherhood. For those who want children, the biological clock still ticks, but with good healthcare, nutrition, and exercise, many can and increasingly do tackle pregnancy in their late thirties and even beyond. As we were writing this, a fifty-six-year-old New York woman gave birth to twins (albeit with a donated egg). The Centers for Disease Control and Prevention reports that 263 children were born to American women between the ages of fifty and fifty-four in 2002; that's up 10 percent from the year prior. While births have declined among women in their twenties, they've increased among women in their thirties and forties (not to mention fifties).[20]

Considered over whole populations, this shift on the woman's side of the mating game makes for some big changes. In every society in which women have access to education, jobs, and fertility control, many are opting out of childbearing completely, or at least leaving it until much later in life. That means they can afford to be choosier and more demanding about the men in their lives. They can even afford to behave "badly" in ways that used to be the preserve of men—smoking, drinking, causing scenes in public places, and having a whole string of sexual partners without committing to any of them.

In times gone by, the mating game was strictly for young first-time-arounders. Of course, there were cases of feckless, divorced, or widowed older men snagging younger women, but they were the exception rather than the rule—the stuff of sensational headlines, especially when they involved celebrities. The film directors Charlie Chaplin and Woody Allen and the rock 'n' roll wild man Jerry Lee Lewis come to mind.

Now the mating game has a lot of players who aren't exactly in the first flush of youth, even allowing for the claim that "fifty is the new thirty." Some have just never taken the plunge, and, having waved good-bye to their mid-thirties, they get the urge for a committed relationship. Others have taken the plunge, sometimes several times, and find themselves more alone than they want to be as a result of death or divorce. Whatever type of single they are, all not-so-young singles face a common difficulty: meeting prospective partners. Unlike younger singles, whose ages and life stages are all comparable, for whom singledom is the norm and opportunities for meeting like-minded others abound, not-so-young singles face a host of problems, particularly regarding access to other eligible singles. According to Kathleen Roldan, the director of dating for Match.com, busy older singles have few chances to meet by chance. "What we hear most from singles is what they are really lacking in their day-to-day lives is access to other singles. It has become more difficult to casually bump into someone who you are going to want to date."[21]

In the not-so-young mating game, too, men used to have the advantage. Even with proper diet, exercise, and a little surgery, the years inevitably take their toll on the body. Men have tended to look for physical attractiveness in their partners, while women have always been more responsive to character attributes such as intelligence, charm, and humor. (Wealth and power have also proved appealing.) This meant that an intelligent, charming, witty older man stood a pretty good chance of finding a soul mate even if he wasn't so presentable physically—and especially if he had money. By contrast, even the most intelligent, charming, and witty older woman would probably struggle to get a second date with any man if she wasn't a pleasure to behold. But now the balance of power has shifted here, too. From celebrities all the way down to ordinary folk, there's an increasing trend toward older women playing the mating game with younger men.

In some cases the difference is just a couple of years, while in others the gap is a lot wider. For example, Britain was held in thrall when two contestants in a make-believe reality TV show fell for each other across a twenty-five-year age gap. Lady Elizabeth Devonport, fifty-eight, and Mark Foxsmith, thirty-three, were play-acting two-hundred-year-old parts in UK Channel Four's *Regency House Party* when they fell in love. The actress Demi Moore and the pop star Madonna are two American celebrities who have fallen into the arms of younger men. And a clear sign of the times appeared in 2003, when the Australian firebrand academic Germaine Greer (born 1939), who made her name with the feminist polemical *The Female Eunuch* in 1971, published *The Boy*, a lavish celebration of young men.

In our view, women haven't just become more empowered and choosy; they've also become downright predatory. Not all of them, granted, but each of us would have no problem pointing to a number of female friends and acquaintances who fit the bill. Regardless of whether marriage and children are top priorities, women seem to have much more of an agenda than do men when it comes to their romantic relationships. Where many men seem perfectly happy to take a relationship as it comes, women are apt to have timetables, conscious or unconscious. They grow dissatisfied if their men aren't on track, whether it has to do with saying "I love you," meeting the family, providing an "appropriate" gift, or getting down on bended knee. Men are constantly measured against women's sense of what should be happening and by when. Depending on the woman, the game book can be incredibly complex, and calling the right plays time after time can be next to impossible.

As women's attitudes and behavior become less predictable, it's difficult for many men to know what to do. Paul Fraser resents the fact that many women make the mating game even more complex by sending mixed messages about who men are supposed to be and how they should act. "Men don't know what women want," he complains, "because women don't know what women want. They say they want men to be more sensitive, but soon get bored of a man who is 'in touch with his feelings.' They want to be respected as equals, but also want men to treat them like a lady. We become more sensitive in our lovemaking, and yet more and more women are admitting to having rape fantasies (is that to feel powerless?). Men are at a loss in how to act around a potential mate. It is like crossing a field of land mines—you never know what approach will blow up in your face."

Tufts University student Rebecca Frank thinks the whole situation is exacerbated by outside forces that claim to know how people should act and think: "There are too many outside factors, including women who analyze every aspect of those relationships (*Sex and the City* phenomenon) and the Dr. Phil-ization of America (men aren't sure what's right and are unwilling to go with their feelings)."

Niels den Otter, twenty-three, an Amsterdam-based sound designer/composer, blames his being single on his obsession with technology, but he also concedes that relationships require a level of finesse that may not come naturally to men. He deems the biggest challenge facing men in their relationships with women "first of all to really respect the woman as a, for instance in rank, 'higher individual.'" The second greatest challenge, he says, once the relationship has started, "is giving each other the space to develop." It's a constant balancing act between trying to give all that's expected without being seen as too intense or smothering. (Granted, many women have the same complaint about men.)

The constant presence of mass (and niche) media in our lives means it's far more difficult to simply act "naturally" without second-guessing oneself. Our friend Bernice Kanner has enjoyed great success with her *Are You Normal?* series of books, including *Are You Normal About Sex, Love, and Relationships?*, precisely because just about all of us worry to some degree or another about whether we are, in fact, normal. Do other people have the same fantasies? The same fears and hang-ups? Am I having sex as much as I'm supposed to? Am I doing it the right way? Would my relationship be considered healthy? With all the glossy media images and stories out there about other people's fabulous lives, it's a wonder any of us can get up in the morning, look ourselves in the mirror, and be satisfied with what looks back.

Women have to deal with a daily onslaught of messages about how they're supposed to look, prioritize their lives, and raise their children, but they still seem to get off more easily than men. At the risk of repeating ourselves, men now live in a fog of negative messages and images. The underlying theme: Can men do anything right? Years of media chronicling the failings of men and the travails of women past and present have reinforced the notion that "all men are bastards."

There are signs, though, that lots of men are fed up with the negative characterizations and think turnabout is fair play. So now we're seeing the spread of the notion that "all women are scheming bitches, especially American women"—a theme that's played over and again through men's discussion forums online. A contributor to mensnewsdaily.com had this to say:

> After 20+ years of social brainwashing to make men feel inadequate (a certain mid-90s copy of TIME magazine with a pig's head on a business man's body and the subtitle "Are Men Pigs?"), you shouldn't be surprised that most well-meaning men have had the confidence intimidated right out of them. I'm one of them. . . . I just don't care anymore. How is someone going to have confidence when they're made to feel like a tool all their life (have you watched any TV lately)?
>
> I'm a considerate guy, and all it ever gets me is taken advantage of. That, and I can go into any coffee shop and hear all these pretty young women talking sh*t about men. I love coffee, but sitting around a place where most of the patrons openly hate me simply because of my equipment has made me buy my own espresso machine and avoid the places. Add to that the fact that quiet men are apparently completely unattractive to modern women, and you have a formula for failure and pain. I don't think ALL American women are like this, just the vast majority.[22]

This was one of the more measured, restrained notes we found floating around in cyberspace. Suffice it to say, there are some pretty hostile men out there—including a good number who are venting about all the hostile women out there.

On a more hopeful note, at least one contributor to a forum on AOL (he asked us to refer to him simply as M. Kelleher) is hoping to chart a new course through the choppy waters of gender relationships today:

> It's really sad that some people still want to attack each other, but society still doesn't do anything to prepare people for adult male-female relationships. What we need now is better preparation for adult life in a two-gender environment. Men need to learn to identify women who are hostile to men and avoid them. Women need to learn to identify men who are hostile to women and avoid them. And we all could improve the way we treat each other, so our work is cut

out for us. Let's not play the "boys against the girls" game—all that leads to is a lot of unhappiness for everyone.

HE SAID, SHE SAID

Our prosumer research confirmed for us that, even as gender roles change, the divide is still out there. Interestingly, there's an equally clear divide within the ranks of males—specifically, with regard to men who are dads and men who aren't. Today's dad, for instance, is significantly more conservative on social issues than his wife and men who aren't parents. We've hypothesized that this has to do with the fact that, even as fathers are being called on to be more nurturing and involved, their traditional role as "protector" has become much more difficult. In addition to all the old threats children have long faced, including substance abuse and hanging around with the "wrong crowd," there is now school violence, inappropriate media content available in the home through multiple channels, and, of course, the threat of terrorism. Dads seem to be the ones trying to hold the line.

Our 2004 survey of nearly 2,000 Americans found there's real disagreement among men and women regarding whether people are entitled to expect regular sex of their partners. **Whereas more than three-quarters of men agreed with that notion, less than two-thirds of women did so. Looking at moms and dads, we found that an overwhelming 81 percent of dads believe men and women are entitled to expect regular sex, while only 65 percent of moms feel the same way. Clearly, a likely avenue for frustration and discord.**

Similarly, men are less likely than women in the United States to consider monogamy the "natural state" for human beings; 60 percent of women agreed with this notion, compared with just 55 percent of men. There was little difference on this score between moms and dads. The real difference lay between the non-dads and others. A minority of men without children in the home (47 percent) agree that it's natural to confine oneself to a single sexual partner.

Despite men's lower levels of agreement with the proposition that monogamy is the natural state, a vast majority of Americans surveyed disagree with the notion that there's nothing wrong with extramarital affairs provided no one gets hurt. There was substantial difference on this question between male and female respondents (13 percent of men agreed, compared with just 4 percent of women), but the numbers were low in both cases.

Two areas in which men's—particularly dads'—conservatism really shines are divorce and religion. Maybe American dads are true romantics, or maybe they've read the statistics about how much better off men are in a stable relationship. Either way, they are the group most likely to regard marriage as for keeps: **An overwhelming 86 percent of dads agree that divorce should be the absolute last resort, whereas only 75 percent of non-dads and moms and 71 percent of non-moms agree.** This split may reflect, in part, married men's understanding that divorcing their spouses might well lead to substantially less contact with their children. But it also likely has to do with dads' religious beliefs.

The United States is a famously churchgoing nation, so it's not surprising that religious beliefs are a factor in many Americans' sexual behavior. What's interesting is that dads are the most affected. Overall, 39 percent of Americans surveyed agree that religion does factor into their sex lives, while a slightly higher 41 percent disagree. However, this balance tilts the other way among American dads—44 percent of them say religion is a factor, while 40 percent say it isn't. This contrasts with non-dads, of whom 38 percent agree and 44 percent disagree. Even more strikingly, it contrasts with American moms: 35 percent of them agree religion is a factor in the bedroom, but 41 percent disagree. Non-moms are more closely balanced, with 40 percent agreeing and 42 percent disagreeing. In other words, American dads are the only one of the four groups with a balance of opinion tilted toward religion as a factor in their sexual behavior.[23]

REINVENTING MARRIAGE, REDEFINING FAMILY

As gender relationships are redefined, it's no surprise that the institution of marriage is changing, too. Conventional marriage is not dead, but it can no longer lay claim to being the norm—at least, not in the traditional form of man and woman of similar age wed at the altar, till-death-do-us-part. One major effect of the increased options and shifting balance of power in the mating game is the increase in cohabitation, living together as a couple without "benefit" of marriage. In the past (at least in some cultures), it was known as living in sin; any children born of the union were referred to as illegitimate, and the situation could only be salvaged, in society's eyes, by the man marrying the woman and "making an honest woman of her." In the modern mating game, cohabitation is neither unusual nor necessarily entered into as an interim arrangement in preparation for marriage. In fact, it's increasingly risky to refer to someone as a person's "husband" or "wife"; many couples make a point of not being married, intend to stay that way, and bridle at the assumption that they're legally wed. "Partner" seems to be the safe and neutral alternative.

Maybe today's higher rate of cohabitation is a sign of confusion about the best way to play the mating game. As one academic sociologist commented on National Public Radio's *Talk of the Nation:* "I see the young people of our culture today trying a different arrangement. It's multiple partners until they find one that seems compatible with them. And that's why we have so many people cohabiting today. They, too, are confused about marriage. . . . And they don't know what a good partner looks like or what a good relationship looks like. So I think they're out trying multiple partners before they make that final commitment. So that's a big change."[24]

The trend toward cohabitation likely stems from a broad variety of factors, including greater acceptance of unwed couples living together, less societal pressure to marry, and the trend toward delayed childbearing. Of course, it also has much to do with women no longer needing a husband for income, protection, and social status. Without those factors at play, getting married may seem nothing more than an old-fashioned formality, something one does or does not do solely out of personal preference.

There's also another trend bolstering people's decisions to delay or avoid altogether the "middle-aisle trek": Conventional families are no longer the only way for people to enjoy the feeling of long-term commitment and support. As singledom in all its varieties through different age groups becomes more widespread, it becomes increasingly possible for singles to develop bonds that are familial in every way except genetically or legally.

For some time now, we've been seeing the emergence of urban "families" and "tribes," and we don't mean "look at me" fashion groupings such as boarders, Goths, and vogueurs. Think *Seinfeld* and

Friends, but without an age ceiling and without the witty-banter requirement. These are people who hang out together and drop by each
other's homes without getting dressed up or even giving advance notice; people who share their wonders and woes over a kitchen counter,
a bar top, or a linen tablecloth.

Ethan Watters's book *Urban Tribes* focuses on unmarried people in
their twenties and thirties who make long-lasting friendship groups
the center of their lives. "Single life in the city is no longer a phase
that needs to be concluded quickly," he says. "With little fanfare,
we've added a developmental stage to adulthood that comes before
marriage—the tribe years."[25]

The trend stands out in our 2004 survey. Among a set of statements relating to friends and family, **the one with which the most
people agreed (88 percent) was that friends can be as much
"family" as blood relatives.** Rates of agreement were virtually the
same among married and unmarried people and among those with
and without children in the household. **There was a gender split (96
percent of women agreed, compared with 87 percent of men),
which confirms the generally held notion that women are more
likely than men to develop deep and meaningful relationships
with people not related by marriage or genetics.**[26]

Clearly the notion of friends as family has widespread acceptance.
This "different ties and different tribes" trend echoes the days before
suburban sprawl made car-borne nuclear families the norm. In older
forms of community, the pace of life was slower and people routinely
bumped into each other at the store and dropped in at the family
home for a chat; kids routinely referred to familiar adults as "uncle"
and "auntie" even when there was no blood tie. One big difference
with today's "friend-families" is that fewer of their members are linked
by blood.

Does a gay union qualify as a conventional marriage and a basis
for a conventional family? In our survey, just 34 percent of U.S. respondents felt able to agree that same-sex partnerships/"marriages"
should be accorded the same status as man-woman marriages, while
49 percent disagreed. On this issue once again, women tend to be
less conservative than men in the United States: 38 percent agreed
compared with 31 percent of men, while 45 percent of women disagreed versus 53 percent of men. The gender gap is even more pro-
nounced in the UK, largely because far more women than men

agreed (52 vs. 37 percent) and far fewer women than men disagreed (29 vs. 45 percent).[27]

Whether or not people regard gay marriage as acceptable, "conventional" probably does the whole notion a disservice. By traditional standards, homosexuality (both male and female) is at best unconventional, and certainly doesn't fit in with traditional notions of what a family is supposed to look like. Yet, as we've seen in the past few years—and particularly leading up to the 2004 U.S. presidential elections—many homosexual couples yearn to give their relationships the official stamp of conventionality. Social conservatives tend to oppose the legalization of gay marriage for many reasons, not least because they believe that it would somehow undermine the institution of marriage. But supporters of gay marriage point out that it's heterosexuals who are undermining marriage by virtue of their high rates of divorce; they argue that giving gay marriage the same rites and status as heterosexual marriage would actually help to reinforce marriage as the "gold standard" of commitment in the mating game.

THE MARRIAGE MILL

In addition to the trend toward later marriage and marriage avoidance, we're also seeing an increase in serial marriages and in so-called starter marriages. Pamela Paul's book *The Starter Marriage and the Future of Matrimony* explores this trend of brief, childless marriages. Young people are getting married in their early and mid-twenties and getting divorced in less than five years. "In 2000 more than four million twenty- to thirty-four-year-olds checked the 'divorced' box," Paul writes. These kids may start out believing in eternal love, but having grown up in an era of widespread divorce, they're quick to disentangle themselves before children and alimony become long-term obligations. Paul cites several motivations for early marriages: some young people want to leave their parents' nest, while others, who are already independently successful, feel marriage will polish them into a "power couple." Peer pressure has a lot to do with it, too: after five stints as a bridesmaid, a young woman's more likely to go after the big white dress herself.

And celebrities make it look so easy. Marriages based on the model of Paul Newman and Joanne Woodward, whose decades-long union inspires admiration and not a little awe, seem few and far between.

Mostly we skim the latest marriage banns on the covers of weeklies at the grocery store checkout and cynically wonder, "Oh, yeah, how long is this one going to last?" We expect marriage among the fashionable to be just that—fashionable. Some young people are no doubt influenced by these brief marriages. When Julia Roberts, Nic Cage, Angelina Jolie, and Drew Barrymore call it quits after a few months, or when Britney Spears marries "just for the hell of it" and then moves for an annulment after only fifty-five hours, it just seems (to some) like the thing to do. After all, these newly divorced celebrities are likely to appear on next month's glossy cover with a new beau in tow. We don't hear about the heartache after the first lurid announcements of a breakup; sorrow is yesterday's news. We might blame our culture of disposability, where everything and anything is subject to obsolescence or replacement, or our culture of ease, which tells us that anything hard to do is probably not worth doing. Or maybe it's our culture of dissatisfaction, in which nothing ultimately answers our ever-growing demands for untarnished happiness.

But one thing's for sure, marriage is still highly prized, or why else would celebrities keep getting in and out of it? It used to be that stars felt obliged to get married for the sake of their careers, and that certainly continues to be the case with politicians. Few seek public office without the highly publicized support of a smartly tailored spouse. Marriage bestows an aura of respectability, maturity, and stability. It declares its members to be desirable, well adjusted, and responsible, which is just what power couples are hoping to project. Men and women raise their individual status when they combine assets, financial and otherwise. They evoke something like clan power on a couple scale. Bill and Hillary Clinton are the most notable power couple, and public responses to their travails in the media point to changing ideas of marriage. After the Monica Lewinsky scandal, the country was divided on Hillary's feelings and motives when she stood by her man. Was she a strong woman and devoted spouse, or a dupe? Did the Clintons have a "marriage of the minds," in which sexual infidelity mattered little, or was it a marriage of power and convenience, in which any and all feelings mattered not at all? New Jersey Governor James McGreevey's 2004 step-down, with his wife still at his side despite his announcement that he is gay, inspired similar debate. Aside from the jokes made regarding Clinton's quibbling about the definition of "sex," a deeper concern lay in his ability to govern ethically.

Could we divide the statesman from the husband? In other words, is marriage an ultimate test of character, and of attitudes toward gender equality? If so, what might Clinton's actions mean for the majority of women who voted for him in the 1996 election in the biggest gender divide in election history? (Fifty-four percent of women, but only 43 percent of men, voted for him.)

Clearly, the rules relating to relationships, marriage, and family are changing. Far fewer of us are bound by strong community or religious ties that set forth a rigid code of conduct. The many, many options available to us as we build our lives and relationships can be the ultimate freedom or the ultimate burden. What's clear is that men no longer have the power or the social and legal authority to call all the shots, and women no longer need to make quite so many sacrifices and adjustments just so they can enjoy the status and security a shiny bauble on their ring fingers used to accord. What remains to be seen is how succeeding generations of men and women will define the male-female relationship and its parameters. After all, they're the people who will be determining the "future of men." The next chapter takes a look at how men are responding to this era of rapidly changing gender expectations.

WHAT TO REMEMBER

1. The metaphorical notions of competitive sports and shopping seem apt ways to describe contemporary practices of dating and mating. And, as is the case with so many other popular practices, the Internet is playing a key role in their evolution. It offers the player/shopper an array of options that come "preselected" against a series of preferences: religious beliefs, politics, range of interests, and so on.

2. The Mars versus Venus divide is all over the mating-game ritual, but it is manifest in some unexpected ways. Foremost among these is the notion that "life partners are necessary to fulfillment": it's more the male opinion—77 percent of men agree, compared with only 64 percent of women. This may well be the ultimate consequence of the influence of "progress" on relationships. That which used to be provided by the male (safety, home and hearth, social status) is now something women are entirely capable of providing themselves. Where man's contribution used to be fundamental to survival, now it's an optional add-on—and one that comes at a price some women aren't willing to pay.

   What's intriguing is that part of the new masculinity, M-ness, is man's recognition that he needs woman—a realization that comes, ironically, during the Era of Female Independence, a time when men can be replaced by boy toys, female lovers, abstinence, and even vibrators. Whereas men still need women, their traditional source of comfort and inspiration, women are increasingly less likely to feel that they need men. And that's changing everything about the rules of the game.

10

HOW ARE MEN HANDLING THE SEA CHANGES?

"**M**an must be pleased; but him to please / Is woman's pleasure." So wrote Victorian poet Coventry Patmore in his widely influential *The Angel in the House.* Like countless nineteenth-century manuals on mores, Patmore's poem sought to delineate the proper spheres of men and women. If man had to risk his mortal soul in the daily grind of a competitive capitalist society, then woman had to be tender of the hearth, providing spiritual and bodily comfort at home.

We tend to forget how tirelessly social and religious leaders of the nineteenth century advocated what are now tiresome and largely obsolete commonplaces, such as "a woman's place is in the home." But we also might take for granted in the twenty-first century that we've struck a gender balance in our daily work and home lives. And to be sure, in the last half century, we have seen enormous changes in the roles women and men play in providing income and care for their families and for each other. But men and women still struggle to define those roles and to negotiate responsibilities. A man must be pleased, but so must a woman, and what counts as satisfaction and fulfillment for each is changing every day.

Consider some of the fundamental changes we've already covered that have taken place since 1950 and that continue today:

- Developments in science and economics and, most important, socio-psychological shifts, mean that, in much of the Western world at least, the female's need for the male has decreased to the point at which his most important function is biological (the ability to procreate). And even that can be outsourced.
- Men's traditional advantages—including strength, greater access to educational and job opportunities, and higher legal and social standing—have been marginalized or even reversed. As we noted in an earlier chapter, as of 1995 fully 10 percent of all U.S. males aged twenty to twenty-nine were either in jail, in prison, on probation, or on parole. (The number of incarcerated men under age twenty-five doubled between 1986 and 1995.)[1] Suicide rates among U.S. men aged twenty-five to thirty-four in 2001 were double those of the early 1980s. Young men aged twenty to twenty-four are seven times more likely than young women to take their own lives.
- As we evolve toward a more global, information-centered society, the stereotypical markers of a man—physical strength and a hunter-and-warrior psyche—have become less relevant and, in the case of the latter, even ill suited to today's work environments. Women's strengths as collaborators and multitaskers, on the other hand, stand them in good stead. In the United States, women's earnings for year-round, full-time work are 75.5 percent of men's, up from 59.4 percent in 1970. Earning parity is even higher in many European countries, including 91 percent in Italy and 95 percent in Portugal.[2]
- Media stereotypes of the contemporary male tend to be negative, very often depicting men as inept buffoons or mocking them for their inflated egos or macho attitudes. Women, in contrast, are often depicted as more competent and intelligent—and certainly as less one-dimensional.

- Masculinity is clearly in transition, with the new balance of power calling for "lighter" versions of maleness that take more account of what used to be deemed female values. On the big screen, men are still heroes, but the new depiction of masculinity looks a lot less like John Wayne and a lot more like Orlando Bloom. Men might still be attracted to stoic, muscle-bound action heroes, but women are rejecting them in favor of the decidedly more beautiful, more sensitive, and less macho "new man."

- To a far greater degree than in the past, it is women who are defining who men ought to be and what behaviors and characteristics are acceptable for them.

- As women are increasingly able to get by without men, men are finding they have to learn new tricks in order to attract a life partner—or, at least, the caliber of partner they want to attract. That means tending to the interior (improved communication skills, greater sensitivity) and exterior (improved grooming, more attention to fashion).

- Where once demands for physical beauty rested disproportionately upon the female, now boys and men are subjected to a media onslaught of idealized depictions of men. Among the results: a 1997 *Psychology Today* study found that 43 percent of men were unhappy with their appearance, up from approximately 14 percent thirty years earlier. In 2003, U.S. men underwent nearly 1.1 million cosmetic surgical procedures, up 31 percent from the year prior. As further evidence of their body-image and control issues, males now account for one in five cases of anorexia nervosa, up from one in ten or fifteen in 1980.

- With sex taking place earlier and marriage taking place later, men and women experience much longer periods of dating and independent living prior to marriage, which may not take place until one's thirties or forties, if at all. (In 2002, 23 percent of women and 54 percent of men aged thirty to thirty-four had never been married, up from just 9 percent and 6 percent, respectively, in 1970.) The fact that women now have these years of independence between birth family and marriage completely changes the dynamics of the husband-wife relationship.

- We're seeing greater understanding that while marriage is good for the male, it's not necessarily good for the female. And our studies have consistently shown that men in the United States and other countries are more inclined to consider a lifelong partnership a requirement for a "fulfilling" life. Apparently, a lot of men are going unfulfilled: In 2000, married-couple households made up just 50.7 percent of the U.S. population, down from nearly 80 percent in the 1950s.

- A perceived lack of positive male role models for boys and young men has reached what some consider a crisis point. Too many boys are getting their cues about what it takes to be a man from entertainment and sports (or from women) rather than from fathers at home or teachers in the classroom.
- Where women talk about individual empowerment, men are feeling less empowered, even emasculated. Much of men's angst these days can be attributed to not knowing the best, most appropriate place to be. Where is the line drawn between emotionally vulnerable and plain old pathetic? Where does attractive confidence end and arrogance begin? Which aspects of chivalry get dates and which the evil eye? At what point does attention to one's physique morph into unflattering narcissism? What the &%$#@ do women want?

We know men are responding to the radical shifts in power, gender roles, and social mores we've experienced in the past few decades, but little attention has been paid to how. Women, most often, are the focus of studies and debates regarding the female incursion into traditionally male enclaves, with researchers virtually ignoring the all-important issue of the male response. Where once the system (social, economic, political) was clearly skewed in favor of men, now the balance is becoming more equitable—or, some would argue, perhaps even favorable to women. The question, then, is How does the reduction of male authority in the classroom, in the workplace, and in the family affect the individual men who must come to terms with it? This chapter explores some of the ways in which men are reacting.

MASCULINITY REDEFINED

To a large extent, this book is an exploration of modern-day masculinity. And by that we mean how men are expected to behave in order to be considered "real men." The notion of "masculinity" wasn't much of an issue until the end of the nineteenth century, probably because that was the time when women first really challenged what it meant to be "feminine." What is considered masculine almost always takes its cue from ideas of femininity; just subtract the female and there stands the male, simple and clear.

We're all familiar with masculine stereotypes, positive and negative. Strength, independence, objectivity, and leadership on the one hand, and aggression, violence, an inability to emote, and general dominance on the other. From statesman to corporate warrior to grease monkey to steed-riding knight to convicted felon, men are thought to exhibit all of these characteristics. It's only the degree to which individual men possess these qualities and the finesse they demonstrate in putting them to use that separate the manly from the brutish.

Changing views, demands, and expectations regarding what it means to be masculine have resulted in a good deal of conflict within and between men, not to mention between men and women. Much of this conflict stems from societal pressure to rein in what many would consider basic (biologically based) male attributes. Overt aggression is now considered a sign of moral turpitude, something men resort to only when they haven't the intellectual or moral strength to prevail in a more civilized manner. Uncommunicativeness is seen as selfish, a personality defect to be overcome; it's seen as hindering relationships both at work and at home. In other words, society's new and widespread presumptions about what it takes to be a socially acceptable man increasingly make men feel they are expected to keep their "manliness" in check. Such, at least, is the position of various men's movements.

It's funny how the problems with us
Always stem from problems with me
Like, I don't pay you enough attention or treat you properly
And because I'M the one who's stubborn that's why WE always disagree
If I could learn to be more open we'd solve our problems easily
Our relationship's a one-way street because I'm crippled emotionally
I'm quick to take but slow to give
I should be less selfish, you decree
Or we might as well forget it, call it quits, it's up to me
And the reason for this dissection of my personality is because I said
"Wait until the commercials" when you said "Make a cup of tea."

—submitted by Paul Fraser in response to our query,
"If you could climb up to the mountaintop and proclaim one
message to the women of this world, what would it be?"

After decades of feminism and increasing opportunities for women, it's not difficult to see how men may be feeling marginalized or even vilified. *Spreading Misandry: The Teaching of Contempt for Men in Popular Culture,* by Paul Nathanson and Katherine K. Young, and Susan Faludi's *Stiffed: The Betrayal of the American Man* are two of the more notable books to have addressed what many perceive to be men's losing streak in the culture wars. It is worth noting that many books on this topic are written or co-written by women, suggesting that women as well as men need a clear and positive concept of maleness in order for them to feel we have achieved gender equity.

In *Spreading Misandry,* Nathanson and Young point out how popular movies and television shows often characterize men as violent or foolish. Women's superior morality and wisdom in these depictions is the latest twist on the life-giving power traditionally associated with women. As noted in chapter 7, myriad shows feature men who are inept, vainly attempting manly endeavors and ultimately trumped by their better halves. What many people fail to note is that the man-as-dunce formula is successful only because men are assumed to be not only strong, but also invincible. We can laugh at their high jinks because we know that, deep down, they are the dominant sex. The question is at what point that assumption becomes a liability. It may well be that men suffer less from their depiction as buffoons than they do from the stereotype that, at their core, they must be invincible.

FIGHTING FOR MEN'S RIGHTS

"Sick of Male Bashing in the Media?" asks a bumper sticker for sale on mensactivism.org. Men's rights groups, found on such websites as patriarchy.com and mensactivism.org, say men feel emasculated by a culture that tends to see women as victims at the hands of men. Virginia Woolf once wrote about how she tried to kill Patmore's "angel," who sat on her shoulder and made her mince words and flatter men. Today, some men think women have turned that "killing" rage on them. Men's rights activists list among their grievances Selective Service registration, excessive child support and alimony, and domestic violence suffered by men. Many of these groups take pains to attempt to debunk "feminist myths" of lower wages for women, high incidence of rape, historical incidences of matriarchal societies, "goddess" mythologies, and other explicit or implicit "male-bashing lore." Nevertheless, it would be inaccurate to say that most men's rights activists are trying to turn the clock back to a patriarchal era in which white men ruled; some include in their philosophies an invitation to gay men and men of color. What they're looking for is a way to assert their right to "masculinity," however they choose to define that, at a time when traditionally masculine traits are demonized, ridiculed, or otherwise attacked.

Just how do men's movements define masculinity? That depends on the group, and some have clearer ideas than others. For "mythopoetic" masculinists such as Robert Bly, author of *Iron John*, men dropped the ball when the tradition of fathers initiating their sons into manhood was broken. According to Bly, "Zeus energy is male authority for the sake of the community." He contends that men need to rediscover what's been lost in an industrialized society and start getting in touch with their inner man. In the 1980s, many followers of Bly's philosophy left their families behind to go on "wildman" retreats to exorcise the wimpy New Age Guy who was threatening to kill off their vital male essence. The common picture we have of these retreats is of men beating their chests and roaring around a fire—the sorts of manly things one simply doesn't do in a suburban living room. Today the Mankind Project continues Bly's philosophy with its New Warrior Training Adventure. Men who take part in the training learn to integrate "the dark and soulful qualities of [their] masculine [natures]" and to "transcend the momentum of toxic masculinity." What's "toxic masculinity"? Fear and weakness and denial. Once these are purged in the company of men, the organizers assert, a man finds "within himself the sacred masculine energy" that "seeds life with passion, zeal and creativity."[3] The "warrior" language used by this group seems less about swords than about honor, something hard to come by in the Western workaday world that advocates competitiveness primarily for material gain. The mythopoetic movements look back to mythological hero cycles: You've got to return home, but as a better man.

In large part, movements such as Bly's focus on men to the exclusion of women. They're not about appeasing or making compromises with women; they're about asserting one's primal manhood (albeit in generally positive ways). And an underlying theme seems to be that it's women and their pesky insistence on being treated as equals that led to this sorry state of emasculation.

Toward the opposite end of the spectrum are men who label themselves "profeminist." These men acknowledge traditional male power and privilege, but rather than attempt to reassert them, they seek to mitigate them. The National Organization for Changing Men (NOCM) and the National Organization for Men Against Sexism (NOMAS) are two groups that attempt to right the wrongs of male society by addressing such issues as domestic violence, rape, and pornography. On one hand, these organizations are trying to overcome the gender divide and get on the same page as women. On the other, the idea of "changing men" assumes a male essence that is bad and must be altered or even eradicated. Does changing men make them more like women, or more fully men? Men involved in profeminist movements would say they're trying to be more fully human, but the adoption of "female" viewpoints is a sore point for men who wish to preserve something essentially "male."

Not all men, of course, go in for "organized" manhood. Some criticize Bly's "feminine" appearance and express discomfort with his notions of acceptable male bonding behavior. Others save most of their scorn for profeminist men: "Let's just say the radical feminists have them by the balls" is a familiar lament. But men do seem to need time with each other, and, for many, the preferred way to bond with other men is the old-fashioned way: over beer and sports, as we discussed in chapter 4, not over bonfires during men-only retreats.

We actually seem to be in the midst of a sort of revival of this type of "boys will be boys" camaraderie, with high-profile examples including the *Ocean's Twelve* trio of merry pranksters, George Clooney, Brad Pitt, and Matt Damon, and actor Ewan McGregor's transcontinental motorcycle trip with his buddy Charley Boorman. Matt Damon's long-term friendship with his *Good Will Hunting* co-writer and co-star, Ben Affleck, has also been widely publicized.

Escaping into male friendships appears to be one important way in which men are dealing with the shift in gender roles and gender identities. Time with buddies reinforces men's notions of what is considered appropriately "male." It allows them to engage in talk and behavior that might not necessarily win the approval of their significant others and other women, and it gives them an opportunity to relax in an environment that is likely to be less judgmental and less fraught with expectation than may be common in their daily (gender mixed) lives.

Thanks to the debut of Spike TV in mid-2003, men can even "get together" in the virtual world of their very own men's television network. Spike TV is described in *TV Guide* as a channel that "inspires and defines the modern man through programming that appeals to his lifestyle interests. This is the one place men can find all the comedy, movies, sports entertainment and innovative originals they want, from a male point of view." The irony of men wanting their own network in a medium dominated by males hasn't been lost on women. As Penn State University student Kaitlyn Andrews-Rice wrote in the *Daily Collegian*, "It seems that men needed a network all to themselves, because owning and making all the decisions about the TV that we consume wasn't enough."[4]

What exactly is the kind of programming that appeals to the modern man's "lifestyle interests"?

Here's the January 2005 "primetime schedule," called @9:

Monday 9:00PM   **WWE Raw**
Spike TV has the most WWE (World Wrestling Entertainment) action available anywhere on TV. Catch all your favorite WWE Superstars and Divas on four different WWE shows!

Tuesday 9:00PM   **I Hate My Job**
This fall Spike is giving eight regular guys the opportunity of a lifetime, to ditch their present "crappy" jobs and go after their dream career.

Wednesday 9:00PM   **The Club**
Ice, one of the only standalone nightclubs in Las Vegas, is on the verge of its first anniversary and the honeymoon is just about over.

Thursday 9:00PM   **Hey!**
From the hit Japanese game show Spring of Trivia. As the esteemed author Isaac Asimov once noted, "Humans are the only animals that enjoy useless knowledge."

Friday 9:00PM   **Untold**
From the tumultuous lives of some of America's best-known athletes, to the brutal world of ultimate fighting, to the extremes amateur body builders will go to perfect their bodies, the new Spike TV series "Untold" brings to light some of the greatest sports stories never told.

As for special programming, Spike aired the much-covered 2004 Video Games Awards and, in January 2005, Autorox, "the awards show that kicks asphalt"—as far as we can tell, the first awards show honoring cars.

A TV lineup that features wrestling and automotive awards shows may not seem to signal a step up on the evolutionary scale. In fact, the lineup reflects many of the stereotypes of what sitcom dads would find attractive on TV—namely, what most women would term mindless entertainment. What's significant about Spike TV isn't so much its content as its very existence. Early in this book, we talked about males traditionally being considered the "default" human beings. Women "need" special programming, special categories on *Jeopardy!*, even special hospitals because they are "different." Different from the norm. Different from men, the standard-issue human beings. What Spike TV represents is an acknowledgment that in some ways men are now the have-nots. The former rulers of the airwaves must create a special retreat where they can watch "their kind of programming" in peace and without apology. It seems to us that Spike TV is a backlash against the network and Hollywood fare we described in chapter 7. Its programs correspond to most of the major forms of current programming (for instance, reality TV, awards shows, "soft" features), but it's given a male bent and presumably is safe from overt male-bashing.

In its second year, the men's network has made an effort to move away from such he-man staples as beer, babes, and fast cars. Keith Brown, Spike TV's vice president of news and documentaries, was hired to add a bit of gravitas to the lineup. "It's all about balance," Brown told the *Asbury Park* (New Jersey) *Press*. "The way I see it, it's as important to deal with men's mental and physical health and issues like finance and politics as it is to deal with escape." He adds, "I'm a firm believer that as men, we are interested in everything. We're not all sports and cars. That's looking at men very one dimensionally. Guys care about everything. Men want substance. They want variety. They want serious content."[5]

In the same article, Brown speaks of the importance of tapping into men's sensitive side—a notion that wouldn't seem to fit with the bulk of the network's programming. He speaks of the very same longing we have seen among our male friends and colleagues for deeper connections and permission to explore those aspects of their personalities that might once have been maligned as "girlish." When Brown was researching his book, *Sacred Bond: Black Men and Their Mothers,* a few years back, he tapped into a wellspring of emotion within the men he interviewed. "When I went on my book tour," he says, "guys would come up to me and talk about how healing this was, to talk about the relationships with their mothers. That experience let me know that there's such depth in men that we don't necessarily have the channels to let out."[6] The rise in male bonding is an important way in which today's men are "letting it out."

THE DADDY DILEMMA

Whether they're part of an organized group or not, men share similar concerns, and a major issue for many in the postfeminist era is fatherhood. Certainly the shift in expectations regarding what fathers are supposed to bring to the family are unprecedented. Some men believe their sex has failed to live up to its responsibilities on the fatherhood front. Bly claims fathers aren't doing their part as role models, while the Mankind Project lists as one of its warrior goals becoming a better, more involved father. Many men's rights activists, on the other hand, think the problem stems from women rather than men. They complain that women get off too easy—they're far more likely to gain custody of the children, which allows them to rake in child support and alimony without giving their exes enough of a chance to be dads.

How are men's attitudes changing toward fatherhood? The British journalist Mark Honigsbaum describes three types of father he regularly sees at the playground after school. There's "Divorced Dad," frantically trying to make up for lost time; "Semi-Attached Dad" or "Sad Dad," a married man who struggles to balance work and fatherhood; and "Fully Involved Dad," a term coined by the British Equal Opportunities Commission, which found that men in two-income households are responsible for approximately a third of childcare for kids under age five.[7]

In the 1960s, British men put in about fifteen minutes a day with their children. That amount has risen to two hours a day, which by today's standards counts as full involvement.[8] While it's certainly an improvement over the sixties and seventies, we might find it worthwhile to remember that before the industrial revolution, the average rural father would have spent a great deal of time indoors with his family, particularly during the dark winter months. Today's fathers, many of whom must work well beyond the standard forty-hour work-week, are caught between the ideal of full involvement and the reality of too few hours left over for family and self.

Whoever or whatever is to blame, modern man has not made nearly the same inroads into parenthood as women have made into the work world. Only one in ten men surveyed in England said they are close to their fathers, according to the writer Steve Biddulph (*The Secret of Happy Children and Manhood: An Action Plan for Changing Men's Lives*). In the United States, 40 percent of children today do not even live with their biological fathers.[9] At the same time, we're seeing more men take the initiative to become stay-at-home dads—some for practical economic reasons, but others because they know their children will benefit tremendously from extended contact with their fathers.

Stay-at-home dads, many of whom resent being called Mr. Mom ("If you're going to call us anything, call us Mr. Dad," suggests one father on slowlane.com, one of many websites devoted to stay-at-home dad support), have picked up where women left off when they joined the workforce. Economic rather than personal reasons often prompt men to stay home, but many wouldn't exchange the experience for the world. Against stereotypes of the maternal instinct, fathers are discovering their own capacity to care for children. Still, it can be difficult to feel like a "man" with diapers and sippy cups in tow. Men who serve as primary caregivers for their children are frequently faced with the question of when they're going to get a "real job." It's harder for stay-at-home dads to get understanding from friends and former colleagues, let alone from inquisitive strangers sharing a park bench. A man who stays at home not only loses income, he loses his status as breadwinner, his traditionally correct role. The assumption is that he is depriving his wife and children of time together by not being "man enough" to pull in a paycheck that allows his wife to stay at home. It's little wonder, then, that many men are unwilling to accept the job.

Full-time dads also must contend with a society that doesn't believe fathers are naturally equipped to be primary caregivers, particularly of infants. One fortyish Floridian we spoke with felt that women he came in contact with, whether at the playground, the supermarket, or the doctor's office, regularly questioned his judgment or scrutinized his interactions with his baby more closely than they would have were he the mother. "There was no assumption on the part of others that I was capable of caring for a baby," he says. "And this despite the fact that I had a background in elementary education and had also been a stay-at-home dad for my first child. Even when I took my daughter to her pediatrician, I was considered somehow peripheral to her life. There was an awkwardness when the nurses asked about the baby's development and feeding and sleeping habits, because they didn't seem to fully believe that I was the one who was tending to her needs while my wife worked. It was an ongoing source of aggravation for me, almost a 'reminder' that I wasn't fulfilling my proper role in life, and I'm sure it's something most other stay-at-home dads have experienced, as well."

Whether or not society is truly ready for dads as primary caregivers, formal efforts are in place in some countries to encourage the practice. In some ways, rather than helping young fathers respond to societal shifts, they're pushing them headlong into the rushing waters. In an effort to keep more men (and women) in the home while their children are young, for instance, the Swedish government instituted a "parental insurance program." In 1990, parents were offered up to fifteen months of regular paid leave. Lots of fathers, though, would sign their time over to their wives, so the government mandated gender-specific months of paid leave. Even with the state backing them up, men were initially disinclined to be stay-at-home dads, even temporarily.[10] This disinclination is even stronger in such countries as the United States, where even maternity leave is abbreviated (three months, unpaid, if you're lucky), and where paternity leave tends to be taken in days rather than weeks or months. Many men face competing pressures—they should be hands-on, fully involved dads, while not giving an inch in the workplace. Yet how often do we read about this in the press? In comparison, there's near-constant coverage of the dilemma women face in trying to juggle home and work. For them, there's sympathy and at least some attempts at solutions. Men are on their own.

From a marketing standpoint, Dad has been ignored by child-centered brands more often than not, with seemingly little recognition that he also does his share of diaper runs and toy-store outings and is involved in deciding what his kids eat. Ignoring Dad's role in nutrition is a particularly dangerous oversight at a time when attitudes and behaviors related to food and nutrition are changing so rapidly. Just recently, we examined organic eating trends in Europe and the United

States, and we discovered that men and women oftentimes tip toward more natural foods upon the birth of their first child, forgoing processed snacks and antibiotic-laden meats once their children begin to eat. The birth of a first child represents an important opportunity for marketers of wholesome foods, and if they ignore Dad it will be to their detriment.

Our former colleague Mark Wnek, now the "Ad Guru" for Britain's *The Independent* and just named chairman and chief creative officer of Lowe New York, built one of the hottest and fastest-growing agencies of the late 1990s. The father of a toddler and newborn, he is optimistic that we've entered an era of devoted, hands-on fatherhood—a time when men will embrace their roles as fathers rather than simply accept them. And that shift, he believes, is already being seen in advertising.

"I think the big über-movement in the world will increasingly be the search for authenticity," Wnek told us. "Unless there is a cataclysmic worldwide spiritual awakening, the powers that be are likely to continue to 'develop' the world at breakneck speed: digging up its treasures, covering it with concrete, manufacturing any and every product and commodity that the imagination can think of (you think there's an overwhelming amount of consumer choice now, you wait). As night follows day, this will increasingly remove people from the 'real'—real craftsmanship, real food without additives, real experiences, real life." And that, in turn, will cause them to search out that which is authentic.

"For men," says Wnek, "the epitome of authenticity is the heart-rendingly guileless stare of their tiny child. This will drag men by the millions back to the home—and all its social and spiritual accoutrements—as life's epicenter, and away from the office. This will in turn create (and already is creating) happy, well-balanced children who will grow up into adults unwilling to kill each other either corporately or on the battlefield."

It seems a utopian vision, and Wnek concedes that his own industry shows few signs of recognizing this new model of male parenthood. "We see this in advertising only every now and then—Volvo does it best, I think, and the Reebok Alan Iverson commercial where he talks about not wanting his children to think he's hard is interesting—but mostly advertising portrays men as hunks or go-getters. Whether this reflects the unreconstructed macho psyches of marketers, admen, or guys in focus groups, I don't know."

THE AGE OF UNEMPOWERMENT

To think of how many changes men have had to absorb in recent decades boggles the mind. Laws that made man the master of his domain at home have been repealed. Women have largely surpassed men in the classroom and have caught up to them in many occupations. There are even signs that women are faring better in the workforce. In a 2003 U.S. survey, for instance, men were less likely than women to say they were motivated to do their jobs; only 75 percent of men said they were, compared with 87 percent of women.[11] If women complain of the glass ceiling, men are often dissatisfied without quite knowing why. **The sociologists Michael Kimmel and Michael Kaufman point out that the "aggregate power" we associate with men, particularly white, middle-class men, "does not translate into an individual sense of feeling empowered."[12]** Men entrenched in a corporate culture may feel just as alienated as women do, without feeling able to complain about it. After all, the business world is supposed to be a man's world, so a man is expected to display all the attributes of a corporate warrior. If he doesn't feel at ease, then something is wrong with *him*, not the system. And if his wife is making more strides than he is, then so much the worse. He's a Stepford Husband.

For the average man, coming to an equitable and mutually satisfying relationship with women continues to present difficulties. The age-old question "What do women want?" is meeting with myriad answers, but not one that satisfies all. The result is that many men are finding they must test out different personae. Scott, a thirty-five-year-old business analyst who asked us not to use his last name, divides himself into two men: Bourbon Scott and Buddha Scott. Bourbon Scott is older; he's the one who grew up remembering his mother bad-mouthing his father, and in his twenties he tried hard to give women what he thought they wanted. "I had difficulty figuring out my role. I thought, they'll respect hard-core frat guys, you know, confident." So Bourbon Scott did his best to be smooth and distant. As Scott grew older, he came to feel that Bourbon Scott was getting in his way. "I decided it's not them, it's not women, who are making me feel uncomfortable. It's me." He didn't become a hardcore Buddhist, but he did start meditating as a way of overcoming his anger against his mother and women in general. But after the

breakup of an eight-year relationship, he's finding it difficult to get involved with the right woman. "I can be anyone's perfect first date.
That's easy. But on a second date there's often silence, which makes
me scared again. You realize there's this person in front of you who
you don't know, and it's hard to go ahead from there." The struggle
for dominance between Buddha Scott and Bourbon Scott may not be
quite as epic as the Mankind Project warrior's, but it's a struggle
nonetheless, and it's a battle being played out in various ways within
many a modern man.

When asked what he's looking for in relationships with women,
Brian, a thirty-four-year-old filmmaker who also asked that his last
name not be used, told us, "I have to be in control." After a pause, he
added, "How misogynistic is that—wow." But control's a big issue for
a lot of men and women. She's gotta have it; he's gotta have it. As
Brian sees it, women are too practiced at trying to appear in control,
and won't admit when they're not. Sounds familiar, doesn't it? It's
what men are daily accused of or ridiculed for. Other things don't
seem to change. Both Scott and Brian think women are always trying
to feel them out as prospective mates by inquiring how much money
they make. As bachelors, they feel they have to pick up the tab, and
are relieved when women offer to chip in. If sex is going to happen, it
won't be confused with gratitude or obligation.

**There's no one-size-fits-all answer to how men are handling
the shifts in gender roles and relations over the past few decades.
Some of the men we spoke with in researching this book are
angry and bitter over what they see as women's lack of respect
for them and for men in general. (Some of the men ranting on
websites are scary angry.) Some are relieved not to have to
shoulder the entire burden of providing for their families. Some
are pleased by what they see as a greater variety of options available to them in terms of acceptable personas, careers, and
lifestyles. And some are nostalgic for the "good old days" when
"men were men, and sheep were scared."**

Most likely, the majority of men feel some combination of all or
most of those sentiments. Sure, there are those on the fringe who are
self-avowed women-haters (most often saving their greatest antipathy
for American women). And there are some who have eagerly shed the
last vestiges of traditional masculinity and embraced their feminine
sides almost to the exclusion of their maleness. Most men, however,

fall comfortably between those two extremes, unhappy about some developments and thrilled about others. *What we expect to see more of in coming decades is men taking the time to sort through their feelings and make clearer decisions about their lives, their priorities, and how they feel about being men.* We may well see a Men's Revolution that advocates not equality (they already have more than that), not a return to traditional gender roles, but recognition of man's contributions and positive characteristics. Aretha Franklin said it best: R-E-S-P-E-C-T. *Cargo* may be on the right track with its SELF ESTEEM T-shirts.

WHAT TO REMEMBER

1. The aggregate power of the white, middle-class straight man, especially in the corporate workplace, does not translate into individual empowerment. Much of the male angst we're seeing today is felt by men who don't know what is considered appropriate male behavior. The frustration is increased by the fact that the women they're hoping to attract, form partnerships with, or simply work with have widely differing views on the subject—and may not even be sure themselves.

2. A good number of men seem to have discovered that the best place—maybe even the only place—to get genuine affirmation of their maleness and of the fact that they're doing okay is from male friendships and friendship groups. In this, men are following the example of women, who have long leaned on each other for support, affirmation, and help with day-to-day struggles.

3. As men grapple with the enormous changes they have had to absorb since the end of World War II, they have finally reached a point at which they want to reassert their pride. Or at least to *feel* pride again. The vast majority of men don't want to turn back the gains of the women's movement—in fact, our studies have found that men are even more loath than women to see women return to the home. Men don't want to take back responsibility to be the sole provider for their households. What they do want is to reclaim their self-respect and a viable voice in the home and in society at large. Not "I am Man, hear me roar," but "I am man, respect me and live and love and work alongside me." They'd like the respect they engender at work to mean something when they clock out.

4. Clearly, the societal shifts we're seeing will persist as men and women continue to grapple with their new roles, what is expected of them, and what changes they want to see. Few people seem to have a clear destination in mind, but men seem far more inclined than in past decades to influence the route. Responsibility for advocating changing gender roles is no longer going to be left solely in the hands of women.

CONCLUSION

M-NESS—
THE BRIGHT FUTURE OF MEN

I t's the first thing the world learns about us—before the toe count, before the slap on the bum that gets us breathing. "Boy or girl?" is the first question on everyone's mind. And regardless of the changes the world—especially the Western world—has seen, a person's sex is still a fundamental aspect of who that person is. What other question rates such obsession? Democrat or Republican? Hindu or Buddhist? Rich or poor? Gay or straight? Compared with all the other aspects of identity—race, nationality, class, sexuality, and so on down the list—sex is still the one that is most fundamental to our understanding of a person. If someone's race is unclear, we're okay. We may even avoid discussion of it to show how comfortable we are with not knowing. Or, if we do ask, we do it directly. But sex? When was the last time you heard someone ask, "Pardon my directness, but are you a man or a woman?" It would be impossible. An embarrassment for the person asking and a humiliation for the person being questioned. Still, all the same, we have to know.

What *has* changed is the turf the answer to that question is expected to cover. Being a man or a woman no longer means what it did a century or two ago. Culturally, women have made swift inroads into the world outside their homes—in academia, in the corporate world, in politics, and just about everywhere else. The shifts in Western society from family-centered agrarian economies to the atomized family

units of the industrial age, all the way to the postindustrial, information-based economies of the second millennium C.E. have consistently broadened the potential of access to power, responsibility, and
prestige for women at the same time that they have rewritten the social bonds of the family. And the votes are in: freedom and family, if
not actually countering each other, do seem at the very least to not automatically support each other. The further we push into the
Information Age, the weaker the bonds of family become. Marriage—
which benefits men universally, but may actually be detrimental to
women, depending on their husbands—now comes later, and the development of urban and suburban "tribe" relationships consisting of
bonds between groups of single men and women of around the same
age frequently fills the gaps.

But the future of sex and gender does not stop with cultural up-
heaval. Women are also filling in the gaps physiologically, sexually,
and reproductively: running faster, getting stronger, gaining in mus-
culature—and fast on the heels of men. This narrowing of sexual difference brings its own surprising changes, with women in "tough"
jobs, women in war. Women virtually everywhere, doing virtually
everything.

Even the power relations that seemed inherent in sex—men as
penetrative and women as receptive—have seen some reversal. Cash-
ing in on an item of hot cultural capital, the female rapper Peaches
performed a number about this shift on her 2003 album, *Fatherfucker*.
"Don't you know it's supposed to feel better for boys?" she asks on
"Back It Up, Boys," an ode to women using strap-ons with their
boyfriends, and taking control in ways that would have made mainstream feminists of the twentieth century blanch.[1]

The change in the identity of the penetrating partner should
come as no surprise: after all, once you can get sperm from a bank—or
over the web—why would you need the penis to be real, and who
cares where it goes? Piece by piece, the male dominance that seemed
so insurmountable prior to the 1950s is being dismantled.

**It's not that men are vanishing or being made meaningless. It
isn't even that the differences between men and women are disappearing. If gender distinctions were even close to extinction,
we'd no longer have the obsessive need to know whether the
person walking by us on the street is male or female.** We still see
those two categories as different, and, to some extent, we still see

them in opposition. But the gap between them has shrunk, and the assumptions we make about each have radically changed. We don't map power onto that split the way we used to. Nor do we make rigid assumptions about success, physical ability, or intelligence based on that divide. It used to be that the male/female split was akin to subject/object, center/margin, important/frivolous. Now we are more likely to make such assumptions based on the characteristics of the *individual* rather than his or her sex.

TOWARD A NEW MASCULINITY: M-NESS

The fact that men have changed and that their role is now less dominant isn't a bad thing, even for men. The economic, cultural, and political shifts we've seen over the past few decades have actually given men more options, just as the women's movement was intended to provide more options for women. Today's men are freer to reimagine and reinvent themselves, and the ones who are most flexible about doing so—the ones who are best able to embrace their M-ness—are the ones who have the best chance of thriving in today's gender environment.

Julius van Heek, a forty-year-old designer living in Chicago, summed up for us how the effects of the women's movement have been different for different types of men. "For one type of man (the old fashioned, conservative)," he explained, "the women's movement has threatened his existence and has exposed his weaknesses. So watch out: desperate (or threatened) people do desperate things. For the other and growing type of man (one who is more well rounded, interested in expanding his horizons), the women's movement has allowed him to be more expressive, whether from an experimental or permanent viewpoint. Look at the volume of men who are willing to try new things, whether it be food, fashion, male makeup, childrearing, or cooking."

We can easily see men as having moved from *essential* to *optional*. Where men were once essential to women in certain capacities, now women can fulfill those functions on their own. The key point to keep in mind is that it's up to each individual male to determine how essential he is in anyone's life and in the world at large. Those men who most readily adapt to the new expectations of culture are the ones most likely to find success. Those who refuse to adapt, who refuse to accept the notion that they are no longer in total control, will find the going much rougher. Maybe not in the boardroom—yet—but certainly in the bedroom. The future of men, they will find, is not about control but about cooperation.

We're already seeing men shift toward this more personal version of manliness. We're seeing it in their intensified male bonding and in their more emotive relationships with women. We're also seeing it in their efforts to be their best selves, whether through attempts at personal growth or simply improved grooming. Underlying so much of this is a sense among men that they want to have some of the things that historically have been the province of women, including true companionship, enduring bonds with their children, and spiritual connectedness. Throughout human history, many men have enjoyed these things, but, for most, they were peripheral to (or even in opposition to) their sense of being a man. Now, men want those things to be at the core of what it means to be male.

Particularly interesting to us as we conducted our research for this book was the fact that whereas most of the women we interviewed felt men were better off in the 1950s compared with today, most of the men vehemently disagreed. Madeline Park, a working mother in her thirties, is one of many women who assumed that men would have preferred life half a century ago. "I think men are worse off," she told us. "They are not necessarily the breadwinners anymore, and I think that hurts their egos. They don't have the obedient wives at home cooking and cleaning, so they have to now pick up half the work. I would imagine that all men would dream for the 1950s mentality." Cathy Lasowski, a single baby boomer based in Paris, agrees. In her view, men are worse off today because "they have to fight more to hold on to power, and they have more confusion/questions about having that power."

While some of the men we talked with conceded that there are more pressures on men today—especially increased competition in the workplace and greater demand to help with household chores— they were more apt to point to the advantages their generation is enjoying. Jimmy Szczepanek, thirty-four, who works in public relations in New York City, feels men are better off today because they are no longer "confined to an unrealistic view of what men are supposed to be." The British writer Paul Fraser, thirty-three, agrees, saying "there is less pressure on men to 'be a man' than in 1950." Tim Dirgins, the husband of Madeline Park, takes the view that men are worse off in terms of career, but better off in terms of family relationships. Dirgins defines a "real man" in 2005 as one who "may not be the primary breadwinner but shares equally in childrearing and housework."

The fact that so many of the men we interviewed consider the major changes brought about by the women's movement—women's full participation in the workforce, men's full participation at home—to be a positive step confirms our hypothesis that what we're seeing take shape today isn't so much the beginning of a new revolution between men and women, but a revolution within individual men. More and more men are resolving to improve their lot by changing their expectations of themselves, of who they want to be as men. They're less interested in proving themselves (to anyone other than themselves) and more intent on having a say in the social and interpersonal shifts taking place. Complacency is no longer cool.

A recurring theme we heard on the topic of Real Men 2005 was that today's man—or at least the most positive examples of today's man—has far more choices in how he lives his life, a gift and also a responsibility. According to Niels den Otter, twenty-three, a sound engineer in the Netherlands, "A real man back in the day was a plain and simple man who had a job (the kind of job didn't matter; the fact that he had a job earned him respect). When he was finished at work—nine till five exactly!—he headed toward home, where his wife was waiting with dinner. Plain and simple. A real man nowadays is doing a lot to accomplish his dreams, not his ideals (we don't want hippies). His life is a constant flow of work, spare time, quality time with wife and kids. I think *flexible* is the right word to use here."

BEYOND THE ABCs . . .
AND ALL THE WAY TO M

Some of the media have touched on this new version of masculinity, but in large part they've dumbed it down to its ABCs: aesthetics, boy toys (from cars to home theaters and turbocharged phones), and companionship. What they've missed is that M-ness isn't merely about men having more. It's also about them reclaiming their space, their sense of worth, and even themselves. Men want to be the ones who define who they are and what's "appropriate" for them, as men, to do, say, and think. And one thing they consider appropriate is that they be treated with respect—first and foremost, by themselves. Men who have embraced this new masculinity know that caring for themselves extends their capacity to care for others—their female partners, male friends, extended family, and pets. And they understand that caring for the whole range of beings who contribute to their emotional lives isn't "womanish" or "unmanly"; it's the fuel that helps drive and sustain them as men. For too long, men were shy about admitting the importance of such ties. Now we're seeing men—including famous men, ranging from George Clooney and Matt Damon to Prince William—celebrate their bonds with other men in a public fashion. They may joke about the bonds, but they are fierce in defense of each other and in defense of their friendships.

On the domestic front, M-ness means being a caregiver and caretaker and companion rather than a controller. And the men who advocate this new definition of masculinity feel strongly that these are values other men should share. The American magazine editor Jim Frank, father of two college students and happily married for twenty-seven years, feels more marriages would be as successful as his if men were more willing to throw off the macho attitudes of the "old" masculinity and embrace the sense of partnership and collaboration than is inherent in the new.

"After childbirth and those necessarily biological functions—like breastfeeding—there's nothing the married man (or any father) shouldn't do that the married or unmarried mother does: changing diapers, feedings in the middle of the night," Frank says. "That's obviously just a small part of it. But it goes across all marriage topics: it's a partnership, so jobs, responsibilities should be divided. Do they have to be equal? That depends on the partners and if they've been smart enough to talk about it and figure out what they will/won't do, do/don't like, etc. It's not about 50-50; it's about fairness. Hey, you live there? You're responsible. And don't give me this 'I bring home the bacon' shit unless you cook it, too. As for the role in a child's life, that's simple. Total involvement. Go to back-to-school night, read bedtime stories, do some of the carpool driving, help make the important decisions. It would be nice if it started with one simple rule: be there. Of course there are job concerns (I've missed more school events, bedtimes, and meals than I'd like), but that's part of the responsibility part, and it isn't about the gender of the person who isn't around. If you've decided to have children (well, yeah, that would be a good start—actually deciding rather than just doing), be prepared to be there, wherever 'there' is. And I can tell you: It's everywhere. It's also the best place to be."

Julius van Heek is a decade younger than Jim Frank, is childless, and is gay, but his definition of the role a man should play within the family is entirely in line with Frank's: "A man ought to balance the needs/wants of his partner and children," van Heek told us. "He ought to be a role model in relation to constructive activity/projects around the house; exhibit structure, responsibility, independence, love; provide/participate in intellectual education and the education required to manage money. He ought to learn how to relate to his children emotionally and be active in the physical bonding (touch) required for his children's future healthy relationships. He has a duty to teach his children about the natural beauty of the human form and how to learn to be comfortable in one's natural skin. This is no different for the woman of the household."

This attitude that men's obligations within the household and toward their children should be no different from women's may seem like common sense, but it's a radical departure from the role men were taught to assume in the past—and even from how many boys are being raised today. Most of the people in our generation, the baby boomer generation, grew up with clear models that said Mr. Brady earned the money and Mrs. Brady took care of the house and shopping (she left a lot of the cleaning and cooking to Alice). Certainly in the middle class, it was unusual to see women who worked outside the home, at least once they married and had their first child. Many elementary schools sent their students home for lunch; there was no question that someone would be there to prepare the meal—or what that person's sex would be. Today, such a system would be unthinkable.

In the Western world especially, it's indisputable that most fathers today feel greater pressure to contribute to their households and the day-to-day care of the children. That's not to say they're all stepping up to the plate, but the dynamics of dual-income households make it unlikely that Mom can do it alone. For many, probably most, dads, this change is a positive one, even if it does add stress to their lives. Jim Frank told us, "The change in gender roles strikes me as better, because I can't imagine coming home from work, being met by June Cleaver in a cocktail dress and frilly apron who hands me a martini at the door, then sitting in my favorite easy chair reading the paper while she cooks. Sounds pretty dull. Not that doing nothing at the end of the day isn't occasionally desirable."

This changed household reality can be found at all levels of society—and in most cultures, even in the East. Consider China, a traditional society long cut off from outside influences. Today, says Tom Doctoroff, chairman of advertising agency JWT's greater China operations, Chinese men are caught in a confusion of messages regarding who and what they should be.

"The Chinese character for 'man' depicts 'power in the field,'" explains Doctoroff. "Angular and bold, the pictogram celebrates testosterone-fueled masculinity." He notes, however, that with men's power and position came enormous responsibility. "The pictogram," he says, "also suggests that men, while ruling the roost, were fully responsible for the material well-being of the clan. Confucianism, the Middle Kingdom's cultural blueprint, is rooted in double-edge patriarchy; men boast power but are also constrained by the yoke of duty. They must 'set up a household and establish a career,' 'be successful at 30,' and, last but not least, 'honor and bring glory to ancestors.'"

Today, the expected role of Chinese men has broadened and become more complex, Doctoroff says, and, as a consequence, many men "are fraught with lingering anxiety and nebulous loss of control." From a marketing standpoint, Doctoroff notes that male bonding has become a way in which men cope with the stress of changed societal pressures. "The disoriented modern man craves retreat; friendship is the ultimate sanctuary," he says. And advertisers are using this male bonding as a touchpoint in their messaging: "Bonds that have stood the test of time, ideally dating back to childhood, or at least high school, fuel the warmth of many alcohol campaigns."

Doctoroff's experiences in Asia have taught him that "marketers have an opportunity to touch the hearts of men by developing products and communications that dull the need to 'cross the river by feeling the stones.'" He recommends six ways for marketers to achieve this: (1) project status, (2) give him tools, (3) release his aggression, (4) help him pass the girl test, (5) leverage friendship, and (6) make him an expert.

IMPLICATIONS FOR MARKETERS

Since marketing is what we do, we can't help but have a few thoughts about the implications of the current state of modern man and M-ness *male'ness n.*

Synonyms: male, masculine, manlike, manly, manful, virile, mannish

These adjectives mean of, relating to, or characteristic of men. *Male* categorizes any living thing by gender or sex: *the male population; a male puppy; a male plant. Masculine* refers to what is considered characteristic of men: *a masculine voice. Manlike* applies to qualities of a man (*manlike fortitude*) or resemblance to a human (*manlike apes*). *Manly* describes qualities regarded as becoming to a man: *manly strength. Manful* suggests bravery and resoluteness: *a manful display of chivalry. Virile* stresses the vigor, power, or sexual potency of an adult male: "The virile figure of Theodore Roosevelt swung down the national highway" (Edward Bok). *Mannish* usually applies to women or their traits, clothing, or actions when they seem masculine: *a mannish suit.*

<u>Source:</u> *The American Heritage® Dictionary of the English Language, 4th ed.* Copyright © 2000 by Houghton Mifflin Company.

M-ness n.

A masculinity that combines the best of traditional manliness (strength, honor, character) with positive traits traditionally associated with females (nurturance, communicativeness, cooperation).

A mode of living that is personalized and gender neutral, without being gender ambivalent. Also known as My-ness. A lifestyle that emphasizes higher-quality emotional and physical pleasures, male pleasures, that come from knowing oneself and one's potential.

for our industry. For anyone in our business, the attitudinal and behavioral shifts that have taken place among men over the past half century are of tremendous significance, whether we're looking at the male consumer as a whole or considering how best to target him in any one category.

As codes of dress and behavior relax, men become freer to push the boundaries of gender, not necessarily seeking greater androgyny but insisting upon a broader definition of that which is considered masculine. It's important to note that while men may be doing more of the same things as women, they're not necessarily doing them in the same way. Stay-at-home dads are thought to be more encouraging of their children's risk-taking, for instance, and studies have found that, in general, male shoppers tend to be more brand loyal and goal-oriented than their female counterparts. The implication is that marketers can't reach and influence them in the same ways they reach and influence women. Men will respond to different messages, different channels of communication, and different incentives.

Consider the health and beauty industry. Product manufacturers, service providers, and retailers would do well to remember that even when shopping for beauty products and treatments, men are making their own rules. In the UK, Boots canceled plans to roll out a chain of male grooming salons after two test sites failed to attract a significant clientele. For many men, intensive grooming is still seen as pampering (that is, a feminine indulgence). Though they may want the same benefits as women (a more youthful appearance, a polished look), men want their grooming choices to be seen as utilitarian rather than self-indulgent. For this reason, companies targeting men may benefit from keeping product names short and to the point. Zirh Skin Nutrition, for instance, markets products with names such as Prevent, Correct, and Scrub.

Today the brands that resonate with men do so because they understand the truth about men in this age of evolving M-ness. In the "post mass" world, brands are finding success in catering to very specific needs—be they emotion or performance based. As every target becomes more complex, new opportunities are created by evaluating, understanding, and addressing consumers' ever-changing constellation of needs.

Consider the example of Gillette: As a well-regarded manufacturer of shaving equipment, the brand can easily move into the broader arena of skin care—whether scent, skin protection, or even youth potions. It has consumers' implicit "permission" to do so because of its solid history of helping to care for men's faces.

It's not just traditionally male brands that can cater to men's new needs, however. Nivea, previously focused on women, can find success with its new range of men's skin-care products because of its heritage in that arena. Where Nivea succeeds, we suspect, is with "authentic" and "efficacy" credentials—the stuff works—versus the "badge value" of the prestige makers, who continue to operate in specialty and/or department stores. From its base in the mass drug/grocery space, Nivea succeeds in making these kinds of products accessible to men who would never think about shopping for them (or paying the prices associated with them) in the "class end" of the retail spectrum.

Among teenagers, girls continue to be the economic force across a broader range of products and services, relative to boys. Fashion and cosmetics continue to have a primary focus on girls, even as boys discover personal appearance matters to them (and to the people they're trying to attract). Conventional wisdom holds that boys' discretionary spending goes to food and entertainment (video games, movies, music). While this may be true, opportunity exists to target the "new male teen" in categories that have traditionally been single-mindedly female.

By and large, business still seems to be lagging behind the cultural reality of how much gender blurring has occurred in traditional female domains. For instance, products related to food preparation, home furnishing and entertaining, and home maintenance (i.e., cleaning) are still generally pitched at women, despite the fact that most of these items have become gender neutral. Two years ago, during interviews with homeowners in Kingston, New York, we were struck by the number of men who told us, unaided, that they were the primary cleaners in their households. They also were quick to name products and tools they prefer, such as Windex, Old English furniture polish, Whisk detergent, Woolite, Dustbusters, and Dirt Devils—all products that historically have been pitched at women but that male homemakers like because they get the job done and have designs with unisex appeal.

Men tend to like packaging (particularly when they're buying a less-than-macho product) that is devoid of frills and to be able to buy the product within their own domain (sitting next to razors, for instance, rather than in the women's beauty aisle). When Tyler Brûlé, the founder of *Wallpaper**, launched a unisex fashion magazine, he used separate covers for men and women. The content of *Spruce* was the same, but men found a more masculine-looking publication sitting next to traditionally male magazines, while women could purchase their own version next to other beauty- and women-focused lifestyle magazines. The modern man may be comfortable in his masculinity, but even he has his limits.

Male grooming is an obvious category in which M-ness is having an impact. But what about cars? There, too, we're seeing a shift. When the Mazda Miata was introduced a decade ago, much was made of the degree to which the engine sound echoed that of the traditional sports car. Nothing like the roar of an engine to get the testosterone flowing. Today's iteration of an automobile performance machine is found not in the two-seat roadster, but in Nissan's stylish Murano SUV (a name borrowed from the world-famous Florentine glass manufacturer) and the higher-end Infiniti FX–35. Traditional male cues, only this time integrated not into a sporty roadster but into the default family car of the early twenty-first century.

Or consider the Dodge Magnum, another SUV, but a more "muscular" version. In its launch advertising, while Mom extols the looks, safety, and practical features of the vehicle, the spot ends with Dad and his infant son peering under the hood, with Dad coaching his boy on the meaning and pronunciation of *Hemi*. (Hemi is a type of engine that someone on a Chrysler website describes as "Mopar in type, V8, hot tempered, native to the United States, carnivorous, eats primarily Mustangs, Camaros, and Corvettes. Also enjoys smoking a good import now and then to relax."[2]) Male bonding starts early. The impact of M-ness can also be seen in the introduction of the heavily retro-focused Ford Mustang (following on the heels of 2003's reintroduction of the Ford Thunderbird, an unabashed attempt to recapture the iconic 1957 version). What's the imagery? It's a setting borrowed from *Field of Dreams*, the 1989 Kevin Costner classic, described in *Video-Hound's Movie Retriever* as "an uplifting mythic fantasy based on WP Kinsella's novel 'Shoeless Joe.' An Iowa corn farmer heeds a mysterious voice that instructs, 'If you build it, they will come.' . . . It's all about chasing a dream, maintaining innocence, finding redemption and reconciling the child with the adult, and celebrating the mythic lure of baseball." Doesn't sound much like a "sports movie," does it?

But Ford takes the imagery even a step further. Who is it that emerges from the cornfield to put the Mustang through its paces in the newly carved cornfield driving range? None other than proto-male Steve McQueen. Innocence. Father-son bonding. Mysticism. And pure alpha male. All in one package. M-ness means men don't have to settle for less.

WHAT'S NEXT: THE FUTURE OF MEN

So, what does the future hold for men?

Renewed respect. We'll see more focused and more organized efforts by men to regain the societal and intrafamily respect they used to take for granted. Husband-bashing, believe it or not, is on its way out—not completely (never completely) and not quickly, but we've finally reached a point at which men are truly fed up with being the butt of every joke, and even women are beginning to see that it's gone overboard. We've seen this trend in spurts and fads such as Promise Keepers and the "surrendered wife" phenomenon. Now we're going to see it move beyond the religious right and other conservative groups, and make it into the average household. And that, in turn, will put television executives and advertising creatives on notice that using men, fathers in particular, for cheap laughs has run its course. It's time to give Dad a break. Just about everyone agrees on that.

Further broadening of what's "masculine." As we've stated already in this conclusion, M-ness, or My-ness, signals a shift in society's definition of what can and should be considered masculine, loosening the reins on male behavior and providing greater choices to those men who refuse to be denied entrance into what has long been considered the "women's world." We're not talking men in dresses and false eyelashes. We're talking about men being able to have open and loving platonic friendships with their male buddies. We're talking about men not being ashamed to admit they like the feel of cashmere or spending an hour getting a facial. We're talking about more men being who they are and doing what they want without fear that they'll be "outed" as unmanly.

Adopting female traits. As men are asked to take on new responsibilities at home and cope with increased competition from the female of the species everywhere else, they will need to develop the skills that have allowed women to succeed in these areas—multitasking and collaboration, for instance. Julius van Heek summed it up nicely: In his view, men have been propped up by women throughout history. Now that women are putting themselves forward, it's up to men to pick up the slack and do for themselves those things that used to be taken care of by the women who supported them. "As I have matured I have come to my personal conclusion that men have not ruled the world in modern times," he said. "They may think they have, but it is either the support of women or the prompting of women who have allowed these men to give the perception that men rule the world. Generally, I believe the veil is being lifted as women's roles have become more visible and/or more accepted as well as respected. I believe that women's power position(s) and how important they are have become more clearly understood by the mass public. . . . [Going forward], men will continue to learn how to become more flexible, better planners, more spontaneous; basically will have to become more well rounded, more like women, particularly those who balance work, home, and life goals. Men will have to become better 'project managers.'"

Letting everyone play. The latter half of the last century saw the strengthening of the civil rights movement in the United States, followed by the women's movement, followed by the gay rights movement. The cumulative effect has been that straight white men, while still dominant, have had no choice but to play nice (or at least more nicely) with new entrants to the game. There's no stuffing the genie back in the bottle, certainly not in the Western world. And that means even more changes to come as the composition of the classroom changes, the composition of the applicant pool changes, and (eventually) the composition of the C-Suite changes. Jimmy Szczepanek anticipates that day: "Physical strength is no longer a defining factor in success," he says, "therefore I think that women will continue to play a more important role in business and politics. In addition, as generations of people grow up with different sets of ideals, there will be more opportunities for others. . . . Adolescents are accepting their homosexuality at earlier ages, which signifies a degree of acceptance. There is an increasing number of African American executives. Therefore, I anticipate a more level playing field and (hopefully) the end of white male rule."

New ways of living and working. As the rules in one area change, the pressure is on to be more flexible in other areas. Cathy Lasowski anticipates "an increasing percentage of men falling behind or beginning to opt for nontraditional ways of working/living (as women increasingly do)." This, in turn, will change the ways men view themselves in relation to their jobs and titles. "Changes in jobs—outsourcing, working at home, less allegiance to a single employer/job—could have an enormous effect on how men see themselves and their 'place,'" Jim Frank asserts. "With luck," he says, "and with more and more women not just entering the workplace but rising within it, men won't have to feel that they are the sole breadwinners, that they must 'provide.' . . . Will the majority of important positions (business, political, economic) be held by men? Yes, but the percentage will shrink. Until there are significant changes in the concept and biology of childbearing, women, unfortunately, will never quite reach equality across all people. Individual cases, absolutely; across 'mankind'? No."

Equality and success redefined. Where we differ from Jim Frank is in our belief that "equality"—if we're looking at it as equal success and status—will increasingly be tied not just to career achievement, but to a broader definition of success that incorporates family, friendship, and life balance. So we believe true equality is within reach of women. As working hours and job stress both increase, there will be a breaking point, and society—multicultural, male *and* female society—will call into question whether what the white, middle-class male historically has decreed to be success still meets our needs and wants. Already, "equality" for many women has less to do with job titles and incomes than with a more fair division of labor and equal access to free time.

Being a Real Man today means knowing and doing what it takes to get what you want, when and how you want it. That may include an attractive partner (male or female), it may include power and wealth, it may include health and physical prowess, it may include extended hours of unhurried time with family and other loved ones. After all, we're living in an era of infinite choice. This is the "Dawning of the Age of M-ness."

Does modern man have a future? Yes, indeed. And he has the power to shape it just as women shaped theirs in the last century. Man's greatest battle is not against women or other men or even changing times. It's against the inertia that falsely tells him that he's on top and will always be on top. It's against the false sense of security that what forever has been will always be. This isn't a battle women will instigate or fight on men's behalf. They've fought their battle—and they've won. Now, it's up to men to fight their own revolution.

NOTES

CHAPTER 1
THE GREAT GENDER SHIFT

1. From www.islam.ru.

CHAPTER 2
ME TARZAN, YOU JANE—THE BIOLOGY OF GENDER

1. Helen Fisher, *Why We Love: The Nature and Chemistry of Romantic Love* (New York: Henry Holt, 2004).
2. Anne Campbell, "Female Competition," *Journal of Sex Research* 41 (2004): 16.
3. Desmond Morris, "Men and Women Are Different for a Reason and We Can Turn That to Our Advantage; Sex, Nature and a Division of Labour," *Sunday Herald Sun* (Australia), May 9, 2004.
4. Desmond Morris, "Shattering of a Sex Myth," *Daily Mail* (London), April 17, 2004.
5. Tim Utton, "Caveman Lives, but Don't Expect Too Much Small Talk," *Daily Mail* (London), December 27, 2003.
6. Ibid.
7. Debbie Cafazzo, "Men and Boys Just Don't Think As Women Do," *The News Tribune* (Jefferson City, MO), October 5, 2003.
8. Kathiann M. Kowalski, "The Truth About Guys and Girls: Is It in Your Head?" *Current Health* 2, January 1, 2004.
9. Utton, "Caveman Lives."
10. Frank Muscarella, "An Evolutionary Perspective on Human Reproduction," *The Journal of Sex Research*, February 2004; Nancy Weaver Teichert, "Longevity Linked to Nurturing," *Deseret Morning News* (Salt Lake City), July 24, 2003.
11. "Why We Owe So Much to Granny," *South Wales Evening Post* (Swansea, Wales), March 11, 2004.

12. Rebekah Devlin, "Behind This Door, It's an R-rated Animal Show," *The Advertiser* (Australia), June 20, 2003.
13. "Biology Is Behind Homosexuality in Sheep," *Health Insurance Week*, April 4, 2004.
14. Pamela Fayerman, "Sex and the Faithful Gerbil," *Vancouver Sun* (Canada), January 4, 2004.
15. Devlin, "Behind This Door."
16. Ibid.
17. Simon Baron-Cohen, *The Essential Difference: Men, Women, and the Extreme Male Brain* (London: Penguin, 2003).
18. Kowalski, "The Truth about Guys and Girls."
19. Gillian Ferguson, "Science Meets Pure Disney in Babyland," *The Scotsman* (Edinburgh), October 11, 2002.
20. Cheryl Cornacchia, "Mosquitoes Dine on Our Scientists," *The Gazette* (Montreal), June 16, 2003.
21. Fayerman, "Sex and the Faithful Gerbil."
22. "U. Va. Researchers Study 'Bearded Women' Syndrome," Associated Press, August 31, 2003.
23. Kate Douglas, "Boy or Girl? Planning a Baby? Think Its Sex Is Down to Chance? Think Again," *New Scientist*, September 14, 2002.
24. Ibid.
25. "Girl Power," *The Economist*, October 21, 2004.
26. Tilly Bagshawe, "Do Toyboys Do It Better?" *Malay Mail* (Kuala Lumpur), November 11, 2002.
27. Campbell, "Female Competition."
28. Neal Matthews, "The Fragile Male," *The San Diego Union-Tribune*, March 12, 2003.
29. Ibid.
30. Morris, "Shattering of a Sex Myth."
31. Matthews, "The Fragile Male."
32. Ibid.
33. Kowalski, "The Truth About Guys and Girls."
34. Matthews, "The Fragile Male."
35. Marla Cone and John Vidal, "Pollution: Out for the Count," *The Guardian* (London), February 15, 1995.
36. Chris Mihill, "Men Producing 50pc [Percent] Less Sperm," *The Guardian* (London), January 3, 1997.
37. Robert Lee Hotz, "Chromosomes Make the Man," *Los Angeles Times*, January 18, 2004.
38. Matthews, "The Fragile Male."
39. Carolina H. J. Tiemessen, Johannes L. H. Evers, Robert S. G. M. Bots, "Tight-Fitting Underwear and Sperm," *The Lancet* 347 (1996).
40. Matthews, "The Fragile Male."

41. Gavin McNett, "Y Are Men Necessary?" www.salon.com, June 5, 2003.
42. Matthews, "The Fragile Male."
43. Dennis Chute, "Male Chromosome Wearing Out," *The Edmonton Journal* (Alberta, Canada), June 13, 2004; Richard Reeves, "Men Remain Stuck in Cages of Their Own Creation," *New Statesman*, August 16, 2004.
44. Steve Jones, *Y: The Descent of Men* (Houghton Mifflin, 2003) quoted in Hotz, "Chromosomes Make the Man."
45. McNett, "Y Are Men Necessary?"
46. Clive Cookson, "Scientists Make Male Mice Redundant in Reproduction," *Financial Times*, April 22, 2004; Carl T. Hall, "Look Moms, no Dad!" *San Francisco Chronicle*, April 22, 2004.
47. Louisa Tam, "Male Pregnancy—A World Reborn?" *South China Morning Post*, October 18, 2003.
48. Campbell, "Female Competition."
49. Bagshawe, "Do Toyboys Do It Better?"
50. Lois Rogers, "Ideal Man Has No Rough Edges," *The Australian*, December 9, 2002.
51. Bagshawe, "Do Toyboys Do It Better?"
52. Rogers, "Ideal Man Has No Rough Edges."

CHAPTER 3
WHAT IS MASCULINITY?

1. Sam Martin, *How to Mow the Lawn: The Lost Art of Being a Man* (London: Bloomsbury, 2003).
2. R. W. Connell, "Masculinities, Change, and Conflict in Global Society: Thinking About the Future of Men's Studies," *The Journal of Men's Studies* 11 (2003).
3. Anthony E. Rotundo, *American Manhood: Transformations in Masculinity from the Revolution to the Modern Era* (New York: Harper, 1993) quoted in Caroline S. Miles, "Representing and Self-Mutilating the Labouring Male Body," *The American Transcendental Quarterly* 18 (2004).
4. "Braudy Tracks Masculinity's Metamorphosis," *Ethnic NewsWatch*, January 7, 2004.
5. Dr. Raj Persaud, "If They Ruled the World: How Do We Change the World for the Better?" *The Herald* (Glasgow), March 16, 2004.
6. Andrew Singleton, Jane Maree Maher, "The 'New Man' Is in the House: Young Men, Social Change, and Housework," *The Journal of Men's Studies* 12 (2004): 227.
7. Cathy Mayer, "Numbers of Rich Single Women on the Increase," *The Western Mail* (Cardiff, Wales), April 13, 2002.

8. Will Woodward, "Girls Still Choose 'Women's Jobs,'" *The Guardian* (London), October 29, 2001.

9. David Briggs, "Does Genetics Make Men Less Religious?" *Orlando Sentinel* (Florida), November 23, 2002; David Briggs, "Keeping the Faith; Research Shows Women Are More Religious Than Men Throughout The World," *The Houston Chronicle*, November 16, 2002.

10. "Prosumer Pulse: The Future of Men: USA," Euro RSCG Worldwide, June 2003.

11. "Spain: Matadors Now Mattify; Men's Lines," *European Cosmetic Markets*, March 1, 2004.

12. "Germany: Not a Pretty Sight; Men's Lines," *European Cosmetic Markets*, March 1, 2004.

13. Harry Wilson, "Here Comes the Groom: The Wedding Industry Is Bonding with the Other Half," *Calgary Herald* (Alberta, Canada), May 2, 2004.

14. *St. James Encyclopedia of Popular Culture* (Gale Group, 2002).

15. John M. Broder, "Schwarzenegger Calls Budget Opponents 'Girlie Men,'" *The New York Times*, July 18, 2004.

16. James Rainey, "The Race to the White House," *The Los Angeles Times*, March 18, 2004.

17. Linley Boniface, "Waiting for the New Man," *The Dominion Post* (Wellington, New Zealand), August 14, 2004.

18. Ruth Laugeson, "Real Men Do Dishes. Yeah Right," *The Sunday Star-Times* (Auckland, New Zealand), August 15, 2004.

19. Peter Collett, *The Book of Tells: How to Read People's Minds from Their Actions* (London: Bantam, 2004) quoted in *Sunday Star Times* (Aukland, New Zealand), July 6, 2003.

20. Michael L. Tan, "Bush the Son, Saddam and Sons," *The Philippine Daily Inquirer* (Manila), March 20, 2003.

21. Mark Steyn, "Bush Is a Terminator, Kerry Is a Girlie Man," *The Spectator* (London), July 31, 2004.

22. Steve Sailer, "Why We Need Macho Men," *The American Enterprise*, September 1, 2003.

23. Ibid.

24. Nigella Lawson, "The Raw and the Half-Baked," *The Guardian* (London), October 14, 1999.

25. Joan Smith, "Sir, You've Made a Man of Me," *The Times* (London), April 22, 2004.

26. Lindsay Tanner, "Lost Party in Need of a New Vision," *The Australian* (Melbourne), September 22, 2003.

27. Khanna Parag, "The Metrosexual Superpower: The Stylish European Union Struts Past the Bumbling United States on the Catwalk of Global Diplomacy," *Foreign Policy*, July/August 2004.

28. Joseph Wilson, "How Saddam Thinks," *San Jose Mercury News* (California), April 30, 2004.

29. "A Regional Tradition of Gender Equity: Shanghai Men in Sydney, Australia," *The Journal of Men's Studies* 12 (2004).
30. Ibid.
31. Cay Crow, "Gender Identity and Sexual Orientation Are Different Concepts," *San-Antonio Express-News* (Texas), February 28, 2004.
32. Harrison G. Pope, Jr., "Steroids," *San Jose Mercury News* (California), March 28, 2004.
33. Dalia Acosta, "Latin America: Sexologists See Little Change in Male 'Macho,'" IPS-Inter Press Service, April 3, 2003.
34. Lars Plantin, Sven-Axel Mansson, Jeremy Kearney, "Talking and Doing Fatherhood: On Fatherhood and Masculinity in Sweden and England," *GenderWatch* 1, (2003).
35. "What Sort of Man Reads Playboy? The Self-Reported Influence of *Playboy* on the Construction of Masculinity," *The Journal of Men's Studies* 11 (2003).
36. Kate Santich, "Do Television Ads Dump on Guys as Incompetent, Weak and Stupid?" *Orlando Sentinel* (Florida), May 22, 2004.
37. Don Butler, "What Turns Young Men into Terrorists?" *Ottawa Citizen* (Canada), April 3, 2004.
38. Ibid.
39. "Braudy Tracks Masculinity's Metamorphosis," *Ethnic NewsWatch*, January 7, 2004.
40. "Gender Immigrant: A Conversation with Jennifer Finney Boylan," *Women's Review of Books*, April 2004.

CHAPTER 4
BEYOND METROSEXUALMANIA: THE ÜBERSEXUAL

1. Mark Simpson, "Here Come the Mirror Men," *The Independent* (London), November 15, 1994.
2. Greg Morago, "For Metrosexuals, No Risk Yet of Being Passé," *The Philadelphia Inquirer*, July 6, 2004.
3. "Prosumer Pulse: The Future of Men: USA," Euro RSCG Worldwide, June 2003.
4. Ibid.
5. Simpson, "Here Come the Mirror Men."
6. Michael Flocker, *The Metrosexual Guide to Style: A Handbook for the Modern Man*, (Da Capo Press, 2003) quoted in Andrew Billen, "Are You Metrosexual?" *The Times* (London), November 27, 2003.
7. Mark Simpson, "MetroDaddy Speaks!" www.salon.com, January 5, 2004.
8. "Prosumer Pulse: The Future of Men: USA," Euro RSCG Worldwide, June 2003.
9. Ibid.
10. Simpson, "MetroDaddy Speaks!"

11. Sarah Wilson, "Metro Man," *Sunday Telegraph Magazine* (Sydney, Australia), July 20, 2003.
12. A. D. Amorosi, "Guys & Dolling Up," *The Philadelphia Inquirer*, December 24, 2003.
13. Ibid.
14. Brian Flemming, "George W. Bush Nose Job Story on Late Show with David Letterman," www.slumdance.com, February 20, 2004.
15. "Move Over Macho Man—and Make Way for Mr. Metrosexual," *Bristol Evening Post* (England), August 21, 2003.
16. Peter McQuaid, "Forget the Metrosexual Movement," *Los Angeles Times Magazine*, September 7, 2003.
17. Wilson, "Metro Man."
18. Aidan Smith, "It's a Man's World (Again!)," *Scotland on Sunday*, June 22, 2003.
19. From www.maximonline.com.
20. Nat Ives, "Maxim Seeks to Portray Itself as Sophisticatedly Macho," *The New York Times*, November 9, 2004.
21. Robert Frick, "The Manly Man's Guide to Makeup and Metrosexuality," *Kiplinger's Personal Finance*, June 2004.
22. Peter Carlson, "The Catazine for Men Whose Passion Is All Consuming," *The Washington Post*, March 23, 2004.
23. Ibid.
24. Kim Campbell, "'Manly' Gets a Makeover," *The Christian Science Monitor*, April 7, 2004.
25. Ibid.
26. Ruha Devanesan, "Selling to Mr. Urban Chic," *The Straits Times* (Singapore), June 29, 2004.
27. Chetna Keer Banerjee, "Metro Versus Retro," *The Tribune* (Chandigarh, India) (online edition), May 4, 2004.
28. John Scott Marchant, "Waxing Goes Unisex in Seoul," *The Korea Herald*, May 7, 2004.
29. Ibid.
30. "Male Call: Do Women Really Want to Date Fancy Guys Who Exfoliate?" *San Jose Mercury News* (California), July 25, 2004.
31. Lionel Seah, "Mark His Word," *The Straits Times* (Singapore), August 10, 2003.
32. Olivia Barker, "Regular Guys Cast a Jaded Eye at 'Metrosexual' Trend," *USA Today*, January 21, 2004.
33. Adam Zwar, "The Wiseguy," *Sunday Herald Sun* (Melbourne, Australia.), February 29, 2004.
34. Ibid.
35. Rachel Donadio, Sheelah Kolhatkar, Anna Schneider-Mayerson, "Stuff It, Emo Boy!" *New York Observer*, July 26, 2004.
36. Ibid.
37. Ibid.

38. Guy Mosel, "A New Bloke on the Block," *Courier Mail* (Queensland, Australia), July 19, 2004.
39. Ibid.
40. Ibid.

CHAPTER 5
MAN AS KING OF THE CASTLE

1. Steven L. Nock, *Marriage in Men's Lives* (New York: Oxford University Press, 1998).
2. Ibid.
3. Ibid.
4. "This fellow that was doing the talking had a hair cut like Tarzan, he walked like Jane and smelled like Cheetah," Ronald Reagan, as quoted on "World News Tonight" (ABC), April 23, 1987.
5. From http://jade.cccd.edu.grooms.goodwife.htm.
6. Helen Andelin, *Fascinating Womanhood* (New York: Bantam, 1992).
7. Jo Freedman, *Women: A Feminist Perspective* (Mountain View, Calif.: Mayfield, 1995).
8. Joan Hoff, *Law, Gender and Injustice: A Legal History of U.S. Women* (New York: New York University Press, 1991).
9. Ibid.
10. Freedman, *Women: A Feminist Perspective.*
11. Hoff, *Law, Gender and Injustice.*
12. From www.infoplease.com.
13. Freedman, *Women: A Feminist Perspective*
14. Ibid.
15. Ibid.
16. Ibid.
17. "The Forgotten Half Revisited: American Youth and Young Families, 1988–2008," American Youth Policy Forum, 2001.
18. National Center for Health Statistics, U.S. Department of Health and Human Services, 2003.
19. *The Social Situation in the European Union* (Brussels: The European Commission, 2003).
20. Barbara Miller Solomon, *In the Company of Educated Women: A History of Women and Higher Education in America* (New Haven, Conn.: Yale University Press, 1985).
21. Mabel Newcomer, *A Century of Higher Education for American Women* (Washington, D.C.: Zenger Publishers, 1975).
22. "More Women Than Men Admitted to Class of '08," *Harvard Gazette*, April 8, 2004.
23. Trip Gabriel, "Stairmasters and the Internet Invade a Staid World; To Attract Younger Alumni, Particularly Women, University Clubs Try to Modernize," *The New York Times*, October 4, 1994.

24. David Stenhouse, "Now That Girls Have the Keys to the Boys' Room, Are Lost Male Enclaves Cause for Real Moping?" *The Scotsman*, February 19, 1998.

25. "Alcohol and Pregnancy Don't Mix: Binge Drinking Among Women 18–44 on the Rise," National Organization on Fetal Alcohol Syndrome report, June 23, 2004.

CHAPTER 6
THE TABLES TURN FOR WOMEN

1. From www.wisdomquotes.com.
2. "Men Find New Role in Politics—Next to Wife," *The Times Union* (Albany, NY), June 28, 2004.
3. "The Kennedy Center Board of Trustees," www.kennedy-center.org.
4. "Boys Losing Ground in Colleges," *St. Louis Post-Dispatch*, August 14, 2003.
5. "The New Gender Gap," *BusinessWeek*, May 26, 2003.
6. Ibid.
7. "The Downsized Male: Sometimes It's Hard to Be a Man," *The Economist*, December 20, 2001.
8. "Your Career Matters: Have Husband, Will Travel—World of the Trailing Spouse Isn't Wives-Only Anymore," *The Wall Street Journal*, February 13, 2001.
9. "Study Finds All States Still Show Wage Gap for Women," Reuters, November 16, 2004.
10. Claudia Goldin, "Gender Gap," *The Concise Encyclopedia of Economics*.
11. "Radcliffe Public Policy Center Study Finds New Generation of Young Men Focusing on Family First," Radcliffe Public Policy Center, May 3, 2000.
12. "61 Percent of Men Want to Be House-Husbands," *The Straits Times* (Singapore), February 11, 2001.
13. "The Most Rewarding Career a Man Could Hope For," *Sunday Herald* (Glasgow, Scotland), October 22, 2000.
14. "Diapers and Drool at This Boot Camp," *The Boston Globe*, June 17, 2001.
15. "Make Room for Daddy," *The Ottawa Citizen*, November 3, 2000.
16. "Dads Lose Out in the Rattle Race; UK Has Worst Paternity Law," *Sunday Mail* (London), June 10, 2001.
17. *Monthly Labor Review*, October 2003.
18. *21st Century Changing Lives Report*, The Future Laboratory, 2004.
19. Deborah Orr, "Mother's Little Helper—The Tax Break," *The Independent* (London), May 18, 2004.
20. Prosumer Pulse 2004: A Global Study—Anticipating Consumer Demand, Euro RSCG Worldwide, 2004.

21. "Americans Are Not Going Broke Over Lattes!" Salon.com, October 13, 2003.
22. "Spanish Machos Opt for 'Women's' Work," Deutsche Presse-Agentur, June 13, 2001.
23. "Nursing Group, Facing Shortage of Recruits, Courts Police Officers and Firefighters," *The New York Times*, July 1, 2001.
24. "Man-Sized Issues; How Men Are Taking on Women's Roles in the Business of Caring," *Scottish Daily Record* (Glasgow), June 19, 2001.
25. "My Boss, My Wife," *Time*, August 27, 2001.
26. Sean French, "Men of the Future, We're Told, Will Be 'Sad, Lonely, Isolated Cases.' For Once, I'm in Advance of the Trend," *New Statesman*, October 25, 1999.
27. Ibid.
28. The number of children that would be born to each woman if she were to live to the end of her childbearing years and bear children at each age in accordance with prevailing age-specific fertility rates.
29. "*Economist* Profiles Differing Demography of United States, Western Europe," *Economist*, August 28, 2002.
30. Melanie Philips, *The Sex Change Society: Feminised Britain and the Neutered Male*, 1999.
31. Carl Zimmer, "The Once and Future Male: Men Will Survive Even After the Pivotal Genes That Make Them Men Disappear—The Evolutionary Front," *Natural History*, September 2002.

CHAPTER 7
MASS MEDIA, ADVERTISING, AND THE MODERN MAN

1. Thomas Chau, "Interview: Johnny Messner on 'Anacondas: The Hunt for the Blood Orchid,'" *Cinema Confidential*, August 23, 2004.
2. Phillip Rhodes, Mike Zimmerman, "The Rock Is Cookin'," *Men's Health*.
3. Neva Chonin, "Listen Up, Hollywood—Is There a Female Version of Spidey for Our Times?" *San Francisco Chronicle*, August 3, 2004.
4. Lev Grossman, "The Problem with Superman," *Time*, May 17, 2004.
5. Wendell Wittler, "Television Grapples with Weighty Matter," MSNBC, October 12, 2004.
6. Rochelle Burbury, David Meagher, "The Many Faces of the New Man," *Australian Financial Review*, December 23, 2003.
7. Kim Campbell, "Manly Gets a Makeover," *Christian Science Monitor*, July 24, 2004.
8. Cintra Wilson, "Men Who Hurt Themselves for a Living," www.salon.com, May 21, 2002.
9. "Doctors Feed Blaine After Stunt," CNN.com, October 20, 2003.

10. Ibid.
11. Ibid.
12. Ibid.

CHAPTER 8
REAL MEN AND THEIR REAL ROLE MODELS

1. Kim Campbell, "Manly Gets a Makeover," *Christian Science Monitor*, July 24, 2004.
2. Rex Jory, "Boys Floundering in a World of Women," *The Advertiser* (Australia), October 23, 2002.
3. "Dearth of Men to Be Role Models," *Telegraph News* (Sydney), March 8, 2004.
4. "The Male Minority: The Percentage of Public School Teachers Who Are Men Is at a 40-Year Low," *The Times Union* (Albany, N.Y.), April 18, 2004.
5. Jory, "Boys Floundering in a World of Women."
6. Bess Twiston Davies, "How the Men in Cassocks Became the Boys in the Hood," *The Times* (London), July 5, 2003.
7. From www.capcollege.bc.ca/dept/cmns/louts.html.
8. Jenel Few, "Odds Are Against Black Boys Eventually Getting College Degrees," *Savannah Morning News* (Georgia), April 9, 2004.
9. Jory, "Boys Floundering in a World of Women."
10. "We Must Find Ways to Give Boys More Exposure to Male Role Models," *Canberra Times* (Australia), February 23, 2004.
11. "New Study Reveals Celebrity Culture Has U.S. Teens Setting Sights High," Euro RSCG MVBMS Teen Study, March 2004.
12. Dan Butler, "What Turns Young Men into Terrorists," *Ottawa Observer*, April 3, 2004.
13. "New Study," Euro RSCG MVBMS Teen Study.
14. From www.ucd.i.e/gsi/pdf/35–1/boys.pdf.
15. William S. Pollack, Ph.D, *Real Boys' Voices* (New York: Penguin Books, 2000), p. 17.
16. Ibid., p. 5.
17. Rebecca Walker, ed., *What Makes a Man: 22 Writers Imagine the Future* (New York: Riverhead Books, 2004), p. 61.
18. Pollack, *Real Boys' Voices*, p. 51.
19. Walker, ed., *What Makes a Man*, p. 171.
20. From www.teenwire.com.
21. Ibid.
22. "We Must Find Ways to Give Boys More Exposure to Male Role Models," *Canberra Times*.
23. Bridget Byrne, "Michael Jackson: An Eccentric Superstar Makes Marketing a Tricky Proposition," *The Los Angeles Times*, October 11, 1987.
24. Ibid.

25. "American Television, Drama." www.glbtq.com.

26. Valerie Seckler, "Skin-Deep Appeals," *WWD*, June 30, 2004.

27. Lee C. Harrington, "Homosexuality on *All My Children:* Transforming the Daytime Landscape," *Journal of Broadcasting and Electronic Media*, June 1, 2003.

28. Ibid.; Steven Capsuto, *Alternate Channels: The Uncensored Story of Gay and Lesbian Images on Radio and Television* (New York: Ballantine Books, 2000).

29. Seckler, "Skin-Deep Appeals."

30. Ibid.

31. "MTV Networks to Launch LOGO," www.viacom, May 25, 2004.

32. Harrington, "Homosexuality on *All My Children.*"

33. David Zurawik, "The Evolution of Man," *The Baltimore Sun*, August 10, 2003.

34. Ibid.

35. Ibid.

36. Craig Wilson, "Gay Taste? Here's Straight Talk," *USA Today*, August 5, 2003.

37. Claire Zulkey, "Running Straight for the Queer Guys," *Chicago Tribune*, October 1, 2003.

38. From www.commercialcloset.org.

39. "It Floats," www.commercialcloset.org.

40. "Sunday Afternoon," www.commercialcloset.org.

41. Sandra Yin, "Coming Out in Print—Industries Seek Out Gay Consumers," *American Demographics*, February 1, 2003.

42. Christopher Bantick, "Beckham Boots It Home," *Hobart Mercury* (Australia), February 13, 2003.

43. Ibid.

CHAPTER 9
NEW RULES FOR THE MATING GAME

1. "Arranged Marriages and the Place They Have in Today's Culture," *Talk of the Nation* (National Public Radio), July 20, 1999.

2. Translated from "Elk voordeel heb z'n nadeel!"

3. Michelle Marks, "Love's Tangled Web; Internet Sites Connect Singles, but Keep an Eye Open for Deception," *The Toronto Sun*, August 13, 2004.

4. Tony Vermeer, "Most Men Go for Blondes—Women Prefer Tall, Wealthy Guys," *The Sunday Telegraph* (Australia), August 1, 2004.

5. Joanne Ostrow, "Whither Ms.? TV 'Reality' Romances Strand Women," *The Denver Post*, February 16, 2003.

6. Jenice Armstrong, "Online Dating Antics," *Philadelphia Daily News*, July 28, 2004.

7. "The Funny Odds of Online Dating," Reuters, June 10, 2004.

8. "Online Dating Services Thrive as Electronic Matchmakers," *Chattanooga Times* (Tennessee), August 6, 2004.

9. "Udate.co.uk Leads in U.K. Internet Dating Services," *Internet Business News*, August 4, 2004.

10. Prosumer Pulse 2004: A Global Study—Anticipating Consumer Demand. Euro RSCG Worldwide.

11. Jupiter Research quoted in Brian Kladko, "Internet Dating Adds Niche to Help Cheaters Connect," *The Record* (Bergen County, N.J.), July 31, 2004.

12. Mary Ethridge, "Broker Attempts Dream Matches; Professionals Too Busy to Go on Own Search Let Lunch Date Do Asking," *Akron Beacon Journal* (Ohio), August 7, 2004.

13. Netty C. Gross, "Sick of Being Single," *The Jerusalem Report*, October 30, 1997.

14. "Men Are from Mars, Women Are on PerfectMatch.com," PR Newswire, August 3, 2004.

15. "Survey Reveals Blind-Date Risk-Takers," *U.K. Newsquest Regional Press* (London), August 3, 2004.

16. Prosumer Pulse 2004. Euro RSCG Worldwide.

17. Tom D'Angelo, "Animal Magnetism: It's a Dog-Meet-Dog, Owner-Meet-Owner World," *USA Today*, August 4, 2004.

18. Julie Shaw, "Finding Love Online Story," *Newark Advocate* (Ohio), February 14, 2003.

19. Liz Hoggard, "The Power of One," *Sunday Telegraph Magazine* (Australia), March 14, 2004.

20. Beth Turner, "Record-Breaking Older Women Give Birth," Parents.com, November 18, 2004.

21. "They Fly to Love, and It Shows," *National Post* (Canada), July 24, 2004.

22. From www.mensnewsdaily.com.

23. Prosumer Pulse 2004. Euro RSCG Worldwide.

24. "Arranged Marriages," *Talk of the Nation*.

25. "The Power of One," *Sunday Telegraph Magazine*.

26. Prosumer Pulse 2004. Euro RSCG Worldwide.

27. Ibid.

CHAPTER 10
HOW ARE MEN HANDLING THE SEA CHANGES?

1. "The Forgotten Half Revisited: American Youth and Young Families, 1988–2008," American Youth Policy Forum, 2001.

2. *The Social Situation in the European Union*, The European Commission, 2003.

3. From www.mankindproject.com/values.htm.

4. Kaitlyn Andrews-Rice, "TV Creates Gender Factions That Unfairly Dictate Society," *Daily Collegian* (Pennsylvania State University), February 6, 2004.
5. Karyn D. Collins, "Seriously, Guys . . . Spike TV Executive Keith Brown Adds Some Serious Content to the Cable Channel's Macho Lineup," *Asbury Park Press* (New Jersey), February 21, 2004.
6. Ibid.
7. Mark Honigsbaum, "Real Lives: Man About the House," *The Observer,* November 30, 2003.
8. Cosmo Landesman, "It's Not All Bad Being a Man," *Sunday Times* (London), May 16, 2004.
9. Merle Rubin, "Mismatch: The Growing Gulf Between Women and Men," *The Los Angeles Times,* April 21, 2003.
10. "Parental Leave and Father Involvement in Child Care: Sweden and the United States," *Journal of Comparative Family Studies,* 33, 3 (2002): 387–400.
11. "Workplace Views by Gender," *USA Today,* October 22, 2003.
12. Kevin Alexander Boon, "Men and Nostalgia for Violence: Culture and Culpability in Chuck Palahniuk's Fight Club," *The Journal of Men's Studies,* 11 (2003): 267.

CONCLUSION
M-NESS—THE BRIGHT FUTURE OF MEN

1. From http://rakugaki.aesiraven.com/yay/.
2. From www.allpar.com/mopar/new-mopar-hemi.html.

INDEX